P9-DGR-372

Largo Sete de Cicades, São Miguel

Portuguese
Homestyle Cooking

ANA PATULEIA ORTINS

INTERLINK BOOKS
An imprint of Interlink Publishing Group, Inc.
New York • Northampton

First published in 2001 by

INTERLINK BOOKS

An imprint of Interlink Publishing Group, Inc.
99 Seventh Avenue • Brooklyn, New York 11215 and
46 Crosby Street • Northampton, Massachusetts 01060
www.interlinkbooks.com

Library of Congress Cataloging-in-Publication Data

Ortins, Ana Patuleia.
Portuguese homestyle cooking / Ana Patuleia Ortins.
p. cm.
Includes bibliographical references and index.
ISBN 1-56656-373-9 (library binding)
1. Cookery, Portuguese. I. Title.
TX723.5.P7 O78 2001
641.59469--dc21
00-012959

Printed and bound in Korea

To request our complete 48-page full-color catalog,
please call us toll free at **1-800-238-LINK,** visit our
website at **www.interlinkbooks.com**, or write to
Interlink Publishing
46 Crosby Street, Northampton, MA 01060
e-mail: sales@interlinkbooks.com

I dedicate *Portuguese Homestyle Cooking* to my father, Rufino Patuleia, whose love and passion for our wonderful Portuguese food is his enduring legacy to me and to my children. Here's to you, Pai!

Meu Pai é um amigo,	*My Father is a friend,*
Que eu nunca esquecerei.	*Whom I never will forget.*
Por que amor igual ao dele	*For love equal to his*
Nunca mais encontrarei.	*Never more will I have met.*

This verse is one of the many quaint Portuguese sayings painted on the artful blue-and-white pottery of Alcobaça, a town north of Lisbon.

View of Óbidos

PREFACE

This book preserves and shares the everyday food of my heritage, introducing it to those who are interested in exploring this soul-comforting, understated peasant food of the Portuguese. It seems not long ago, *Portuguese Homestyle Cooking* was not even a passing thought, but events in life often make us change direction, if only temporarily. Some years ago, it occurred to me that treasured family recipes of my heritage would be lost to our children if I failed to record them. As a first-generation Portuguese-American, I knew these recipes needed to be captured on paper, preserved not only for my children but for future generations of descendants of Portuguese immigrants—before the recipes become Americanized.

What was to be a simple notebook of family recipes soon expanded to include common, yet popular, everyday homestyle dishes of our extended family and Portuguese friends. Before I knew it, my thoughts of writing this book were echoed aloud by my brother Rufino Jr. and encouraged by others. Today, Portuguese food is still relatively unknown outside Portugal. Many confuse it with Spanish fare, and still more toss it into books and articles as an aside to Spanish cooking. I feel that it is time for Portuguese food to stand on its own and be more closely examined for itself. With an overview of the diverse influences of the cuisine, this book is a guide to the heart-warming recipes of authentic Portuguese food.

For questions or comments, contact the author at: ana@portuguesecooking.com.

ACKNOWLEDGEMENTS

W hen *Portuguese Homestyle Cooking* was yet in its infancy, the enthusiasm and support that arose from family, relatives, friends, colleagues, and strangers was overwhelming. This book would not have been possible without the help of those listed here. There are not enough words to express the tremendous appreciation I have for everyone, in Portugal and America, who contributed in some way, big or small, to make this book a reality; some have assisted in nearly every phase of this book.

Words have not yet been invented that could possibly thank my husband Philip enough. In his own quiet way, he urged me onward repeatedly with his tremendous patience and boundless good nature—through the researching, proofreading, the many and sometimes repeated testing, the tasting dinners. My thanks especially for picking up the slack when I was totally immersed and, most of all, for believing in me and this book.

Thank you with much love and affection to my daughter Nancy for her diligent editing; son-in-law, Michael Savage, always a willing taste tester; my son Marc for his enthusiasm and generous help with photography; and his dear friend Sara Zegzdryn for her testing, to all of them for their suggestions, creativity, critiques, and constant support and patience. Heart-filled thank-you to "Titi," my aunt Ana Patuleia Valente, for being there from the beginning and for the wonderful cooking lessons, and to my uncle Ilidio Valente for being a valuable source of history, discussions, and tastings and to my mother Evelyn, for answering my many questions.

To Aureolinda Bettencourt, Alvarina Boga, "Mother" Julia Fernandes, Olinda Fernandes, Dilia Luz, and Isaura Nogueira—I want to thank you immensely for not only sharing your heirloom recipes and standing with me as we tested them, but for your patience every time I stuck a measuring spoon or cup under your hand, for answering my questions, and for explaining the unspoken Portuguese touches that are sometimes forgotten.

Thanks to my testers and tasters, who not only gave their time and provided me with feedback that helps even the novice home cook, but who also offered their family recipes: Pat Almeida, Lark and Bob Bolduc, John and Barbara Ciman, Dolores and John Figueiredo, Mary Gil, Catherine and Bill Hosman, Missy McKinnon, Joe and Marguerite Mendonca, Laraine and Bob Ortins, Mary and Tony Dos Santos. To Mike Benson for his assistance with photography. Many, many hugs to my friend and computer troubleshooter, Mike Bassichis for his timely assistance.

So many of you not only offered up your treasured family recipes and the little secret tricks that you do, the helpful hints, and patience while I measured and recorded, but were a great source of information as well. Thank you for sharing it all—Lucinda Almeida, Edelberto Ataide, Edite Biscaia, Deolinda Bettencourt, Elsa Bettencourt, Fatima Bettencourt, Senhorinha Bettencourt, Antonio Cardosa, Leonia Clarimundo; the kitchen crew of Club Luis de Camões of Peabody, Massachusetts; Maria and Rogerio Coimbra, Jose and Ismailda Coelho of Lisbon, Portugal; Alberto F. Cunha of Lisbon Portugal; Evelyn Ortins Cunha, Manuel Cunha, Sonia Cunha, Lili Oliveira Ferreira of Lisbon, Portugal; Maria Fidalgo, Adelaide Figueira, Agapito Figueira, Holy Ghost Society of Peabody, Massachusetts (Irmanda de Açoreana do Espirito Santo); Fatima Lima, Teresa Mendonca, Rich Nunes, Jennifer Nunes, Connie Oliveira, Antonio and Noelia Ortins, Arthur Ortins, Denise Ortins, Dorothy Ortins, Joseph and Jeannette Ortins, Maria de Luz Ortins, Rose Pais, Teresa Coutinho Patuleia, Elena Pavick, Mario Pinto, Lucia Rebelo, Antonio Rosa, Alvarinha Silva, Eliodoro Silva, John F. Silva, Manuel and Maria Silva, Manuel C. Silva, Fernanda and Gaspar Simões, and Juliana Sylvester.

I would like to thank Pat Kelly, who not only was the first to get involved, but whose encouragement, proofreading, and advice were very instrumental in my pursuing this expanded project that went beyond a simple community cookbook. Profound gratitude to Jackie Ankeles, Luis Azevedo, Alfonso Barclamonte; to Linda Bassett for her constant push, suggestions, and tremendous help; Antonio Bragança, Antonio Cardosa, Ken Costa, Mario and Lucia Costa, Eduardo M. Dias, Lisa Ekus, Joan Irons, William LeBlond, Jeanne Lemelin, Giorgio Manzana, Rux Martin, Linda Mendonca, Carlos Pinto, Jorge Ramos and the Portuguese Trade Commission, Beth Riely, Greg Repucci, Mary Rodrigues, John Selski, Ernest Vieira—all who have given invaluable information, advice, product testing, cultural history, contacts, or proofreading—and much more.

Many thanks to Jack Couto and especially Augusto Gabriel, both from Whitehall Imports, for their tremendous help in sharing their knowledge of Portuguese wines and the latest trends in the Portuguese wine industry.

Thank you to professional bakers Alex Couto, owner of Central Bakery, Peabody, Massachusetts, retired baker Manuel Galopim, to John Silva owner of Danversport Bakery, Danvers, Massachusetts, for their invaluable help and patience and to Lourival Mello, an enormous thank you for suggestions and technical imput.

Last, but not least, I would like to thank the staff at Interlink Publishing, especially Michel Moushabeck, Juliana Spear, Moira Megargee, and Pam Thompson for having enthusiastic faith in this project and giving me the opportunity to make it a reality. It has been a pleasure to work with all of you.

x

INTRODUCTION

My family's origins are in the Alto Alentejo province, just south of Ponte Sor, in a small town originally called Aldeia das Laranjeiras, Grove of Oranges. However, name changes were neither unusual nor difficult to accomplish, according to my grandfather, who liked to tell the story of how Aldeia das Laranjeiras became known as Galveias. There were two neighbors, so the story goes, one of whom owned hens, the other, a rooster. When the owner of the hens complained that the rooster was bothering his hens, the owner of the rooster was said to have replied, "Can I help it if my rooster (*gallo*) sees (*veia*)?"

Like so many others, my grandfather Jose Nunes Patuleia came to the United States by way of Ellis Island, seeking a better life for his family. He left Galveias in the winter of 1920 and settled in Peabody, Massachusetts, where he was joined by my grandmother, father, and aunt in 1937. Wherever they settled, Portuguese immigrants transplanted their love of family, food, wine, friendship, and hospitality, and their strong religious beliefs from which they drew their courage and perseverance. I remember that any visitor to our home was always invited to share our meal or, at the very least, to have something to drink. It was not unusual for my father to offer a guest his last beer or glass of wine. "Come in, come in," was a standard greeting in our home. No matter how meager our dinner might be, unexpected guests were always invited to sit down and join us. Friends never left our home empty-

Grandmother Theresa and Aunt Ana's arrival in the United States, 1937

handed, either, especially in the summertime. They would take with them a bag heavy with sun-ripened tomatoes and other vegetables from the garden. Pai (Dad) was even known to climb our pear tree to pick the ripened fruit for our guests. Sharing what we have been blessed with, however meager, is who we are.

As a child, I often stood by my father's side in the kitchen as he prepared dinner. "Watch how I do this, so you learn," he would say in his imperfect English. For past generations it was expected training: watch and learn. I was a willing student, my zest for learning was surpassed only by my father's pleasure in teaching me all he knew—something he enjoyed almost as much as he enjoyed soccer! Along with Pai's teaching, I absorbed his passion for cooking and eating wonderful food, for sharing it with others, and for savoring the taste of their satisfaction as keenly as the food offered. This book is my way of sharing his passion and handing on my culinary heritage.

Traditional Portuguese dishes blend the flavors and techniques of many cultures, dating back centuries. Phoenicians, Turks, Moors, and Arabs are just a few of the peoples who left their mark on what is now Portuguese cuisine. From the Arab countries around the Mediterranean came wheat, rice, citrus fruits, almonds, sugar, saffron, and salt. In Portuguese cooking, braising is done the Arabian way: meat is cooked in a liquid *before* it is seared; in the Western, the meat is seared first. Almond trees, introduced into the Algarve region of southern Portugal by the Moors, bloom so profusely during the winter that the effect is what my father called "Portuguese snow." Phoenicians brought wine and olives, and the Turks taught us the uses of sugar. Although other ingredients essential to Portuguese cuisine are common to Mediterranean countries—olive oil, onions, bay leaves, garlic, fresh coriander, paprika, chili peppers, and red sweet peppers—the ways these ingredients are used are what makes Portuguese fare unique.

Its location on the edge of the Atlantic Ocean played a large part in Portugal's decision to take to the sea. Access to the sea led to the discovery of new lands and exciting new ingredients, creating unprecedented trade opportunities. From the east, the Orient and Indies brought Portuguese cooks tea and a variety of spices including cloves, cinnamon, curry, and nutmeg. Voyages west to the Americas filled ships with tropical fruit, corn, tomatoes, green peppers, and potatoes, giving bright new colors and flavors to traditional dishes. Coffee is believed to have come originally from Ethiopia and eventually spread by Portuguese sailors to Brazil. These influences during the era of the Discoveries fed the evolution of a cuisine.

My father's immigration photograph, 1936

Today, native legumes and leafy greens are still used abundantly in soups and stews. Kale, fresh fennel, and baby turnip tops—a few of the greens that lend distinct flavor to soups—are lightly sautéed and seasoned, or mixed with rice to create tasty side dishes. Red and white kidney beans, chickpeas, pinto, and broad beans not only provide body to sustaining soups, but make interesting accompaniments to main courses. Some dishes combine meat and shellfish. Easy-to-prepare seafood dishes, luscious egg- and sugar-rich desserts, and the way certain spices and herbs are used to flavor foods, give the cuisine its character. And last but not least, infusions of wine and garlic give meat a comforting taste that is unmistakably Portuguese.

Even though the country is small, there are some regional culinary differences. Most obviously, the food of the mainland and that of the Portuguese Azores—lying almost halfway between Portugal and the United States—are quite different. The cheeses in the Azores are made mostly with cow's milk, while the mainland uses sheep's and goat's milk. There is greater use of beef and butter in the islands as well. The recipe for Tripe Stew (*Dobrada*, page 105), is more likely in the Azores to be spicier and to contain kidney beans; its Continental cousin uses lima beans, has a thicker texture, and is milder in spice. The overall flavor of Azorean-style cooking is spicier than mainland fare. On the mainland, seafood use is heaviest along the coast, especially in the southern region of the Algarve. To the northwest, surrounding Lisbon, there is a fair mix of regional dishes. In the north, around the city of Oporto, bean stews like *dobrada* and *feijoada,* stand out. If you go to Beira Alta, boiled dinners are very common, and more frequent use of lamb.

The cuisine I learned at home is that of the Alentejo area, known for its delicious pork, as well as for it wheat, its regal olive groves and picturesque cork trees. A signature of this region is Sweet Red Pepper Paste, *massa de pimentão* (recipe on page 166), which flavors sausages, and the popular Carne de Porco à Alentejana (page 98), a noteworthy dish of fried, marinated pork meat with clams, which is said to have originated during the era of the Inquisition. *Côentros* (cilantro, Chinese parsley, or fresh coriander) is used especially in the Alentejo. The primary fat in soups is olive oil, but other dishes from this region use lard or pork fat. Other culinary offerings from the Alentejo include *açordas* (bread soups) and sweet egg desserts.

My grandparents enjoy a picnic with friends, 1940s

Portuguese cooking has always been resourceful and creative, the recipes easy to make from scratch. As in the old country, here in America traditional culinary methods were handed down from mother to daughter or shared among family and friends through watching, helping, and tasting. Naturally, this method of passing on recipes means that each dish has many variations. Daughters might not have paid close attention, or perhaps they followed their own tastes. Recipes were rarely written down; instructions were universally imprecise; measurements always inexact. Just how much is a "handful"? Measured by whose hand? Additionally, when immigrants first settled in a new land, some traditional methods and recipes were changed of necessity because certain ingredients were simply not available.

Most Portuguese recipes are, as we say, *"com gusto"*—to your liking. No matter what ingredients are specified for a dish, individual quantities are assumed to be according to one's personal preference. This encourages culinary creativity. The recipes included here have been collected over the years from relatives and friends and are presented as they would be prepared in a Portuguese home. To standardize these heirlooms, ingredients have been measured and recipes tested carefully. With the increased availability of traditional ingredients, the dishes can be prepared authentically. Still variations and substitutions have been noted for times when traditional ingredients cannot be found. I encourage you to first cook the recipes as presented, then change the quantities of ingredients *com gusto*.

In the pages that follow, I describe the basic methods of cooking, traditional marinades, and spices most often found in Portuguese cooking, as well as breads and desserts. The instructions are detailed and easy to follow. An informational chapter about Portuguese wine includes a description of the traditional method of making wine at home. These recipes—from different regions of mainland Portugal, the Azores, and the United States—are an introduction to authentic, homestyle Portuguese food at its best—heartwarming, flavorful, delicious! After all, no matter what area, region, or island we as a people came from, *"somos todos Portugueses,"* we are all Portuguese.

São Miguel, Azores

1

INGREDIENTS, METHODS,
& EQUIPMENT

INGREDIENTS

When Portuguese immigrants came to the United States, bringing their culinary traditions with them, some had never traveled outside their home regions in Portugal. Here they met for the first time Portuguese from other provinces and from the Azores. Their regional versions of seafood, meat, and vegetable dishes were compared, shared, and carried on. Seafood dishes were adjusted to use fish available in American markets. Fortunately, many immigrants brought with them the seeds of familiar varieties of tomatoes, kale, wild fennel, herbs, and spices, which enabled them to continue cooking in their traditional manner.

Onions, garlic, tomatoes, paprika, bay leaves, red pepper paste, cumin, chili peppers, parsley, cilantro, olive oil, vinegar, and wine are the common flavorful ingredients that, when combined with meats, fish, and vegetables, distinguish this food from any other. Components in a well-known dish may vary slightly from region to region, town to town, or cook to cook, and should not be altered in order to retain their authenticity. Certain ingredients are inherent to Portuguese cooking—such as *linguiça, chourico,* and red pepper paste. While I encourage substitutions when necessary, keep in mind if you substitute a different ethnic ingredient—for example, kielbasa instead of *linguiça*—the dish can no longer be considered authentic Portuguese cooking; it is now fusion. In presenting recipes that attempt to remain true to authentic Portuguese homestyle fare, I have avoided suggesting substitutes that would alter the Portuguese taste of the food. Substituting some canned or frozen ingredients for fresh ones can be done, however, without seriously compromising quality or taste. The essential ingredients are simple and readily available to almost everyone.

The quality of ingredients is reflected in the taste of the dish. Use the freshest ingredients possible. When preparing fresh vegetables and herbs, be sure to rinse them well in cold running water, removing any particles of soil and tiny insects. Trim the bruises, potato eyes, garlic germ sprouts, celery threads, and mottled leaves of greens. Rinse well and blot dry. The following ingredients (in alphabetical order) are the most fundamental to the Portuguese kitchen.

2

Bread

Traditionally baked in wood-fired ovens, bread is a constant element in any Portuguese meal; it is the one food item that is eaten every day. Since as early as the Middle Ages, bread provided basic sustenance. From the Romans came wheat, which was made into a bread that the Portuguese liked very much. Ever since the first Feast in honor of the Holy Ghost, bread—considered to represent the body of Christ—is still the major ingredient, with meat, in the celebratory Soup of the Holy Ghost (page 42). Today, crisp crusts, delicate flavors, and textures varying from dense and chewy to cotton-like, are characteristic of Portuguese breads. Most Portuguese bakeries in the United States carry the following breads, but many bakeries now sell crusty artisan or European peasant-style breads that make good substitutes.

Corn Bread (*pão de milho or broa*) Years ago, traditional corn bread was made of ground corn, water, and salt. This resulted in a very hard crusted bread with a slightly moist interior. Today's bread is made with a combination of wheat flour and cornmeal—some prefer white cornmeal to yellow. The crisp crust is softer than that of the old corn bread, but the texture is still slightly moist, open-grained, and dense. Corn bread, eaten both in the Azores and in continental Portugal, is produced in many Portuguese-American bakeries, some of which have switched from cornmeal to corn flour to save time in production (page 175).

Crusty Rolls (*papo-secos*) These rolls, made with wheat flour (page 181), are frequently served with grilled sausage; *presunto*, a salt-cured ham; sautéed medallions of marinated meat; fresh sardines; or cheese. The name *papo-seco* denotes the crusty puffed-up shape of these tasty rolls.

Flat Bread (*pão estendido*) This baked bread and the fried version, *pão de sertã* (page 177) hail back to the time before breads were leavened. Both combine wheat and corn flours. *Pão estendido* (page 178) can be baked on an oven stone, producing a crusty, somewhat thin bread; *pão de sertã* is pan-fried in a cast-iron skillet.

Homestyle Bread (*pão caseiro*) This popular home-made country bread has a crispy crust, a cotton-like texture, and an earthy flavor. Made with a *fermente* (sponge) and wheat flour, this bread is fat-free (page 179).

Cheese

The different regions of Portugal have homemade cheeses with their own distinct flavors. Variations in climate, soil, native pasture grasses, and what the sheep and goats eat in those pastures all influence a region's cheese. Made primarily from sheep's and goat's milk, the cheeses range in flavor from mild to intensely sharp. Textures range from soft and creamy to semihard. The very mature cheeses are grated. Typically eaten with fruit or bread, before or after a meal, these cheeses are intrinsic to the Portuguese diet.

Many cheeses are named after the towns of their origin. Some of the cheeses are made by small-scale producers and are not exported. Artisan cheeses like Azeitão, from the town of the same name, are imported in very small quantities. A few of the more popular Portuguese cheeses can be found in Portuguese grocery stores here in the United States and Europe.

Blue Island Cheese (*queijo da Ilha Azul*) The island of Faial (the "blue island"), in the Azores, produces this cheese. Light yellow in color, it has a semisoft texture and a mild, smooth flavor.

Cheese from the Mountain Ridge (*queijo da serra*) Wrapped in linen cloth, this cheese comes from the high mountain plateaus of mainland Portugal. Intensely flavored, with a creamy texture, *queijo da serra* requires a spoon for eating. As it ages, the texture becomes harder. It is sold in whole wheels only, starting at about 2½ pounds. The hefty price tag relegates it to holidays and other special occasions. In spite of this, it is Portugal's most popular sheep's-milk cheese.

Cheese of St. Michael (*queijo da São Miquel*) This specialty cheese from the island of St. Michael in the Azores is made from cow's milk. It has a semisoft texture and a mild flavor.

Cheese of St. George (*queijo da São Jorge*) Sliced or grated, this popular semihard cheese made from cow's milk comes from the island of São Jorge. This cheese delivers a spicy flavor.

Fresh Cheese (*requeijão/queijo fresco*) Azorean and continental Portuguese make this semisoft white cheese, which has a delicate texture and mild flavor. Traditionally it was made with sheep's milk, but is also made with cow's milk (page 160). It is also used to make sweet cheese tarts, *queijadas* (page 212).

Goat Cheese of Palhais (*queijo de cabra—Palhais*) This excellent and slightly salty goat cheese is from Palhais on mainland Portugal. The semisoft texture gives way to a smooth mouth feel and a slightly tangy flavor.

Chili Peppers

When a recipe calls for *piripiri*, it means chili peppers. Peppers are referred to according to the form to be used. Chili peppers can be dried, crushed hot red peppers, known as *piripiri moida* or *malegueta seca*; a paste of crushed hot red peppers, *massa de piripiri*. There is also a hot sauce, *molho de piripiri*, which is similar to American Tabasco sauce. Another form is tiny chili peppers, *malaquetas*, that have been pickled in vinegar. The form of the pepper can be switched for another, based on personal preference, availability, the particular dish being prepared, and aesthetics. They are, for the most part, interchangeable, so feel free to change the form listed in a recipe for another. Portuguese cooking may not be as hot and spicy as Spanish, but we do like to add a zing or two to some dishes. You should be able to find one form or another among the pickled peppers and hot sauces in your supermarket.

Dried Crushed Red Pepper (*piripiri moido* or *malagueta seca*) This hot spice is prepared by drying chili peppers and crumbling them. The flakes are sprinkled with a light hand into stews, seafood dishes, and added to the seasoning of some sausages.

Hot Pepper Paste (*massa de piripiri* or *massa de malagueta*) The hot pepper paste is slightly different from one cook to another, but it is made primarily of chili peppers and salt (page 167). Some preparations include a touch of sweet red pepper, lemon juice, perhaps a small amount of garlic, and olive oil.

Hot Pepper Sauce (*molho de piripiri* or *molho picante*) This is a thinner sauce, very similar to Tabasco or any of the hot pepper sauces in American supermarkets. It is made with chili peppers (*malagueta*), vinegar, and salt. For a zesty twist, add a splash of this hot pepper sauce to

4

melted butter or mix with a small amount of olive oil for dipping boiled lobster meat. Tabasco sauce is a perfect substitute.

Citrus

The flavors of lemon and orange go beyond enhancing the desserts of Portugal. Their juices are used to flavor pork roasts, tripe, even the *farinheira* sausage of the Alentejo region. The zest (colored portion of the peel), is traditionally used whole or grated, perfuming cakes, sweet breads, or puddings. Pure lemon or orange extract may be substituted in desserts.

Cornmeal

Both yellow and white cornmeal is used in bread making. The grind can range from fine to coarse. Some markets now sell corn flour, yellow or white, which is finer than fine cornmeal. The recipes in this book usually call for corn flour because the results are more pleasing to modern tasters. Cornmeal or flour must be "scalded"—combined with boiling water—before being incorporated into the dough.

Eggs

Eggs are a frequent component of Portuguese cooking, most notably in our desserts. Poached eggs appear in bread soups and in dishes of legumes and sausage. Hard-boiled eggs are used not only as a garnish but as an accompaniment to various savory dishes. Desserts are rich with eggs, especially the traditional sweet breads and puddings. Large-sized eggs are used for the recipes in this book.

Hard-Boiling Eggs

For perfect hard-boiled eggs every time, I highly recommend the method from Julia Child's book, *The Way to Cook*. This is the best method I have ever used:

Place the eggs in a small saucepan and cover with cold water. Cover and bring to a boil. Remove the pan from the heat and keep covered for 17 minutes. Drain the hot water from the pan and immediately shake the pan back and forth to crack the egg shells. Then cover with cold water. Peel the eggs immediately and quickly. Rinse any tiny shells off and set the eggs aside. This allows the sulfur gases, which are caused by a chemical reaction during the cooking process, to escape, thereby preventing that grayish-green ring from forming around the yolk.

5

Fats

In Portuguese cooking the traditional fats are salt pork, bacon, lard, olive oil, and butter. Each fat plays a special role. In the Alentejo area, for example, bacon fat and lard are commonly used in frying and stewing, while olive oil, rather than meat stock, provides the flavor in soups. The Azoreans, lacking readily available olive oil, traditionally used lard as their primary fat. When corn oil became available in the Azores, it grew in popularity especially for frying, but olive oil is more commonly used for frying on the mainland. Butter, which at one time was considered to be a luxury

reserved for the wealthy, is used moderately for frying beef, dotting the tops of pork roasts or chicken, and for cooking rice. Butter is used more widely in baking. Although aware of the healthier choice of cholesterol-free olive oil, some Portuguese cooks in Portugal and the United States continue to use lard or salt pork in certain dishes that would lose their original character otherwise. Fat substitutions can be made, but with a loss of traditional flavor. Olive oil makes the best substitute for lard and bacon.

Lard (*gordura* or *banha de porco*) An animal fat, lard was once used extensively as a cooking medium and as a preservative. Lard imparts a distinctive flavor to sautéed dishes, but is generally regarded as unhealthy. Olive oil, a healthier traditional fat, preserves the Portuguese flavor of dishes.

Olive Oil (*azeite*) Portuguese olive oil is aromatic, fruity, and as intensely flavored as it is rich in color. The imported Saloio and Victor Guedes brands are most readily found in ethnic markets. Mono-unsaturated olive oil is cholesterol free. If you have difficulty finding Portuguese olive oil, Spanish and Italian extra-virgin and virgin olive oil are good substitutes.

Salt Pork (*toucinho*) Pork fat, preserved in salt, was traditionally fried to render lard. The crispy fried rinds or cracklings, called *torresmos,* are considered a delicious snack, familiar in the southern United States. Pieces of raw salt pork are added to some stews and soups for flavor. Smoked bacon is considered an acceptable substitute.

Herbs

The following herbs are the ones used most often in Portuguese cooking. For the most part, they are readily available to cooks in North America.

Bay Leaves (*loureiro*) Also known as laurel, this aromatic herb is often used in European cooking. In Portugal, where it grows profusely, it was often planted as a hedge to delineate property boundaries—a practice that continues in some areas. The dried leaves flavor soups, stews, and braises. Remove the whole leaf before serving a dish.

Cilantro (*coentros*) Also called Chinese parsley or fresh coriander, it is available in dried and seed form (coriander). Fresh cilantro leaves flavor Portuguese seafood dishes, salads, vegetables, and rice dishes. This herb resembles parsley, but it has a sweet, lemon scent. I find the dried form to be flavorless and strongly recommend using fresh cilantro whenever possible. Try growing it in your garden. (See Parsley.)

Garlic (*alho*) An aromatic herb, garlic is indispensable in Portuguese cooking. It imparts its flavor to soups and stews and is essential to *escabeche* or *molhanga*, the garlic-flavored vinegar sauce served with fried fish (recipes on pages 170–71). To use garlic, press the heel of your palm firmly against the entire garlic bulb, the "head." The pressure will cause the individual cloves to separate from the head. Next, use the flat side of a large knife blade to press the garlic clove. This flattens the clove, separating the skin from the meat. In the middle of the clove, you might see a green sprout, known as the germ, which has a bitter taste. Remove and discard the sprout. When you sauté garlic, you should cook it only until it is lightly golden and releases its aroma. Fresh garlic is used whole, sliced, or as a paste made with a mortar and pestle. I recommend using only fresh garlic for best flavor. When recipes in this book call for garlic, use large cloves. (One clove, finely chopped, equals about one generous teaspoonful.) Use two cloves for each one called for, if the cloves are small. The purple-skinned Italian garlic is the variety I recommend.

Wild Marjoram (*manjerona*) This herb, a close cousin of oregano, grows wild in Portugal. With a spicy, sweet scent, it is primarily used for curing olives. It is sometimes used in other dishes. Oregano can be substituted.

Parsley (*salsa*) This herb is available in two varieties—flat and curly. Curly parsley is often used by chefs as a garnish. Flat-leaf parsley, sometimes referred to as Italian parsley, has a stronger flavor and is most likely found infusing stews, seafood, and vegetable dishes. It is rich in vitamin C and is touted as a breath freshener. Parsley may be purchased fresh or dried. I often take a good amount of fresh flat-leaf parsley, rinse it, pat it dry, and chop it; then I seal it tightly in plastic wrap and store it in the freezer. Freezing retains the flavor and color of parsley better than drying. (Fresh cilantro can be stored this way, too.) Handy in the winter when gardens have been put to bed and fresh parsley or cilantro is hard to come by, this method also works well for storing any herbs left over from preparing a recipe.

7

Used primarily in soups, leafy greens provide the highest amount of vitamin K and give us vitamin C and folic acid. In most dishes, cabbage, spinach, kale, baby turnip greens—even mustard greens—are often interchangeable.

Kale (*couve*) When they came to this country, many Portuguese immigrants brought seeds to grow familiar crops, which they carefully cultivated in their backyard gardens. My father planted a variety of kale called *couve talo branco*, or "white-stalk kale," similar to collards. The broad, flat leaves, almost ten inches wide, are best in soups and salt-cod dishes. *Galega*, a taller kale, is used for Green Broth Soup, *Caldo Verde* (page 23). On the Portuguese mainland, the flat, broad-leaf variety is common. A curly-leaf version, typical of the Azores, is similar to the kale grown in the United States and found in the produce aisles of many supermarkets. Portuguese kale resembles cabbage and collard greens, both in flavor and in its bluish-green color. *Cavalo verde vates* kale can also be successfully grown in the United States. Kale can be

picked as late as November and it freezes well. When I have used up all of my fall harvest of kale, I buy fresh collard greens.

Except for *Caldo Verde*, kale is usually torn, not cut. To do this in the Portuguese manner, take a leaf of the greens in one hand. Using your thumb and first two fingers of the other hand, pull off pieces of kale about one to two inches in size from the main rib and between the fibrous branches of the leaf, until only the skeleton of the leaf remains. Repeat with the remaining leaves until enough has been torn for the dish you are preparing.

Cabbage (*repolho*) When a Portuguese recipe calls for cabbage, the Savoy variety, which we refer to as *lombarda*, with its crinkled leaves and sweeter taste, is most preferred.

Wild Fennel or **Anise** (*funcho*) This licorice-flavored, feathery-leafed green is especially prized by the Azorean Portuguese. It is a wild, bulbless variety that grows profusely in their gardens and is intrinsic to the Azorean Fennel Soup, *Sopa de Funcho* (page 32).

To prepare any of these greens for cooking, place greens in a clean sink and rinse with several changes of cold water, with special attention to the underside of the leaves. Rinsing the kale greens thoroughly while rubbing the top side of the leaves against each other is a time-honored technique believed to remove not only the grayish-white bloom on the leaves, but also the bitterness. Lift the greens out to drain in a colander or on toweling. Any grit should fall to the bottom of the sink. To prevent any grit from settling back onto the greens, do not allow the sink to drain while greens are still in the water.

8

Legumes

Legumes are well represented in Portuguese cooking, not only in soups and stews, but in salads as well. Dried beans (*feijão seco*)—cranberry, black-eyed peas, roman, fava, butter, kidney, and chickpeas (garbanzos)—are high in fiber, protein, and carbohydrates. They can be used interchangeably in many soups and stews. Dried beans are best for flavor, but in a pinch, good-quality canned beans (Progresso or Goya brands, for example) are acceptable substitutes.

To use dried beans, rinse them well in a bowl of cool water. Pick over the beans, removing small stones and deformed, broken, and shriveled beans, as well as any that float. Soak in fresh cool water sufficient to cover the beans by 2 to 3 inches. Soak them at least 8 hours or overnight in the refrigerator. I usually set them to soak before retiring for the night to use the following afternoon. Chickpeas, which can be much harder than most dried legumes, require longer soaking (at least 15 hours) and cooking times (1½ to 2 hours), and sometimes additional water may need to be added during the cooking process.

To cook dried beans, drain the soaking water and rinse the beans. Place the beans and enough fresh water to cover them by 2 inches in a saucepan. When preparing legumes, make sure they are always completely submerged in water during the cooking process. Cover the pan and bring the ingredients to a boil over high heat. Reduce the heat to a slow simmer. Cook until the beans are very tender (about 45 minutes to 1 hour) and mash easily when pressed with a fork. To avoid tough beans, *do not add salt* until the beans are nearly done.

1¼ cup dried beans = 1 pound dried beans

½ pound dried beans = 2½ cups cooked beans

A 1-pound, 3-ounce can of beans equals approximately 1 cup dried beans before soaking or 2 cups of cooked beans. (If you choose to use canned beans, do not drain and rinse them before using unless they are going into a salad.)

Health Note: Be especially careful with fava broad beans, which are toxic unless cooked thoroughly. According to a Michigan State University extension service bulletin (March 9, 1998), fava beans, which look like large overgrown pea pods, "are edible only when they are very young and immature... Some people are allergic to raw fava beans." The beans contain vicine, which causes a toxic allergic reaction that can be fatal to some people of Mediterranean descent.

Olives

Olives (*azeitonas*) accompany nearly every meal in a traditional Portuguese home. Regal olive groves dot the landscape of the Alentejo region, and much of the country produces black olives that are cured in water, salt, and wild marjoram or oregano. Three varieties are imported to the United States. A large, black, mild-tasting olive; a smaller black olive with a sharper bite, carrying a more traditional Portuguese flavor; and green sharp-flavored olives.

Onions

It is no wonder that onions are cherished in Portugal. They are the main ingredient for the *refogado*, an aromatic, sautéed mixture which is the base of many stews and soups. All-purpose yellow and Spanish onions are common kitchen staples.

Refogado

Refogado describes in one word both the method and the aromatic foundation on which stews, seafood dishes, and many soups are based. "*Faz um refogado*" (make a *refogado*) is an instruction understood as the first step to many recipes. In that single step, the cook sautés onions in olive oil and may add one or all of the following: garlic, bay leaf, paprika, or tomatoes. In the recipes that follow, when I speak of cooking the tomato after it has been added to sautéed onions "until it is partially dissolved," I mean cooked down until the vegetables are softened and the flavors are married to each other. We often say that we know when we are in a Portuguese home because of the aroma of *refogado* that fills the kitchen.

Potatoes

Russets, Red Bliss, New White, Maine, Prince Edward Island, and Yukon Gold varieties of potatoes are popular with Portuguese cooks in the United States. Russets are especially favored for frying, while red-skinned or new potatoes give the best flavor and texture in Portuguese boiled dinners, baked dishes, and roasted. Mealy potatoes work well in soups that require puréeing; I prefer to use Maine potatoes or sometimes the Yukon Gold variety in soups. Avoid buying potatoes that have any sign of green color to them. The green color indicates the presence of a toxin. Remove potatoes from any plastic packaging and store in a cool, dry place away from light.

Presunto

Presunto is a lean, spice-and-salt-cured ham, very much like the Italian prosciutto di Parma. It is cut into small cubes and added to soups and stews or simply sliced and eaten with bread, accompanied by wine. Other than in a Portuguese specialty store, it can be difficult to obtain in the United States. The very lean Italian Parma ham is a perfect substitute.

Rice

Both long-grained rice and short-grained rice are used in Portuguese cooking. Long-grained rice is used for most savory dishes while the shorter grains are used in soups and for traditional rice puddings. Here in the United States, some Portuguese cooks use converted rice in place of the regular long-grain rice because they like its fluffiness.

Salt Cod

Salt cod (bacalhau) *is a dry, salt-cured codfish that must be reconstituted before use. Traditionally, cod was salted aboard the fishing boats; back on shore, the salted fish were laid out in the sun to dry. This method preserved the fish for a long time. Portuguese cooking makes frequent use of salt cod.*

Purchasing and Preparing Salt Cod

The best salt cod comes from the cold waters of Norway, but it is becoming increasingly available in North American markets. Portuguese cooks prefer large fillets of salt cod, containing bones and skin, which are removed after the fish is soaked or cooked. These fillets give maximum flavor. Salt cod fillets are available boned and skinned. They can also be purchased in smaller pieces, packed either in wooden boxes or on foam trays, wrapped in plastic.

The day or two before the fish is to be used, rinse and cut the fillets into approximately 4-inch pieces or the size called for by your recipe. Place them in a large bowl and cover by at least 2 inches with cold tap water. Soak the codfish, refrigerated, for 16 to 24, even 36 hours if need be, changing the water several times to re-hydrate the fish and remove some of the salt. To prepare a codfish dish for tomorrow night's dinner, for example, start soaking the cod late this afternoon, changing the water 2 to 3 times before you retire for the evening and 4 more times tomorrow before using.

If you are preparing large fillets that have skin and bones, soaking make take as long as 48 hours. Frequent changes of water hasten the process. Smaller pieces of fish (about ½ pound) may take 16 to 24 hours or as little as 10 hours if you change the water frequently. Near the end of the soaking period, taste a small piece of the fish. If it is still too salty for your taste, change the water again and soak it longer. If you are soaking more than 2 pounds of fish, use more than one bowl. Remember that salt can always be added back in at the end of cooking, but if too much salt remains after the presoak, the finished dish will be irredeemably salty. At the end of soaking, the fish should have a mild taste of salt. There is a fine line between removing too much and not enough of the salt. If the fish is oversoaked, flavor is lost, resulting in a tasteless piece of fish. Bear in mind soaking times vary not only with the amount of fish but the degree of saltiness, which varies from batch to bach. The times are given merely as a guide.

Precooking Salt Cod

Some recipes call for the previously soaked salt cod to be precooked or poached before it is used in the dish. The following method is the one I prefer, and recommend, for most cod dishes.

1. Bring a pan of water, large enough to accommodate the fish, to a full boil. Turn off the heat.
2. Rinse the presoaked fish again and add to the pan. Cover and allow to sit for 15 to 30 minutes (depending on the thickness of the fish), until the cod is opaque or flakes easily. Remove the smaller pieces as they become opaque.
3. Drain the cod, discard bones and skin, if present, and place the fish in a bowl. Cover with scalded milk. Cover the bowl and let stand for 1 hour. Drain, taste again for salt, and use the fish as needed.

Note: Soaking the fish in scalded milk is a trick I learned in Portugal. The milk helps the fish retain its moisture and tenderness. Not all Portuguese cooks soak the cod this way, however. I do it both ways: I do not use milk when I make Codfish Cakes (page 61), but I find it improves baked salt cod dishes to which little or no extra moisture is added.

Sausages

Flavorful smoked sausages are part of the fabric of Portuguese cooking. A variety of sausages, made with various cuts of pork and by-products, are popular any time of the year. Pork meat is cut into pieces and infused with a marinade or seasoning before being stuffed into casings and smoked. Sausages are commonly grilled, added in slices or chunks to soups, seafood, poultry, and even beef dishes. Since the sausage is already cooked during smoking, it needs only to be heated through; overcooking can dry out sausage. Chapter 5 describes the common sausage types (page 127) and contains instructions for sausage-making with specific recipes.

Seafood

The Portuguese have always taken advantage of the availability of different varieties of fish and shellfish. Many Portuguese Americans live near the coasts in the United States and still make a living from the sea. Others buy haddock, scrod, fresh tuna, halibut, and other white fish in fish markets.

Cockles (*amêijoas*) These tiny sweet clams from the waters off of Portugal are traditionally used in Pork with Clams Alentejo-Style (page 98). They are difficult to find in the United States. I suggest small littleneck clams, which make an excellent substitute.

Sardines (*sardinhas*) Sardines are a naturally oily fish with a flavor similar to mackerel, but milder. They are a healthful source of calcium and beneficial fatty acids. Americans generally are familiar only with canned sardines, packed in olive or vegetable oil (now soy and canola oils, too). The canned sardines are great in sandwiches. Fresh sardines that are 2 to 3 inches in size are called *petingas*. They are easily pan-fried or baked and eaten bones and all. Larger sardines (5 to 6 inches) are baked or grilled over charcoal. Fresh (or fast-frozen) sardines are necessary for the recipes in this book; canned sardines cannot be substituted.

Tinker Mackerel (*carapaus*) These little fish of the mackerel family are usually gutted, salted, and fried. Larger ones, called *chicharro*, are more oily and are likely to be grilled.

Cleaning or Dressing Fish

1. Using a pair of kitchen scissors, cut off the fins at the top, sides, and belly of the fish.
2. With the edge of one scissor blade, scrape off the scales.
3. Place the point of the scissors at the belly fin, and snip along the ridge of the belly to the vent, located midway toward the tail. With your index finger, reach inside the belly and pull out and discard the innards of the fish.
4. Rinse well and pat dry, ready for your intended preparation.

When Portugal took to the sea centuries ago, its explorers had no idea what lay ahead. At that time, the spice trade depended on overland routes that were dangerous because of thieves and costly because of high tariffs at foreign borders. The discovery of an alternate route—by sea—that avoided the overland dangers, turned out to be more than the country had hoped for. Portugal became Europe's marketplace for spices. In those times, only the wealthy could afford the costly imports. Today, we have access to the widest range of spices imaginable in our global market. The following spices are traditional in Portuguese cooking.

Cinnamon (*canela*) A sweet, spicy, and aromatic spice, cinnamon is used mostly in desserts. It comes in stick and powdered forms. The stick form is commonly used to scent puddings during the cooking process. The powdered version is blended into mixtures and sprinkled onto dishes. There are different varieties of cinnamon. Two of the most popular are Ceylon, a subtle-flavored cinnamon, and Cassia, which has a stronger flavor and darker color. For decorating Sweet Rice Pudding (page 195), I prefer the Ceylon cinnamon. When I rub the ground spice of Ceylon between my fingers, the release of the cinnamon is easier to control.

Cumin (*cominhos*) This pungent spice is used in vinegar sauces and seafood and meat dishes. Sometimes it is used to season Portuguese blood sausages. Cumin, when used judiciously, is well suited to certain dishes. It is a love-it or hate-it spice that one might need to acquire a taste for. Although it is traditionally used in seed form and ground with a mortar and pestle, cumin powder can be used instead, reducing the amount called for by half.

Curry Powder (*caril*) This mixture of spices is used occasionally to season seafood and meat, giving color in addition to flavor.

Nutmeg (*noz-moscada*) Nutmeg is used in moderation for seasoning meat stews, vinegar sauces, and *tortas* (a Portuguese omelette snack). It is not very often used in desserts. Best when freshly ground, only a small amount is needed to flavor a dish.

Paprika (*colorau*) Hungarian sweet paprika is not Portuguese in origin, but it should be. Used for centuries by the Portuguese, paprika is typically used in some regions of Portugal in dishes that other regions flavor with red pepper paste, *massa de pimentão*. Sometimes, it is used in combination with *massa de pimentão*. Today Spanish and Portuguese paprika is also used.

Pepper (*pimenta*) The fruit of tropical plants, white and black pepper corns are not related to chili peppers. Freshly ground pepper is best. White is preferred in white sauce and in fish dishes where black specks might be unattractive. White pepper gives a subtle but hotter flavor than black. The choice is a matter of personal taste.

Safflower (*açafrôa*) Transplanted here with seeds from Portugal, *carthamus tinctorius* is an annual that grows in many Portuguese gardens in the United States. The plant has prickly-edged oval leaves on stalks that are two to three feet tall. The globe-shaped flower has maroon threadlike petals with yellow tips. Under the thin petals, a white sphere holds the seeds, promising next season's harvest. It is the petals, which are first dried and then crushed, that are used to flavor some Portuguese dishes. Safflower is high in linoleic acid, one of the essential fatty acids. Do not confuse safflower with saffron, which comes from a crocus flower. Those who are allergic to ragweed may be severely allergic to safflower as well. Saffron or paprika can be used as a substitute.

Saffron (*açafrão*) This spice is popular, especially in Spanish cooking. The harvested stigmas of the crocus flower add yellow color and subtle flavor. Crumble and soak in a bit of water for 15 minutes before using.

Salt (*sal*) Coarse sea salt or kosher salt will bring out the best flavor of ingredients. Coarse salt does not contain additives to keep it from caking. The amount of salt given in these recipes is based on the Portuguese palate. Also, equal measures of table salt and coarse salt are not equally salty, because the coarse salt is less dense. So be sure to adjust the amount of salt to your liking—smaller amounts if you're using table salt—and taste as you season. Salt should be added toward the end of cooking, after any juice or broth has had time to reduce. Dishes that contain sausages, salt cod, or canned substitutions should be tasted before you add salt. Reserve the table salt for baking.

13

Tomatoes

Another important ingredient in making a *refogado* (see page 10), tomatoes impart a distinctive flavor to the base of some stews and seafood dishes. Meaty, red, ripe, flavorful tomatoes that are peeled and chopped, work well in most Portuguese recipes. It is not essential to remove the seeds. It is a matter of personal preference. The seeds carry much of the flavor, and I prefer to remove them only for aesthetic reasons in certain dishes. When flavorful tomatoes are not available, especially in winter, high-quality canned tomatoes or a small amount of tomato paste can be used. Ever since tomato paste became available to them, many Portuguese cooks use it readily for its concentrated tomato flavor.

Heart of the Ox/Bull (*coração de boi/toro*) This tomato, named for its large heart shape, is a popular Portuguese variety. Like other varieties of vegetables grown in the homeland, *coração de boi* tomatoes were brought here by Portuguese immigrants and cultivated. A meaty tomato with outstanding flavor and minimal seeds, it is grown in many Portuguese-American home gardens. The familiar American favorite beefsteak or Italian plum tomatoes also yield good results in Portuguese dishes.

Peeling Tomatoes

To peel a tomato easily, cut an X through the bottom skin. Dip tomato into boiling water for 10 seconds. Plunge into a bowl of ice water. Skins should easily peel from the tomato. Another method works when the tomatoes are very ripe and slightly soft. Rub the edge of the blade of a paring knife over the skin. With the point of the knife, gently pierce one end of the tomato and peel off the skin. If you wish to remove the seeds, cut the tomatoes horizontally and gently squeeze the seeds out. Slice plum tomatoes vertically to remove the seeds. Another method to remove tomato skin is with a vegetable peeler—a method I have used in a pinch if the tomato skin isn't quite soft.

Vinegar

Vinegar plays a part in the dressing of salad, marinades, and vinegar sauces. Both red wine vinegar and white wine vinegar are used. Apple cider vinegar, which my uncle Ilidio claims was introduced to Portugal after World War II, is now popular as well and used for salads as an alternative to wine vinegar.

Wine

Just as necessary as bread and soup, wine has its place in the Portuguese meal. However, wine is more than a beverage. It is intrinsic to the wine and garlic marinades (pages 168–69) that are used to flavor meats and fish. (See Chapter 10.)

SEASONING METHODS

Throughout this book, you will notice certain recurring spice and seasoning combinations, although the amounts may differ or another variable may be added, giving each recipe its own character. The following are a few typical combinations of spices and seasonings.

Herb and Spice Paste This heady, aromatic combination is one of the first things I learned to make at my father's elbow. The mixture is used to season meats and poultry. Garlic is mashed with a mortar and pestle, blended with coarse salt, crumbled bay leaf, a light touch of Sweet Red Pepper Paste (*Massa de Pimentão*), parsley, olive oil, and freshly ground pepper. This blending of seasonings is the hallmark of Portuguese cuisine, especially in the Alentejo region. Some regions use paprika and coarse salt in place of *massa de pimentão*. Other regions may include cumin, safflower, or other spice. Proportions vary according to personal taste. Although the ingredients sound rather ordinary, they interact with the main ingredient being seasoned and produce something extraordinary. (Recipe page 166).

Sweet Red Pepper Paste (*massa de pimentão*) This is a paste of sweet red peppers that have been cured in coarse salt. It is a traditional ingredient, most popular in the Alentejo province. Often used to flavor meats, especially pork dishes, it is also an ingredient in the basic herb and spice paste (above) and in the Alentejo's *linguiça* sausage. Although there is no substitute for *massa de pimentão,* some regions use paprika in its place.

Wine and Garlic Marinades (*vinho d'alho*) Marinating is a common method of seasoning and tenderizing meats and fish. Amounts of wine and garlic vary according to individual preferences (recipes, pages 168–69). Sometimes a marinade is used in combination with a seasoning paste.

EQUIPMENT

Very few special items are needed for creating Portuguese dishes in your own kitchen. I am one in a small group of Portuguese cooks who gather once a month to prepare a dinner for about 200 people for our monthly social. Before we begin, one cook usually asks the others if they are ready. With a sheepish smile a fellow cook replies, "I have my knife—that is all I need," as the paring knife is produced. As much as we joke about it, it is almost literally true. A Portuguese cook, it is said, needs little more than her hands and a sharp, trusty paring knife. The "knife" is nothing more than a squared-off, 1-inch wide by 4-inch long carbon blade with a round wooden handle. This style of paring knife, owned by many Portuguese, is a utility knife, commonly used by leather workers, like my father, to trim hides in the leather industry. These knives are still available today. I purchased mine in a local hardware store. A few pots, a mortar and pestle, sieve, and bowls, of course, make up the rest. The following more up-to-date items make Portuguese cooking a breeze. I encourage you to use the additional modern conveniences of food processors, electric mixers, and the like, to make your cooking easier.

Cheese Molds Although some kitchen specialty shops carry ceramic molds with perforated bottoms for making cheese, molds for making fresh cheese can be fashioned inexpensively at home. Use plastic food containers (for example, deli takeout containers, margarine tubs) in any size up to one pound. For the Fresh Cheese (page 160), you will need containers to hold approximately two pounds of cheese. With the tip of a razor-sharp craft or utility knife, cut slashes in the bottom and around the sides to allow the whey to drain from the curd. Clean fruit or tunafish cans can also be used. Simply remove the lids from both ends of the can and with a metal punch, make holes in the sides.

Colander or Sieve If you don't own a food mill, pull out this common kitchen tool. Place over the pot and use a fork or spoon to press vegetables or beans through the holes. Use cooking liquid to keep things moving. A fine-mesh sieve is perfect for making cheese; a baker's sieve is even better. Make sure the sieves are of stainless steel.

Food Mill In the evolution of kitchen equipment, the food mill, which we call a *passador* ("pass through"), replaced the colander and fork for puréeing. It is a labor-saving tool when it comes to puréeing vegetables, especially legumes, in Portuguese soups. It has a perforated bottom and some sort of blade that is cranked to press the meaty parts of vegetables or legumes through while screening back seeds and skins. To use, simply place a food mill over a pot or bowl. Ladle cooked ingredients into the food mill, turn the hand crank to process through, adding broth or other recipe liquid as needed. There are many types available at kitchen specialty shops.

Hand-held Blender This appliance the Portuguese call *varinha mágica,* "magic wand," lets you purée seedless and skinless ingredients right in the container they are cooked or served in. To purée soup, remove the pan from the heat, place the blade end of the blender into the pot and process until desired texture is achieved. Return the pan to the stove and continue with the recipe. Available at kitchen specialty shops.

Kale Cutter A hand-cranked device that clamps to the table, it is used primarily to cut kale into a fine chiffonnade for the soup known as *Caldo Verde* (page 23). This handy kitchen tool "shaves" the greens into perfect thin slivers in seconds. Available at Portuguese markets, usually through special order.

Meat Grinder A hand-cranked meat grinder that clamps to the table or a grinder attachment to a freestanding electric mixer is very useful in making codfish cakes and sausages. It is available in kitchen shops.

Mortar and Pestle The mortar, a small bowl, and pestle, a short, dowel-shaped tool, are used to pound and blend ingredients such as spices together. They are made in various sizes out of wood, stone, or marble. It is an indispensable tool. Mashing and blending garlic with other ingredients using a mortar and pestle produces a paste that is significantly different from what a food processor will whip up. The food processor, or the chef's knife, simply cuts the garlic, but the pestle mashes one element into another, pulverizing them and releasing their essences, and then marrying the flavors thoroughly. It is the Portuguese cook's secret tool for seasoning main ingredients. In a pinch, use a small or medium (preferably wooden) bowl with a fork or the smoothed end of a short wooden dowel.

"LITTLE TASTES" ~ *Petiscos*

Appetizers as we call them today, were not traditionally part of a Portuguese family meal. As my Uncle Ilidio would say, "What was an appetizer? The people were poor; there wasn't any such thing as an appetizer." After a hard day's work, appetites did not need stimulation. What was served were simple starters or accompaniments. In most Portuguese homes, bread and olives are still always on the table. Roasted peppers, marinated lupini beans (*tremoços*), sautéed *linguiça* sausage, or fresh cheese may be included. A few slices of *presunto,* a salt-cured ham (like Italian prosciutto), with bread, or perhaps a wedge of melon, would be served. The following list are recipes that lend themselves to a light course or snack, and can be used as *petiscos,* "little tastes." Savory pastries, *salgados,* can also be included on the appetizer table.

Shrimp Soup with White Beans, page 37

2

SOUPS

Sopas

Light or hearty, soup has always been a mainstay of the Portguese diet. When I was growing up, soup and bread were served in our house every day. Sometimes, we had the same delicious soup for supper we had had for lunch. Created from the most humble ingredients, classic soups, soups with strange names, and nameless soups, were the lifeline to survival for many of Portugal's poor and especially Portuguese immigrants. Soups in Portugal, especially the Alentejo region, began with bread, olive oil, water, and garlic. This became a bread soup known as *Açorda* (page 43). Variations were created by adding native wild plants gathered in the field. *Sopa de Pedra* (page 38), my grandfather told me, is a soup that actually began with a stone! (The story of stone soup is retold on page 38.)

In the peasant kitchen, it is unusual for stock to be made ahead. Any meat, poultry, or fish flavor is obtained when the ingredient is used as part of the dish itself. Water is the primary liquid ingredient. Sometimes wine is added. If by chance there is broth remaining from a stew or braise, frugal cooks use it for making soup. In the hands of my great-grandmother Ana, an ounce of necessity and a pinch of creativity would transform the aromatic broth remaining from a Portuguese boiled dinner, *Cozido à Portuguesa* (page 117), or the liquid from cooking beans, into a flavorful soup. Actually, many soups began as the "soup of the pot," or *sopa de panela* as my grandmother would call it. In the old days, the recipe was according to whatever ingredients were on hand, as with any pot luck soup or "soup of the day"—pasta, beans, diced leftover vegetables from the boiled dinner or diced fresh vegetables. Today, I chill leftover broth, remove and discard any solidified fat, and strain the liquid. The ingredients are then combined with the reserved broth, creating a satisfying meal; no additional seasoning is necessary. Nothing is wasted.

Preparations for some soups begin with soaking legumes or salting meats a day ahead. Some start with a base of potatoes, beans, or other vegetables puréed with water. The addition of chopped vegetables gives texture to the soup, and starches (potatoes, rice, bread, and beans) add body. It is very common for potatoes, rice, and beans to be served together in some combination, either in the same meal or even in the same soup, to make it more substantial.

We know that if our children are picky eaters when it comes to vegetables, they will at least get their nutrients from our soups. Our vegetarian friends also enjoy these soups simply by eliminating any sausage or other meat.

For a satisfying and nourishing meal, ladle out a bowl of hearty soup and cut some thick slices from a crusty wheat bread or dense cornbread loaf. Add some regional olives and wine. *Boa apetite!*

Vegetable Soup
Sopa de Legumes
Serves 6

Sopa de legumes, *nicknamed simply Portuguese soup or* sopa à Portuguesa, *by Portuguese-Americans, is one of the more popular soups served in our homes. This version is that of my friend Isaura Nogueira, who includes pork ribs with carrots, green beans, white kidney beans, cabbage, and kale. The ribs add depth of flavor while the combination of vegetables deliver full texture to this nutritious soup. This soup can be easily transformed into a cholesterol-free vegetarian dish by omitting the pork and adding an extra tablespoon of olive oil to the pot.*

Day ahead:
½ pound (1¼ cups) dried white kidney beans
1 pound meaty pork ribs
2 tablespoons coarse salt

1. Soak the beans overnight in enough water to cover by 2 inches, about 4 cups.
2. Rub the pork ribs with the salt, cover, and refrigerate.

Next day, for the broth:
12 cups water
2 medium starchy potatoes, peeled and cut into 1-inch cubes (about 2 cups)
1 medium carrot (6 to 7 inches long), peeled, and roughly chopped (about ½ cup)
1 medium very ripe tomato, peeled, seeded, and coarsely chopped (about 1 cup)

1. Wipe excess salt from the meat and place in a 5-quart stockpot. Drain and rinse the beans. Add to the pot with the 12 cups of fresh water, potatoes, carrot, and tomatoes. Cover and bring to a boil over high heat.
2. Reduce the heat and simmer for approximately 40 minutes or until the vegetables are very tender and the meat is nearly falling off the bones.
3. Remove the pork ribs to a platter, cover, and set aside in a warm place. Using a food mill, purée the vegetables with the broth to a smooth consistency.

For the soup:
¾ pound fresh flat-leaf kale or collard greens, rinsed, trimmed of thick middle rib, and coarsely chopped (about 4 cups) (page 8)
3 cups coarsely chopped Savoy cabbage
½ pound green beans, cut into ¼-inch pieces (about 2 cups)
1 large onion, finely chopped (about 1½ cups)
1 medium carrot, coarsely chopped (about ½ cup)
½ cup pasta (such as elbow macaroni)
3 tablespoons olive oil
1 tablespoon coarse salt or to taste
⅛ teaspoon black pepper

1. Bring the puréed broth to a boil over medium-high heat. Add the kale, cabbage, green beans, onion, carrot, pasta, olive oil, salt, and pepper. Reduce the heat to medium-low. Cover and gently simmer for about 15 minutes, until the vegetables are tender and the pasta is cooked.
2. Remove the meat from the bones, cut into serving-size pieces, and serve on the side. Provide plenty of crusty country bread to dip in the broth.

Note: The meat can also be returned to the pot instead of being served on the side.

21

THE ART OF CHIFFONNADE

One of the soups most associated with Portuguese cooking is Green Broth Soup, caldo verde. Equally important as the standardized ingredients of caldo verde, is the chiffonnade, greens cut into grass-like slivers—the signature of this soup. When our children were young, they would even ask for "grass soup," which raised an eyebrow or two when other parents learned from their children what Nancy and Marc were having for dinner.

I learned the art of chiffonnade by watching my father. After rinsing the kale and trimming the thick middle rib, he stacked several leaves and rolled them up tightly, lengthwise. Holding this log-shaped bundle in one hand and taking up a sharp knife with the other, he cut very thin slivers of kale—as if paring an apple— until we had enough for the soup. In all the years that I have used this method, I have had innumerable "green thumbs," but I have never cut myself. I doubt any culinary instructor would encourage this method. It does, however, give new meaning to the expression "green thumb." I recommend the safer use of a cutting board and a sharp chef knife or kale cutter (page 16). (If you use a cutting board to cut greens into chiffonnade, make diagonal cuts; otherwise, any long strands of greens will need to be torn or cut into 2-inch pieces. A kale cutter cuts the greens to just the right size.)

22

Green Broth Soup

Green Broth Soup

Caldo Verde

Serves 4 to 6

Although oral history places the origin of this soup in the northern Minho province of Portugal, it is enjoyed throughout the country. The traditional ingredients of potatoes, Galega kale (page 8), olive oil, and sautéed linguiça, a mild Portuguese smoked sausage, mingle in a hot pot to create this classic named for the color of the broth. Variations in the ratio of water to potatoes are evident from region to region and cook to cook. The soup should have a body like light cream. If it is too thick, thin it with a small amount of water, about ½ cup. The puréed potato broth with a very fine chiffonnade of kale is the signature of this soup. My family enjoys this dish with plenty of kale, but feel free to add less if you wish. Ladle the soup into bowls and serve, as tradition dictates, with a single slice of sautéed linguiça floating in the broth.

6 cups water

5 medium Maine or Yukon Gold or other starchy potatoes, peeled and quartered (about 5 cups)

1 small yellow onion, finely chopped (about ½ cup)

1 tablespoon coarse salt or to taste

1 bunch (1½ pounds before trimming) flat-leaf kale or collard greens

5 tablespoons olive oil

¼ pound *chouriço* or *linguiça* (page 12), sliced very thin (scant ¼-inch thick)

1. In a 4-quart stockpot, combine the water, potatoes, and onion. Cover and bring to a boil over high heat. Reduce the heat to medium-low, season with salt, then simmer until the potatoes are very tender, 20 to 30 minutes.

2. Meanwhile, trim the kale leaves of the thick central stem at the back of the leaf. Rinse the leaves well in a sink full of cool water. Lift out to drain. Read over the instructions on the previous page for how to properly cut the kale. Be sure that the strands of kale are no greater than a couple of inches in length. Continue cutting until you have about 6 cups. Set aside.

3. When the potatoes are cooked, purée the contents of the soup pot to a smooth consistency. Return to a boil.

4. Add the reserved greens and the olive oil. Simmer until the greens are bright green and tender, but not mushy, approximately 5 minutes.

5. In a skillet, brown the sausage slices, turning to color both sides and reserve.

6. Serve the soup in the traditional manner with one slice of the sausage added to each bowl. Any extra sausage is served on the side.

Tip: Most Portuguese soups thicken as they cool because of the starch they contain. Once they are reheated, the broth loosens up. It's okay, though, to add a small amount of water, if necessary, to help it along.

Note: Adjust the amount of kale or collard greens and potatoes to your preference.

23

Kale Soup
Sopa de Couves
Serves 8 to 10

Sumptuous and heart warming, this soup hits the spot on a cold winter's night or after a long day's work. My father always added yellow turnip, called rutabaga in some parts of North America, to this classic Portuguese soup. If yellow turnip is unavailable, use white turnip. Be sure to peel the turnip of its waxy coating. My Aunt Ana likes to include carrots for additional flavor. In the Alentejo where beef was scarce, my grandmother used the more plentiful lamb or pork for this dish. In the United States, she frequently alternated them with the beef shin included here. The kale is traditionally torn into pieces (page 8), but you can chop it. My family uses Maine potatoes for this soup, but Red Bliss or new potatoes hold their shape better. The choice lies with the texture you prefer.

1 pound (2½ cups) dried red kidney beans soaked overnight in enough water to cover by 2 inches

3 pounds beef shinbone, trimmed of excess fat

1 medium onion, coarsely chopped (about 1 cup)

2 garlic cloves, finely chopped

1 bay leaf

12 cups water (3 quarts)

1½ cups cubed yellow turnip (rutabaga) (1-inch cubes)

¾ pound *salpicão* or *chouriço* (page 12)

3 medium Maine, Red Bliss, or new potatoes, peeled and cut into 1-inch cubes (about 2½ to 3 cups)

1 to 2 carrots, peeled and sliced into ¼-inch slices (about 1 cup) (optional)

¼ teaspoon dry crushed red pepper (page 4) (optional)

¼ cup pasta, such as elbow macaroni

1 bunch (1½ pounds) fresh kale or collard greens, rinsed, trimmed of center rib, and torn into 1- to 2-inch pieces (page 8)

¼ cup olive oil

1 tablespoon coarse salt or to taste

¼ teaspoon black pepper

1. Drain and rinse the beans.

2. In a 5-quart stockpot, place the beans, beef shin, onions, garlic, and bay leaf. Pour in approximately 3 quarts of water or enough to cover the beef by about 1 inch. Cover, bring to a boil, then reduce the heat to medium-low. Simmer the beef and beans, occasionally skimming from the broth any impurities, for 1½ hours.

3. When the beans are very tender, remove about 1 cup to a small dish. Mash the beans with a fork, adding some of the broth, then return the paste to the pot. (If you do not like bean skins floating in the broth, pass the beans through a food mill, sieve, or colander, adding some of the broth as necessary. The skins should be all that remains in the colander or food mill. Return the beans to the pot.)

4. Add the turnip to the pot. Return the broth to a boil, then reduce the heat and simmer for 20 minutes.

5. If using *salpicão,* you may need to first trim a metal clip from one end of the sausage and the casing string from the other before cooking. Add with the potatoes, carrots, and crushed red pepper. Continue to simmer until the vegetables are almost cooked, about 20 minutes.

24

6. Add the pasta, kale, olive oil, salt, and pepper to the pot, and simmer for about 15 to 20 minutes. Soup is ready when the pasta is done and the kale is tender.

7. Remove the beef shin from the pot, trim away and discard any gristle and fat, along with the bone. Cut the meat into pieces. Remove the sausage from the pot and cut into chunks. If *salpicão* is used, peel and discard the casing before cutting sausage. Serve the meat on the side, as part of a second course, or return it to the pot and heat through. Serve hot with plenty of crusty bread to dip in the broth.

Tip: Adding the kale about 5 minutes before adding the pasta ensures tender kale and more *al dente* pasta, if that is your preference.

Note: *Salpicão* is the one sausage that, for some reason, needs to have the casing removed before serving. The reason seems to have been long forgotten; it is just one of those culinary quirks.

São Miguel, Azores

Turnip Green Soup with Rice

Sopa de Nabiça com Arroz

Serves 6

Very young, tender turnip greens are essential to this distinctive soup. Loaded with nutrients, the greens add unique flavor. The chouriço *sausage provides the right counterpoint for the slightly bitter leaves.*

3 tablespoons olive oil

1 small onion, finely chopped (about ½ cup)

1 clove garlic, finely chopped

4 cups water

2 medium Maine or Yukon Gold potatoes, peeled and coarsely chopped (about 2 cups)

1 tablespoon short-grain rice

¼ pound *chouriço* (page 12), cut into ½-inch slices

2 teaspoons coarse salt or to taste

¼ teaspoon pepper or to taste

½ teaspoon dry crushed red pepper (optional)

3 cups tender turnip greens, coarsely chopped

1. Heat the olive oil in a 4-quart stockpot. Add the onions and sauté over medium-high heat until soft and translucent, about 5 minutes. Toss in the garlic, cooking until slightly aromatic, about one minute.

2. Add the water and the potatoes. Cover and bring to a boil. Reduce the heat to medium-low and simmer until the potatoes are very tender, 20 to 30 minutes. Use a slotted spoon to remove the potatoes to a dish. Coarsely mash the potatoes with a fork and return to the broth. Or, for a smooth consistency, purée the entire contents of the pot. A hand-held blender makes the job easy.

3. Return the soup to a boil. Add the rice, *chouriço*, and seasoning. Reduce the heat, cover, and simmer for 15 minutes, until the rice is not quite done.

4. Add the greens. Re-cover and continue simmering until the rice is done and the greens are just tender, about 7 to 10 minutes. Serve hot, accompanied by olives and plenty of crusty bread.

Variation: Mustard greens and broccoli rabe make excellent substitutes for the turnip greens in this recipe. My father would harvest the mustard greens from his garden in the spring when they were especially young and tender. Some of his friends used broccoli rabe. To use, rinse the greens well in cold water. Discard any mottled or older leaves. Chop and add when the rice is nearly done. Cover and simmer for just 5 minutes. These tender greens cook quickly.

Chicken Feet

In the earlier years of my marriage, chicken feet became difficult to find in supermarkets. Fortunately, my friend Nancy had a son who was learning animal husbandry at a local agricultural school. Every spring, chickens were slaughtered for market, and the chickens' feet were discarded. When I mentioned this "little dilemma" of mine to Nancy, she offered the services of her son Joe. Expecting a few chicken feet, try to imagine my surprise and excitement when Joe brought me a bag of ninety-eight—that's right, ninety-eight chicken feet. Word reached my husband's secretary that I had a mother load of chicken feet in my freezer. She quickly called me and asked, with controlled excitement, "You've got chicken feet?" "Yes," I replied. "Would you like some?" The answer was clear, and the very next day my husband found himself driving down Route 128 in disbelief—transporting a load of chicken feet.

Chicken Broth

Canja
Serves 6

When my father and I sat down to eat this simple chicken soup, which appeared frequently on the Sunday dinner table, he always included the chicken feet. We would make little deals about who would get such choice parts! Can you guess who got the feet? (Hint: Dad was easily charmed.) The name canja is Asian (Concani or Malay), which suggests that the recipe was picked up by navigators during the era of discovery. Like other peoples, the Portuguese turn to chicken soup for comfort when they feel under the weather. The simplicity of the ingredients allow the full flavor of the chicken to come through. Sometimes my grandmother used a whole chicken. I can still see her, removing the chicken from her large white enamel soup pot, before it was completely cooked. She added additional spices, draped the chicken with bacon, and finished roasting it in the oven. Her canja would be just the broth, a very small amount of pasta or rice, and the gizzard, heart, and feet of the chicken. The roasted chicken served as the second course. When a whole roasted chicken was not planned for dinner, my grandmother made this soup with chicken pieces. She deboned the meat after cooking and added some chicken meat to the soup as well.

2½ pounds chicken pieces (legs, thighs, backs, necks)
chicken gizzard and heart
2 chicken feet, rubbed with coarse salt and
    rinsed well
6 cups water
½ cup short-grain rice or pasta (such as elbow
    macaroni)
1 tablespoon coarse salt or to taste
¼ teaspoon white pepper
lemon wedges (optional)
sprigs of mint for garnish

1. In a 4-quart stockpot, place the chicken pieces, gizzard, heart, and chicken feet, with 6 cups of water or enough water to cover the chicken by 1 inch. Cover and bring to a boil over high heat. Reduce the heat and simmer until the chicken is tender and nearly falling off the bone. Skim the broth of impurities as needed, about 25 minutes.
2. With the exception of the giblets and chicken feet, remove the chicken from the pot. Reserve the meat to serve on the side or use in another dish, except for a small amount called for in step 4.

3. Bring the broth to a boil again, then add rice or pasta if desired. Season with salt and pepper. Reduce the heat to medium-low and simmer about 20 minutes, until the rice is done—less time if using pasta.
4. Meanwhile, remove the meat from the bones and hand-shred enough to yield about 1 cup. When the pasta or rice is cooked, add the shredded chicken back to the soup. Heat through and serve with a mint leaf and a wedge of lemon.

Variation: A squirt of lemon juice often found its way to my father's bowl of *canja*. I, on the other hand, didn't appreciate its tangy flavor until I was older. It is an optional condiment to this dish.

Note: Chicken feet are a delicacy in many countries. They can be purchased today, fresh or frozen, at specialty or ethnic food stores. They are usually sold with the outside skin (a darker yellow) removed, revealing the pale yellow color, and with the nails trimmed. When cooked, the best part is the ball of the foot. Try it; you just might find it absolutely enticing.

27

Bean Soup

Sopa de Feijão

Serves 6

The simple and traditional Sopa de Feijão, *in the style of my father's hometown of Galveias, is one of the first soups my father taught me to prepare. He would set a colander over the soup pot and let me force the beans through the holes, using just a fork and some water. The lighter bean broth and the additional flavor of cilantro sets this one apart from other kale soups.*

½ pound (1¼ cups) dried red kidney or roman beans, soaked overnight in enough water to cover by 2 inches (about 4 cups)

6 cups water

1 bunch (about 1½ pounds before trimming) kale, rinsed and trimmed of thick center rib

3 cloves garlic, finely chopped

1 bay leaf

4 tablespoons olive oil

1 tablespoon finely chopped cilantro

1 tablespoon coarse salt or to taste

½ teaspoon black pepper

1. Drain and rinse the beans. Set aside.
2. Place the beans in a 4-quart stockpot with 6 cups of water. Cover and bring to a boil. Reduce the heat to medium-low and simmer for 1 hour or until the beans are very tender (easily mashed with a fork).
3. Stack the kale leaves, a few at a time, on top of one another. Roll lengthwise and slice crosswise into ½-inch-wide strips—like chiffonnade but wider. Cut the strips again, crosswise, into shorter lengths (about 2 inches). Set aside.
4. Remove about half of the beans from the stockpot and some of the cooking liquid. Use a food mill, colander, or sieve set over a bowl to process the beans; only bean skins should remain. Discard the skins and return the puréed beans to the stockpot with the garlic, bay leaf, and olive oil.
5. Return the soup to a boil. Add the kale, cilantro, salt, and pepper. Re-cover, reduce the heat, and simmer about 10 to 15 minutes, until the kale is tender, but not mushy. This soup can be served simply with crusty country bread and olives.

Tip: For best quality, don't use a hand-held blender to purée soups with beans. The little pieces of bean skins do not feel particularly good in the mouth.

Variations: Use white kidney beans (my grandfather's favorite), in place of red kidney beans. Flouting tradition, my father often added a small chunk of sausage to the pot.

28

Bean Soup with Tomato
Sopa de Feijão com Tomate
Serves 4 to 6

Rich with fiber and flavor, this soup has a wonderful body to it, which thickens as it cools. When our children, Nancy and Marc, were young, they would always ask me to make this soup. The thickness of the soup made it easier for them to feed themselves without spilling very much broth. The beans can be prepared in advance, making short time of the remaining preparations.

½ pound (1¼ cups) kidney beans, soaked overnight in enough water to cover by 2 inches (about 4 cups)

6 cups water

¼ cup olive oil

1 small onion, finely chopped (about ½ cup)

1 small very ripe tomato, peeled, seeded, and coarsely chopped (about ½ cup)

1 teaspoon sweet paprika

1 bay leaf

1 clove of garlic, finely chopped

1 large boiling (Maine) potato, cut into ½-inch cubes (about 1 cup)

¼ to ½ cup rice or elbow pasta

1 tablespoon finely chopped parsley

2 teaspoons coarse salt or to taste

½ teaspoon pepper

1. Drain and rinse the beans.

2. Into a 2-quart saucepan, place the beans with 3½ cups of the fresh water, enough to cover by 2 inches. Place the covered pot over medium-high heat and bring to a boil. Reduce the heat and simmer until the beans are very tender, about 40 minutes. Reserve with cooking liquid.

3. Heat the oil in a 3-quart stockpot and sauté the onion until soft and translucent, about 5 minutes. Add the tomato, paprika, bay leaf, and garlic. Cover and simmer until the tomato becomes soft and partially dissolved, about 15 minutes.

4. Set a food mill over the pot and purée half or all of the kidney beans into the pot, using the reserved cooking liquid and remaining fresh water. Add any unpuréed beans with the potatoes to the pot, cover, and bring to a boil.

5. Toss in the rice or pasta, parsley, salt, and pepper. Reduce the heat, cover, and simmer until the potatoes and rice or pasta are done, 25 to 30 minutes. Serve with plenty of crusty bread for dipping in the broth.

Variation: My Aunt Ana would sometimes skip the rice or pasta and potatoes. Instead she would add 2 cups of roughly cubed winter squash at step 4. I sometimes take this variation one step further and add roughly chopped fresh spinach in the last five minutes of cooking.

29

Carrot Soup
Sopa de Cenoura
Serves 6

With freshly harvested carrots, this is a truly wonderful dish that is easy to make and loaded with vitamin A. It's perfect in the fall and makes a delectable first course dish for a Thanksgiving dinner. A friend in Torres Vedras, a town north of Lisbon, made this unique soup for me and my husband while we were honeymooning in Portugal. I consider it unique because a straightforward puréed soup that does not require other ingredients to give it additional texture is unusual in Portuguese cooking.

4 tablespoons olive oil
1 small onion, coarsely chopped (about ½ cup)
¼ cup very ripe tomato, peeled, seeded, and
  coarsely chopped
1 clove garlic, left whole
1 pound carrots, peeled, and coarsely chopped
1 medium white sweet potato, peeled and
  chopped into 1-inch pieces (about 1 cup)
1 cup peeled and roughly chopped yellow turnip
  (rutabaga)
4 cups water
1 tablespoon coarse salt or to taste
⅛ teaspoon white pepper

1. Heat 2 tablespoons of the oil in a 4-quart stockpot over medium-high heat. Add and sauté the onion until a light golden color. Stir in the tomato and garlic. Reduce the heat to medium-low. Cover and continue cooking until the tomato is soft and partially dissolved, about 15 minutes.
2. Put in the carrots, sweet potato, and turnip. Pour in the water, cover, and bring to a boil over medium-high heat. Reduce the heat and simmer until the vegetables are very tender, about 30 to 40 minutes. Remove the pot from the heat and purée the soup (a hand-blender works well).
3. Stir in the remaining oil and season with salt and pepper. Bring the soup back to a boil, reduce the heat, and simmer for 2 more minutes, then serve.

Note: Regular white potatoes are typically used for this soup, but one day I found myself with only white sweet potatoes in my bin. Taught to use what I had on hand, I added one to the pot. The result was wonderful. Since then, I use a white sweet potato for this recipe; I like the way it rounds out the flavors. Try it both ways and see which you prefer.

Tip: For entertaining or special occasions, I dress this dish up with a drizzle of heavy cream.

Variation: For a change in color and texture, in step 3 add ¾ pound fresh spinach, coarsely chopped. Simmer for 5 minutes until the spinach is just tender.

Clockwise from top left: Chickpea Soup with Spinach (page 39), Carrot Soup (page 30), Shrimp Soup with White Beans (page 37), Green Broth Soup (page 23).

Fennel Soup

Sopa de Funcho

Serves 6 to 8

The Azorean Portuguese speak with great delight of this dish. Licorice flavor dominates this soup, and it is the Azoreans' most common use for fennel. The slightly sweet flavor comes from the feathery fennel leaves. The variety of fennel found in most supermarkets (sometimes incorrectly labeled anise), has a large, somewhat flattened white bulb at the base of the leafy stems. This is a good substitute for the wild version. Unfortunately, some markets remove most of the leafy stalks from the plant. Shop around for bulbs with the most greens. If you have the benefit of a local farmers' market, you may find fennel bulbs with the fine leaves still intact. Lucia Rebelo, who is from Terceira (the "third" island to be discovered in the Azores), adds pig's knuckles for extra flavor. I prefer the less fatty ribs of pork. My uncle Joe Ortins says his mother, who was born on the island of Graciosa, added some carrots to the broth. You can also make this soup without any meat. The following version was inspired by my husband's cousin, Evelyn Ortins Cunha, who is a natural cook.

Day ahead:

½ pound (1½ cups) dried white kidney beans
1 pound pork ribs or pig's knuckle

1. Soak beans overnight in enough water to cover by 2 inches.
2. Rub the meat with 2 tablespoons coarse salt and chill overnight.

Next day:

8 cups water
2 dense bunches feathery fennel leaves or 2 fennel (anise) bulbs with green leaves
1 medium onion, finely chopped (about 1 cup)
5 cloves garlic, finely chopped
1 bay leaf
⅛ teaspoon ground cloves
⅛ teaspoon black pepper
3 Savoy cabbage leaves coarsely chopped (about 1 cup) (optional)
3 large new potatoes, peeled and cut into 1-inch cubes (about 3 cups)
1 bunch scallions, dark green stems removed, thinly sliced crosswise (about ½ cup)
3 tablespoons olive oil
½ pound *linguiça* (page 12), cut into ⅛-inch rounds

1. Drain and rinse the beans. Set aside.
2. Wipe any excess salt from the ribs and place in a 4-quart stockpot with the beans and water. Cover, place over medium-high heat, and bring to a boil. Reduce the heat and simmer until the meat is tender and the beans are easily mashed (about 1 hour). Occasionally skim the surface of any impurities.
3. Meanwhile, trim and discard coarse stems from the fine feathery fennel leaves. Finely chop enough leaves to yield 2 cups. (If you are using fennel bulbs, discard the outer layer. Separate sections of the bulbs, rinse well, and coarsely chop) Set fennel aside.
4. Add the onion, garlic, bay leaf, cloves, and black pepper to the pot. Simmer 5 minutes, then toss in the fennel leaves, and chopped bulb if using, along with the cabbage, potatoes, scallions, olive oil, and sausage. Return the soup to a boil, reduce the heat to medium-low, and continue to simmer until the potatoes are done and the cabbage is tender, about 20 minutes. Usually this soup needs no additional salt, but taste and season to your preference.

Health Note: Replace the salt pork with an additional 2 tablespoons of olive oil.

Onion Soup
Sopa de Cebola
Serves 4 to 6

My grandmother Teresa's tasty version of onion soup is lightly flavored with tomato and quite different from the French variety. She would fry the onions until just translucent, but I like to bring out the sweetness of the onions by sautéing them until they are golden.

3 tablespoons olive oil

3 medium onions, thinly sliced (about 3 cups)

1 small very ripe tomato, peeled, seeded, and finely chopped (about a scant ½ cup)

½ teaspoon paprika

1 bay leaf

4 cups water

2 medium starchy potatoes, peeled and cut roughly into ½-inch cubes (about 2 cups)

1 tablespoon finely chopped parsley

1 tablespoon coarse salt or to taste

¼ teaspoon pepper

eggs, 1 per person

4 to 6 slices day-old country bread, toasted or fried in olive oil

1. Heat the olive oil in a 3-quart saucepan over medium-high heat. Add and sauté the onion until translucent or lightly golden, about 15 minutes.

2. Put in the tomato, paprika, and bay leaf and cover. Cook over medium-low heat, stirring occasionally, until the tomato becomes soft and mixture is partially dissolved, about 15 minutes.

3. Add the water, potatoes, parsley, salt, and pepper. Cover and bring to a boil. Reduce the heat and simmer until the potatoes are tender but not mushy.

4. Place a slice of toasted or fried bread into each soup bowl. Ladle the soup over the bread. To each bowl, add a raw egg, allowing it to poach in the piping hot broth. It takes 2 to 3 minutes for the eggs to cook.

5. Serve with an extra sprinkle of finely chopped parsley.

Tip: Before adding the raw egg, break it into a small bowl. Slide the egg into the soup, keeping small pieces of shell from mixing in with the soup. Eggs may also be softly poached separately and then added to the soup bowls.

Variation: Omit the tomato, eggs, and croutons. Remove the bay leaf and puree ingredients before adding ½ cup short-grain rice or rice-shaped pasta (orzo). Cook until tender. Garnish with finely chopped coriander.

33

Green Bean and Linguiça Soup with Tomato

Sopa de Feijão Verde e Linguiça com Tomate

Serves 4 to 6

For the best flavor, the freshest green beans should be used for this soup. My father-in-law took great satisfaction in adding his homemade linguiça *sausage to this, his favorite soup.*

3 tablespoons olive oil

½ pound *linguiça* (page 12), cut in ½-inch slices (about 2 cups)

1 large onion, thinly sliced (about 1½ cups)

2 medium very ripe tomatoes, peeled, seeded, and coarsely chopped (about 2 cups)

2 cloves garlic, finely chopped

4 cups water

2 large new (waxy) potatoes, peeled and cut into ½-inch cubes (about 2 cups)

½ cup red wine

1 tablespoon finely chopped parsley

1 to 2 teaspoons coarse salt or to taste

⅛ teaspoon pepper

1 pound fresh string beans, trimmed and cut into 1-inch pieces (about 4 cups)

1. Heat the olive oil in a 4-quart stockpot over medium-high heat. Add and lightly brown the sausage slices, turning to color both sides. Remove the sausage from the pan and reserve.

2. Put in the onion and sauté until light golden.

3. Reduce the heat to medium-low. Add the tomatoes with the garlic. Stir, cover, and cook until the garlic is aromatic and the tomatoes are soft and partially dissolved, about 15 minutes.

4. Add the water, potatoes, wine, parsley, salt, and pepper. Re-cover and bring to a boil over medium-high heat. Reduce the heat and simmer for 15 minutes.

5. Add the green beans and continue to simmer until the potatoes and green beans are tender, 10 to 15 minutes. Return the sausage to the pan. Heat through and serve with plenty of bread to dip in the broth.

Kale Soup with Peas

Sopa de Couve com Ervilhas

Serves 6

My friend Olinda Fernandes created this sopa de panela *(soup of the pot or pot luck) one day. It's an interesting twist on pea soup. Chicken and sausage flavor its broth, which tastes even better the next day. Many Portuguese cooks take advantage of what is on hand to create delicious soups. Tomorrow's* sopa de panela *most likely will be different.*

7 cups water

1 chicken leg, rinsed well in cold water

1 large Red Bliss or new potato, peeled and cut into 1-inch cubes (about 1½ cups)

½ pound *linguiça* or *chouriço* (page 12)

1 carrot, peeled, cut into 1-inch chunks (about 1 cup)

½ cup dry split peas

½ cup finely chopped onion

1 clove garlic, finely chopped

2 tablespoons rice

2 tablespoons elbow macaroni or other short pasta

1 teaspoon coarse salt or to taste

¼ teaspoon pepper

1½ pounds greens—collards or kale—rinsed, trimmed, and torn into 1- to 2-inch pieces (about 3½ cups) (page 8)

1. In a 5-quart stockpot, combine all the ingredients except the rice, macaroni, salt, pepper, and greens, adding extra water, if needed, so that the ingredients are completely covered by 1 inch. Cover and bring to a boil over medium-high heat. Reduce the heat and simmer over medium-low until the chicken is nearly falling off the bone, about 30 to 40 minutes.

2. Remove the chicken and sausage from the pot, and set aside to cool. Bone the chicken legs. Reserve the meat and discard the bones. Cut the sausage in chunks and reserve.

3. Purée the remaining contents of the pot, cover, and return the soup to a boil. Stir in the rice, macaroni, salt, and pepper. Reduce the heat and simmer for 12 minutes.

4. Add the greens and simmer until they are tender and the macaroni is cooked, 10 to 15 minutes. Return the chicken and sausage to the pot in the last few minutes of cooking to heat through.

Tip: A hand-held blender makes puréeing this soup easy.

35

Gazpacho Galveias-Style
Gaspacho de Galveias
Serves 4 to 6

Made in the style of my father's hometown, Galveias, this simple soup is satisfying on a sultry summer evening. My grandfather enjoyed it very much, especially with fresh cilantro. This gazpacho is different from most because it doesn't include tomatoes. The ingredients should be well chilled. For extra crunchy texture, toast the bread cubes before adding to the soup.

3 cloves garlic, finely chopped

2 teaspoons coarse salt or to taste

1 small onion, finely chopped (about ½ cup)

1 small cucumber, peeled, seeded, and coarsely chopped (about 1 cup)

1 green pepper, coarsely chopped (about 1 cup)

¼ cup wine vinegar

¼ cup olive oil

3 cups very cold water

¼ pound *linguiça* (page 12), cut into ¼-inch thick rounds (optional)

2 to 3 cups hard, day-old Portuguese bread, cut into cubes (or substitute any crusty country bread)

2 tablespoons finely chopped fresh cilantro

1. Using a mortar and pestle, mash the garlic with the salt, making a paste. Place the garlic paste in a large mixing bowl with the onion, cucumber, pepper and vinegar.

2. Blend the ingredients well while drizzling in the olive oil. Pour in the water as needed, stir, and chill well. The soup should be fairly thick.

3. Just before serving, briefly sauté the sausage slices. To serve, ladle the soup into chilled soup bowls and top with the bread cubes and slices of sausage. Garnish with finely chopped fresh cilantro.

Note: If you don't have any day-old bread, cut fresh bread into rough cubes and toast in the oven.

Shrimp Soup with White Beans
Sopa de Camarão com Feijão Branco
Serves 6

The fragrance and flavor of this soup excites the senses. This family favorite includes beans, which give the soup body. You can, however, completely eliminate the beans if you wish to have a lighter soup. Serve this dish as a first course or as a light meal.

¼ pound (¾ cup) dried white kidney beans, soaked overnight in enough water to cover by 2 inches (about 3 cups)

6 cups water

¾ pound small raw shrimp, peeled and deveined (reserve the shells)

¼ cup olive oil

1 small onion, finely chopped (about a scant ½ cup)

1 bay leaf

1 large very ripe tomato, peeled, seeded, and finely chopped (about 1 cup)

2 cloves garlic, finely chopped

½ cup white wine (optional)

2 tablespoons finely chopped fresh cilantro

2 teaspoons coarse salt or to taste

1 teaspoon hot pepper sauce (page 5)

¼ teaspoon white pepper

4 thick slices of toasted Portuguese or other crusty European-style bread

1. Drain the beans from the soaking water and rinse. Add the beans to a 2- quart pot with 3 cups of fresh water, covering the beans by 2 inches. Cover and bring to a boil over high heat. Reduce the heat to medium-low and simmer until the beans are easily mashed with a fork, about 45 to 60 minutes. Reserve with cooking liquid.

2. Meanwhile, briefly rinse the shrimp shells and combine with the remaining 3 cups of water in a 1-quart pan. Cover, bring to a boil over medium-high heat then reduce the heat and simmer for 20 minutes. Strain the broth into another container, pressing the shells to extract the cooking water. Discard the shells.

3. Heat the oil in a 2½-quart saucepan over medium-high heat. Add and sauté the onion until soft and translucent, about 5 minutes. Add the bay leaf, tomato, and garlic. Cover and continue to cook over medium-low heat until the tomatoes have become soft and partially dissolved, about 15 minutes.

4. Pour in the wine, if using, simmer for one minute, and remove the pot from the heat.

5. Set a food mill over the pot. Process the cooked beans, using the cooking liquid of the beans and the reserved shrimp broth. Cover and bring to a boil, then reduce the heat to medium-low.

6. Add the shrimp, ½ tablespoon of the cilantro, followed by the salt, hot pepper sauce, and pepper. Re-cover and simmer gently for 3 minutes, until the shrimp are just opaque.

7. Place one slice of the toasted bread in each soup bowl. Ladle the soup over it. Garnish with remaining cilantro and serve immediately.

Tip: This soup can also be made ahead through step 5. Just before serving, bring up to temperature and continue with step 6. This prevents the shrimp from becoming overcooked.

Variations: For added texture, leave some or all of the beans whole and add 2 cups coarsely chopped spinach with the shrimp. Simmer gently for 3 minutes. To prepare as a lighter soup, eliminate the beans entirely, cook the shrimp shells in 6 cups of water, and follow the directions up to step 4. Then strain the broth, bring to a medium simmer and continue with step 6.

THE STORY OF STONE SOUP

According to one Portuguese version of the universal folk tale, *sopa de pedra* was created by a monk who traveled the countryside in search of a meal. Knocking on door after door, he asked in vain for food. None of the villagers had a scrap to spare. Finally, in desperation, the monk approached one more family and asked to borrow a large kettle. A puzzled lady of the house complied. He took out a stone from his sack and placed it in the empty kettle. He asked if she could spare a little water. At once, the helpful villager brought a pot of water and added it to the empty kettle. "How much better this soup would taste if only I had an onion," cried the monk. Quickly, the woman gave him an onion for the pot. "What wonderful flavor garlic would add to my soup," the monk said. The women's daughter brought him a fistful of garlic. And so it continued, until the monk had filled his kettle with tasty ingredients provided by the unsuspecting family, and the enticing aroma of stone soup filled the air. Leaving them with the stone with which to make their own batch, he left.

Stone Soup
Sopa de Pedra
Serves 8 to 10

As a little girl, after listening to the story of Stone Soup as told by my grandfather, I used to think of the whole beans as being little stones. Use a different variety of dried beans if you prefer, but leave them whole. This version is loosely adapted from my grandmother's recipe, which my aunt taught me. The less spicy chouriço *sausage may be substituted for the* salpicão.

1 cup dried red kidney beans, soaked overnight in enough water to cover by 2 inches (about 3 cups)

8 cups water

½ pound *chouriço* or *salpicão* (page 12), thickly sliced

1 bay leaf

1 small white or yellow turnip, cut into ½-inch cubes (about 2 cups)

2 medium potatoes, cut into ½-inch cubes (about 2 cups)

1 medium onion, coarsely chopped (about 1 cup)

2 small carrots, peeled and coarsely chopped (about ¾ cup)

¼ cup finely chopped parsley

2 tablespoons coarse salt or to taste

2 cloves garlic, coarsely chopped

½ teaspoon black pepper

1½ cups coarsely chopped Savoy cabbage

1. Drain and rinse the beans, then place in a 5-quart stockpot. Add the water, sausage, and bay leaf to the pot. Cover and bring to a boil over medium-high heat. Reduce the heat and simmer over medium-low for 15 minutes, skimming off any impurities. When the sausage is tender, remove from the pot. Remove the casing and cut into medium cubes and reserve.

2. Add the remaining ingredients except the cabbage. Simmer 45 minutes.

3. Toss in the cabbage and simmer until tender, about 10 to 15 minutes. Return the reserved sausage to the pot, heat through, and serve the soup hot with plenty of crusty bread.

Note: Variations to the soup are as numerous as the story itself. The addition of pig's feet or knuckles is one common version.

38

Chickpea Soup with Spinach
Sopa de Grão de Bico com Espinafres
Serves 6

Soups made with chickpeas are common in Mediterranean countries. This dish of the Alentejo area takes ordinary chickpeas and turns them into an extraordinary soup with a simple, comforting, and nutty flavor. This version is adapted from my grandmother's recipe as taught to me by my Aunt Ana. Chickpeas require longer soaking than most dried beans. I recommend soaking them at least 15 hours before cooking.

1 pound (2½ cups) chickpeas, soaked at least 15 hours in enough water to cover by 2 inches

5 tablespoons olive oil

1 small onion, finely chopped (about ½ cup)

4 large garlic cloves, finely chopped

1 bay leaf

12 cups water

¼ cup rice

1½ tablespoons coarse salt or to taste

¼ teaspoon white pepper

2 tablespoons finely chopped fresh cilantro

½ pound spinach, rinsed, trimmed, and coarsely chopped (optional)

½ pound *linguiça* (page 12), cut into ¼-inch rounds

1. Drain and rinse the chickpeas, then set aside. Heat 4 tablespoons of the oil in a 4-quart saucepan over medium-high heat. Add the onion and sauté until soft and translucent, about 5 minutes. Add the garlic and bay leaf, cooking until the garlic releases its aroma, about 1 minute.

2. Add the chickpeas to the pot with 12 cups of fresh water. Cover, bring to a boil over high heat, then reduce the heat to medium-low. Simmer until the chickpeas are very tender and easily mashed, about 1½ to 2 hours.

3. Use the back of a fork or large spoon to press the chickpeas against the sides of the pot. They should mash easily, which will allow the skins to float to the surface of the broth. Remove the skins with a slotted spoon and discard.

4. Remove the bay leaf. Strain the chickpeas, reserving the broth. Remove any remaining skins.

5. Set a food mill, sieve, or colander over the soup pot. Press the chickpeas through the holes, adding a little of the broth to create a smooth consistency. (If you are using a blender, work in small batches, and then strain the soup.)

6. Return the soup to a boil. Add the rice, salt, and pepper. Cover, reduce the heat, and simmer, stirring frequently, until the rice is almost done, about 20 minutes.

7. Add the cilantro and the spinach. Stir well and simmer for another 5 minutes or until the rice is cooked.

8. Meanwhile, sauté the sausage with 1 tablespoon of the oil in a small skillet, until lightly brown, turning to color both sides. Ladle the soup into bowls and garnish with a few slices of the sausage.

Variation: Omit the spinach leaves and serve as an elegant first course.

39

FEAST OF THE HOLY GHOST — *Festa do Espírito Santo*

In the Azores, there are nearly as many religious celebrations as there are weeks in the year. When immigrants from the Azores came to the United States, they continued to celebrate the Feast of the Holy Ghost. It remains the quintessential festival of the Azores.

My earliest childhood memory is the taste of the soup of the Holy Ghost, *sopa de Espirito Santo.* It was the meal of thanksgiving following the beautiful procession and Mass on the Feast of the Holy Ghost. I understood that the event had great significance as I walked in the procession, wearing a white gown and carrying a bouquet of red roses. Various groups, including children dressed as saints, were cordoned off with yards of red ribbon. One lucky young woman was chosen Empress of the Procession and reverently carried the crown of the Holy Ghost.

The author (center) in the Holy Ghost Procession, Peabody, Massachusetts, 1957

Oral tradition bases the Azorean festival on two religious experiences. In the sixteenth century, the king of Germany vowed to end poverty in Europe by feeding the poor. The king of Portugal refused to help. In secret, Queen (Santa) Isabella brought food to the poor against her husband's decree. When she was caught, her only recourse was a prayer to the Holy Ghost. She dropped the ends of her apron and the food miraculously transformed into red roses. Realizing the power of the Holy Ghost, she ordered that a silver dove, representing the Holy Ghost, be added to the top of her crown, thereby dedicating her royal symbol to the service of a higher power.

The second experience happened when Spain refused to give up control of the Azores. A nobleman, sent by Portugal to take charge of removing the Spaniards, was falsely accused of treason and jailed. His prayers to the Holy Ghost for exoneration were answered. Shoeless and having the appearance of a peasant, he offered a meal to all the poor, in thanksgiving, serving them himself.

Since then, the Portuguese, particularly those from the Azores, have continued to offer *novenas* and *promessas* (promises of pious offerings) to the Holy Ghost during the seven weeks following Easter. Pentecost Sunday, the feast of the Holy Ghost, concludes the season with a procession to the church, a Mass, and the crowning of individuals whose prayers have been answered, followed by the celebratory meal of thanksgiving.

The first time the feast was celebrated in Peabody, Massachusetts, was on May 16, 1916. It has been held there every year since. The meal begins with the time-honored *sopa do Espirito Santo,* a heady concoction of meats, greens, and stock perfumed with garlic and *linguiça* sausage. Some families have their meal of thanksgiving at home instead of eating at the church hall. Sometimes the soup is followed by *carne assada,* beef braised with tomato, wine, bacon, and allspice (see recipe on page 113). Other families serve *alcatra,* a dish for which the island of Terceira is especially known. It is a delectable meal of marinated meat cooked in a special unglazed red-clay pot (see recipe on page 115). Either rice or *batatas assadas* (potatoes roasted with aromatic spices) are served alongside the meat with fresh crusty bread. Each island, town, and family has its own variation of the thanksgiving meal—the soup of the Holy Ghost is the constant component.

Soup of the Holy Ghost, page 42

41

Soup of the Holy Ghost

Sopa do Espírito Santo

Serves 6

This soup is also served at other times of thanksgiving when prayers have been answered. Edelberto Ataide from Graciosa in the Azores is the chief cook for our gatherings at church. He shared this recipe with me. It can easily be doubled or tripled; he often prepares it for more than 200 people.

1 small onion, finely chopped (about ½ cup)
5 garlic cloves, peeled and left whole
1 bay leaf
½ cup white wine
10 cups water
1 small fowl, about 1½ to 2 pounds
¼ pound smoked bacon, roughly chopped
½ pound beef shoulder bone
½ pound beef brisket or chuck
½ pound *linguiça* (page 12)
¼ pound beef liver (traditional, but optional)
1 pound Red Bliss potatoes, peeled and cut into
    1-inch cubes
2 teaspoons coarse salt or to taste
3 allspice berries (preferably Jamaican)
1 pound kale or collard greens, rinsed, trimmed
    of main rib, leaves torn into 1- to 2-inch pieces
1 small head (about 5 inches in diameter) Savoy
    cabbage, cored, cut into quarters
3 sprigs of mint
5 to 10 ounces day-old Portuguese country bread
    or other crusty sourdough bread

1. In a 5-quart stockpot, combine the onion, garlic, bay leaves, wine, and 8 cups of the water. Bring to a boil over medium-high heat.

2. Add the fowl, bacon, beef shoulder bone, beef brisket, and sausage and return to a boil. Reduce the heat and simmer the meat until nearly tender, occasionally skimming off impurities, about 1 hour.

3. If including the beef liver, in a separate pan, bring the remaining 2 cups of water to a low simmer. Add and poach the liver in the hot water until just tender and slightly pink in the center, about 5 minutes. Remove and set aside.

4. As the meats and fowl become tender, remove from the pot. Reserve and keep warm. Strain the broth, then return it to the pot. Add the potatoes, salt, and allspice. Bring the ingredients to a boil over medium-high heat. Reduce the heat to medium-low and simmer for about 10 minutes. Add the kale and cabbage, and gently simmer for another 15 minutes. Turn off the heat. Add one sprig of the mint, cover, and let stand for 5 minutes.

5. Meanwhile, cut the reserved chicken into serving pieces. Remove from the beef the bone and any fat or gristle and discard. Cut the beef into serving pieces and place on a serving platter with the chicken. Dice the liver, if using, and place in a dish to serve separately.

6. To serve, place a few torn pieces of the bread in a soup tureen. Ladle in some of the broth and let it rest 5 minutes so the bread absorbs some liquid. Fill the tureen with additional soup. Garnish the top with the remaining sprigs of mint. Place an additional bread slice in each soup bowl and ladle the soup over it. Serve the meat as a second course with buttered rice.

Variation: On the island of Terceira, cinnamon lightly spices their version of this soup, and potatoes and kale are omitted.

42

BREAD SOUPS AND PANADAS
Açordas and Migas

My father once explained to me that, in Portugal, bread was usually baked once or twice a week. By the end of the week, any remaining bread would be hard. For many of the less fortunate Portuguese, sometimes it was all they had to eat by the week's end. It is understandable why wastefulness is not part of the Portuguese character. Taught by the Arabs, the Portuguese made the uneatable stale bread into meager but tasty dishes known as *açordas* and *migas.* Eventually those who fared better added salt cod or shrimp to the *açordas.* Although *açorda* can be eaten any time of day, when I was growing up we usually enjoyed it on Saturday or Sunday mornings as a late breakfast or a light meal, served with olives and maybe some wine.

Açorda is a soup of stale dense bread moistened with boiling water or broth and flavored with garlic and cilantro (*coentros*). The bread soaks up most of the broth and becomes very wet. *Migas,* on the other hand, has a dryer texture, like bread stuffing without the turkey. Although the finished result lacks a broth, it is made the same as the *açorda* in that the bread is moistened. A lot less liquid is used, however, and the seasoning is different. Some versions are even sautéed in a skillet to give the *migas* a golden crust. Too much liquid will cause excessive sticking to the pan.

When a dish calls for bread to be incorporated with liquid ingredients, typical American-style bread should not be used. If you cannot obtain the Portuguese peasant-style bread known as *caseiro,* use other crusty European peasant-style breads—Italian, French, or Greek, for example. The texture should be somewhat dense with an open grain, not cottony like the "Italian" loaves sold in plastic on supermarket shelves. Today, many specialty bakeries sell delicious rustic European peasant-style breads and rolls.

Thinking about the *migas* and *açordas* brings back memories of my father going out to his garden and returning with freshly cut cilantro (*coentros*). When he picked this herb, he would enter the kitchen sniffing the wonderful leaves, and exclaim, "I love this!" or "Smell, smell!" as he waved the fresh coriander under my mother's nose. My mother waved it off—she didn't like coriander at all. Not everyone does, but if you do, you'll know what my father meant.

43

Bread Soup Alentejo-Style

Açorda à Alentejana

Serves 4

According to oral history, this very old and most basic of the bread soups goes back to the days when the Moors occupied the Alentejo region. Garlic, olive oil, and a fistful of chopped fresh cilantro season boiling water. Broken pieces of stale bread, the amount of which can be very little or quite a bit, are then added to the aromatic broth. The bread absorbs the flavorful broth and softens..

1 tablespoon coarse salt or to taste
4 cloves garlic, coarsely chopped
¼ cup olive oil
½ cup finely chopped cilantro
1 quart boiling water
4 cups torn stale Portuguese or other dense bread
4 eggs

1. Using a mortar and pestle, mash the garlic with the salt, forming a paste.

2. In the bottom of a large bowl, combine the mashed garlic with the olive oil and cilantro. Gradually stir in half the water.

3. Tear the bread into medium-sized pieces (2 to 3 inches). Toss in as little or as much of the bread as you wish. Allow it to soak up some water for about 5 minutes. Add more water, if necessary, so that mixture is not dry. Mix gently. There should be a decent amount of broth although the ratio of liquid to bread is a matter of preference.

4. Break eggs one at a time, into a small bowl, then slide them into the large serving bowl, making a space between the pieces of bread, and allow them to poach in the hot broth, about 5 minutes. Make sure that the broth is piping hot so it cooks the eggs.

5. Ladle the soup into individual bowls, including an egg in each one. Serve immediately.

Note: The eggs can be boiled or poached separately and added to the individual soup bowls.

44

Bread Soup with Salt Cod

Açorda de Bacalhau

Serves 4

After I was married, my father would often call me on the phone and ask in his broken English, "You get the smell?" He didn't need to explain. I would simply reply, "I'll be right there." There wasn't any doubt that I was about to enjoy an açorda de bacalhau. The aroma of the fresh cilantro and fish that filled the kitchen met me as I entered the house. Begin this dish one day ahead with the simple soaking of the salt cod and be sure to taste the soaked cod for salt before cooking. Soak longer, if necessary, in a fresh change of water.

¼ pound salt cod, soaked in several changes of
   cold water, 16 to 24 hours, refrigerated*
1 quart water
4 tablespoons olive oil
4 garlic cloves, coarsely chopped
½ green pepper, coarsely chopped (optional)
½ cup finely chopped fresh cilantro
4 cups torn stale bread (use a dense and crusty
   European-style bread)
4 eggs

1. Bring the water to a boil and turn off the heat. Remove the fish from the soaking water, rinse, and add to the hot water. Cover and allow to poach for 10 to 15 minutes, until the fish flakes easily.
2. Using a mortar and pestle, mash the garlic, forming a paste. In the bottom of a large serving bowl, combine the garlic paste with the olive oil. Mix in the green pepper and cilantro.
3. Transfer the codfish to a dish, reserving the hot liquid. Remove and discard any bones and skin. Break the fish into pieces. Add to the serving bowl.
4. Pour in approximately 2 cups of the hot fish broth. Add the bread chunks to the bowl, letting the bread soak up the broth. Add a bit more liquid if mixture is too dry. Stir gently. The mixture should be a fairly thick soup but not dry; there should be some broth.

*See salt cod instructions on page 11.

5. Break the eggs into the serving bowl. Spoon the hot liquid over the eggs and let them poach for 5 minutes. The broth must be hot enough to cook the eggs. Reheat if necessary.
6. Ladle the *açorda* into individual bowls, including an egg in each. Serve immediately.

Note: The eggs can be poached or soft-boiled separately. Peel soft-boiled eggs carefully so as not to break them open. Add one to each individual bowl.

Reminder: Be sure to taste before adding salt to any dish that involves salt cod, waiting until the very end of preparation. Page 11 describes in detail how to prepare salt cod; sometimes soaking can take 24 to 36 hours or longer. Usually additional salt is not needed.

When my grandfather came home from his morning errands, he liked to have what I would call an *açorda de café,* or "coffee soup." My grandmother would place some day-old bread in a large soup bowl and sprinkle the bread with sugar. Over this she poured his coffee, to which milk had already been added. She was careful not to add too much liquid. Sometimes my grandfather preferred to use just hot milk and sugar on his bread, which he would call *sopa de leite* or "milk soup."

45

Cat's Panada
Migas Gatas
Serves 4

Although migas *is often flavored with rendered bacon fat, spices, and sautéed* linguiça *sausage, there are versions like this one that are closer to an* açorda. *My Uncle Ilidio Valente, who often prepares this dish when left to his own devices, shares his recipe. How this dish got its name is not quite clear. Perhaps the name was created because cats like fish, or the creator was in a whimsical mood. This version of* migas, *a garlic lover's delight, is not cooked over heat. The hot broth from cooking the fish brings the mixture together.*

1 pound salt cod, soaked in several changes of
    cold water, 16 to 24 hours, refrigerated*

4 cups water

1 round loaf (about 12 ounces) day-old country
    bread, cut in 1-inch slices, heavy crusts removed

6 cloves garlic, thinly sliced, or enough to cover
    about 80 percent of each bread slice

olive oil to drizzle

wine vinegar or cider vinegar to drizzle

¼ teaspoon black pepper or to taste

salt to taste (if needed)

*See salt cod instructions on page 11.

1. Drain and discard the soaking water from fish. In a medium saucepan, bring 4 cups of fresh water to a boil and turn off the heat. Add the fish and poach for 15 minutes.

2. In the bottom of a 3-inch-deep 9 x 13-inch dish, place a layer of bread slices (about 2 large slices). Place slices of garlic fairly evenly over the bread, almost covering it. Make a second layer of bread and again cover with garlic slices. Follow with a third layer.

3. Remove the fish from the water and set aside until it is cool enough to handle. Gradually pour enough of the cooking liquid (about 2 cups) over the bread slices. Let stand, covered, for about 5 minutes, allowing the bread to absorb the water. Drain off any liquid that has not been absorbed. (If the bread seems to be too wet, add additional bread in small amounts, to absorb the liquid.) The bread should be somewhat dry; it should not be sopping wet. Using a fork, mash the bread and garlic.

4. Remove any skin and bones from the cod. Shred the fish. It should yield about 2 cups, loosely packed. Scatter on top of the bread mixture. Gently mix everything together, folding the ingredients to blend and form a ball. The texture should be like bread stuffing or thick mashed potatoes.

5. Drizzle with oil and vinegar and season with black pepper to taste. Spoon into individual bowls and serve with olives. With a green salad, this makes a tasty lunch.

Panada Alentejo-Style
Migas à Alentejana
Serves 4

Pork ribs or cubed pieces of pork meat are flavored with the traditional sweet red pepper paste (massa de pimentão) *in this old favorite of the Alentejo. Today's nonstick skillets are wonderful for making* migas. *The cast-iron skillet, however, imparts extra flavor. Lard, salt pork, and bacon are traditional fats for this dish, but I find olive oil to be a perfect health-conscious substitute.*

Day ahead:

1 pound pork tenderloin, pork butt, or
    pork ribs, or any combination
4 cloves garlic, coarsely chopped
1 bay leaf
1 tablespoon Sweet Red Pepper Paste, *Massa de
    Pimentão* (page 166)

1. If using butt or tenderloin, trim excess fat, gristle, and the thin silvery muscle called sinew. Cut the meat into 2-inch cubes. If using ribs, cut between the bones to separate the ribs. Place meat cubes and/or ribs in a large bowl. Add the garlic, bay leaf, and sweet red pepper paste. Turn the meat to coat evenly with the seasoning. Cover and marinate overnight.

Next day:

½ cup olive oil or ¼ cup lard or ¼ pound lean
    salt pork or bacon
2 cups boiling water (amount depends on the
    dryness of the bread)
12 ounces hard peasant-style bread, heavy crusts
    removed, roughly torn into pieces

1. Heat the olive oil or melt the lard in a large cast-iron pan. If you are using salt pork or bacon, fry it in the skillet until the pieces are crisp and the fat has been rendered. Remove the solid pieces.

Discard the bay leaf from the meat. In the hot fat, fry the meat a few pieces at a time over medium-high heat until nicely browned on all sides and cooked through, about 10 minutes. Remove the meat to a platter and keep warm.

2. Using the same frying pan, drain off all but 2 tablespoons of fat and set the pan aside.

3. Place the bread in a large bowl and gradually add enough boiling water so that the bread is just moist—not sopping wet (too much liquid makes it stick to the pan). Lightly mash to mix. It should be the consistency of bread stuffing. Reheat the frying pan. Add the bread to the pan and cook, mashing it again to incorporate the pan juices.

4. Using a wooden spoon, fold the mixture into itself, and cook it until the excess moisture has evaporated and the mixture comes together.

5. Shake the pan back and forth to form the mixture into a log shape, using the spoon to help it along. When the bread is a nice light golden color, roll it out of the pan (as you would roll out an omelette) onto a serving platter and arrange the meat around the bread. Serve immediately.

Note: A nonstick pan makes turning the moist bread easier and prevents the mixture from sticking to the pan.

47

Clams with Potatoes and Chouriço, *page 56*

3

SEAFOOD

Frutos do Mar

The location of Portugal, on the Atlantic, and its Azores Islands, have for centuries provided the country with access to an abundant variety of seafood, especially along the coast. Portuguese cooks took advantage of bountiful catches and created unique and flavorful meals. Today, many of these same tasty recipes are prepared in the United States by Portuguese immigrants and their families in much the same manner as they did in Portugal.

Some types of fish that the Portuguese are accustomed to using in Portugal are not readily available in the United States; substitutions are made with fish common in American markets. For example, *caldeirada,* which is a fish stew, in Portugal might contain conger eel, mullet, skate, and sea bass. Here in the United States we might use pollock, cusk, salmon, red snapper, and halibut. The one fish for which there is no acceptable substitute is salt cod. Ironically, cod, that most utilized fish in Portugal, is obtained outside Portuguese waters. Once viewed as fish of the poor, salt cod eventually became highly esteemed.

Seafood—especially salt cod, shellfish, and sardines—is fundamental to the Portuguese diet. There are countless dishes for salt cod—*bacalhau* in Portuguese. This versatile fish, after it is reconstituted in water, can be poached, fried, grilled, or baked in a casserole. A long-standing favorite of my family, as for many Portuguese, is *Bacalhau à Gomes da Sá*. This traditional dish combines poached salt cod with boiled potatoes and sautéed onions; it is baked and then garnished with black olives and slices of hard-boiled egg.

Other Portuguese favorites include *amêijoas na cataplana*, which is typically made with sweet cockles in the Algarve region of southern Portugal. In North America, littleneck clams, soft-shell clams, or even mussels, can be used to prepare this heady concoction of onions, white wine, sweet pepper, savory sausage, and lots of garlic, herbs, and spices. There are *lagosta fervida*, lobsters boiled in herb- and spice-infused water. The flavorful result leaves little need for melted butter.

Fillets of light fish like flounder and hake are likely to be quickly pan-fried then imbibed or drizzled with the tangy aromatic vinegar sauce *molhanga*, suggesting the Portuguese-Azorean influence. This treat is eaten hot or at room temperature.

Finally, sardines—fresh, not canned—that are simply cooked over a charcoal grill are always a hit whenever they are served. Sardines preserved in brine—originally to survive trips to the Portuguese interior—are a good source both of calcium and healthful fatty acids. They are often served with boiled potatoes and drizzled with oil and vinegar.

The dishes in this chapter can be accompanied by a simple green salad or sautéed greens, olives, crusty peasant bread, and of course, a chilled bottle of crisp *vinho verde,* Portuguese "green" wine (see Chapter 10). Some types of red wine go nicely with fish; the choice depends on the preparation of the dish. Whether they are grilled, baked, stewed, or fried, seafood dishes—made from whitefish, sardines, shellfish, or salt cod—are simply flavored with spices, scented with herbs like cilantro or parsley, and perhaps given a drizzle of oil and vinegar or splash of piquant *molhanga*. Plan ahead for dishes that require marinating, soaking (as salt cod), or purging (the process of removing sand from shellfish).

50

Pan-Fried Fish Fillets

Filetes de Peixe Frito na Frigideira

Serves 4 to 6

Many Portuguese cooks fry their fish without flour or egg. The oil is simply heated until it is hot but not so that it is smoking. The fish is quickly fried. Others fry their fish with a very light coating of seasoned fine yellow or white corn flour. My friend Olinda Fernandes, from Mangualda in northern Portugal, shares her simple marinade for fish. Here I have combined it with my father's seasoned corn flour, giving a flavorful twist to fried fish. I like the flavor of noncholesterol olive oil for frying fish, but if you prefer to use canola, corn, or other vegetable oil, keep in mind the difference in taste.

2 pounds flounder, hake, sole, or haddock fillets, skins intact

6 to 8 cloves garlic, finely chopped

1 cup lemon juice (white wine vinegar or white wine can be substituted)

1 cup yellow corn flour

1 tablespoon paprika

½ teaspoon coarse salt or to taste

¼ teaspoon white pepper

2 tablespoons finely chopped fresh parsley or cilantro

2 eggs lightly beaten

olive oil for frying

1. Rinse the fish and pat dry. Place the fish fillets in a glass dish and season each side with the garlic. Pour the lemon juice over the fish and marinate it for 1 hour.

2. Meanwhile, in shallow plate or on a sheet of waxed paper (for easy cleanup), combine the corn flour, paprika, salt, and pepper. Blend well and set aside.

3. Drain the fish from the marinade and transfer to another dish. Set aside.

4. Combine the fresh herbs with beaten eggs.

5. Dip the fish into the seasoned flour, lightly coating it. Shake off any excess flour and then dip the fish into the beaten eggs. Pan-fry immediately in hot olive oil for little more than 1 minute per side for the flounder, a little longer for thicker fillets, until golden. Serve with hot Tomato Rice (page 147), Sautéed Greens (page 154), and vinegar sauce (*escabeche* or *molhanga,* page 171).

51

Marinated Fish
Pescada em Vinho d'Alhos
Serves 4

Adding cider vinegar to the marinade gives this dish extra zing. Marinate no more than 1 hour before cooking.

6 cloves garlic, finely chopped
1 teaspoon coarse salt
1 cup white wine or lemon juice
2 tablespoons cider vinegar
2 tablespoons olive oil
1 bay leaf
¼ scant teaspoon white pepper
2 pounds hake or red snapper fillets with skins
    intact (or use halibut or swordfish, if grilling)
2 teaspoons paprika
1 cup yellow or white corn flour
2 eggs, lightly beaten (optional)
olive or corn oil as needed for frying

1. Using a mortar and pestle, mash the garlic with the salt, forming a paste. Transfer the paste to a 9 x 13-inch ceramic or glass dish and whisk in the wine or lemon juice, and vinegar, followed by the olive oil, bay leaf, and pepper.
2. Rinse the fish with water and pat dry. Add the fish to the marinade, turn to coat and refrigerate, covered, for 1 hour, turning occasionally.
3. Drain the marinade from the fish. If you are grilling the fish, reserve the marinade (see Variation that follows). Mix the paprika and cornflour. Coat the fish with the corn flour. Shake off excess any excess. Dip the fish into the beaten eggs, if using.
4. Immediately fry the fish in very hot oil until golden (about 2 minutes per side, depending on the thickness of the fish) or desired doneness. Place on a serving platter, cover lightly, and keep warm. Serve the fish with vinegar sauce (page 171). Boiled potatoes drizzled with some of the vinegar sauce are a traditional accompaniment.

Variation: If you prefer to grill your fish, use steaks that are 1 inch thick. Cook over very hot charcoal and baste periodically with the reserved marinade heated in a saucepan. Cook for about 5 minutes per side, turning only once.

Note: Another way fried fish is enjoyed is when it's fresh off the boat. Then it is sometimes cleaned and cut into chunks, seasoned as in the recipe above, and deep fried.

Sardines and Babies

Most cultures have their particular method for predicting the sex of unborn children. I was sixteen years old when I was a witness to the Portuguese method. My family was attending an outdoor summer dance held at our social club, the Club Luis de Camões. On this summer's night, grilled sardines were guaranteed to be served. With us on this particular evening was a dear family friend, Elena, who was very much in the family way. No sooner did she finish eating her sardine, when my father snapped up the fish's skeletal remains and threw them onto the grill. His friends pronounced if the skeleton jumped, Elena would be sure to have a girl. Well, the fish's skeleton jumped, and a few weeks later Elena gave birth to a beautiful baby girl.

Grilled Sardines
Sardinhas Assadas na Brasa
Serves 4 to 6

Grilled sardines have always been one of my favorite dishes. Eating grilled sardines al fresco on a warm summer's night with friends is a very simple and pleasurable way to wind down. We like to bring a brazier along on picnics lunches so we can cook sardines. An oily fish, sardines are similar to large smelt but more moist and flavorful, though not as strong as mackerel. Fresh sardines are best, of course, but frozen ones can be substituted without appreciable loss of flavor. Do not substitute canned sardines (see page 12). Unless you can find fresh ones, purchase frozen sardines in one-pound bags and thaw in the refrigerator before use. Be sure the grill is sufficiently hot before adding the fish; the coals should be covered with white ash. Using a clean, preheated grill rack will make the fish easier to turn. Watch for flames flaring up. Judicious rearrangement of the fish usually solves this problem.

Grilled sardines are commonly served with a salad of tomatoes, onions, and peppers drizzled with oil and vinegar or a vinegar sauce, a dish of black olives, and boiled potatoes or Feijão Frade *(page 148). The best way to eat grilled sardines is to pick them apart with your fingers and eat them with bread. Tinker mackerel, called* carapau *by the Portuguese, are usually fried, and the larger mackerel, called* chicharro *by the Azoreans, are commonly grilled. You can marinate grilled sardines as follows: fillet the cooked fish, remove the center bones, and transfer the fillets to a shallow dish. Add* escabeche *sauce (page 171) and refrigerate. Serve chilled or at room temperature.*

53

1 pound fresh or thawed frozen sardines (usually found in ethnic food shops if your fish market doesn't have them)
coarse salt

1. There isn't any need to gut sardines for charcoal grilling, and there are different opinions about scaling them. I don't scale sardines unless I bake them. Rinse sardines with cold water and salt them with a coating of salt, layering them in a colander or slanted plate to allow water to drain off. Let the salted sardines sit for an hour in the refrigerator.
2. Wipe off any excess salt and grill over white-hot coals until the skin blisters and is somewhat charred and the eyes are opaque, about 3 minutes on each side. Serve with boiled potatoes and a salad of sliced onions, sweet peppers, and tomatoes, accompanied by olive oil and vinegar for drizzling—and of course, bread and olives.

Tip: If you plan to grill additional items like chicken or beef, grill the sardines last so that the flavor does not affect the other foods. We usually reserve a small cast-iron grill specifically for cooking sardines.

Baked Sardines
Sardinhas no Forno
Serves 4 to 6

Before baking sardines, scale and gut them and remove the fins (page 12). I first prepared sardines this way—guided by my father—when I was eight. It is very easy to do. The following recipe for sardines can be used for baking other fish as well.

2 cups yellow corn flour
2 tablespoons paprika
¼ cup finely chopped parsley
½ tablespoon finely chopped garlic
½ tablespoon coarse salt
1 dozen large sardines, fresh or frozen, scaled, gutted (page 12)
3 eggs, lightly beaten (optional)
olive oil to drizzle

Preheat the oven to 350 degrees F.

1. Combine the dry ingredients, mixing well.
2. Rinse the fish and pat dry. Dip the fish in the corn-flour mixture, shaking off excess. Dip the fish into the egg and immediately place on a lightly oiled baking sheet. Repeat with remaining fish, placing head to tail on the sheet pan. Drizzle the tops of the fish with olive oil.
3. Bake for 20 to 30 minutes or until medium golden.
4. Garnish with additional chopped parsley. Serve with boiled potatoes, Vinegar Sauce (page 171), and Sautéed Greens (page 154).

Note: You can omit the egg and just give the fish a thin coating of corn flour followed by a drizzling of olive oil.

Purging and Cleaning Fresh Clams

When I can obtain freshly dug clams from a clam digger, or if I dig the clams myself, I grab a bucket of fresh seawater and soak the clams overnight or several hours so that they will purge themselves of sand and grit. Saltwater works faster and better. The clams are then refrigerated until needed. To those cooks who have access to fresh saltwater, I recommend this method whether the clams are freshly dug or purchased from a fish market. You will be amazed at how well it works.

Another popular method is to soak the shellfish in a large bowl of cold salted fresh water to which a tablespoon of dry mustard or hot pepper sauce have been added. Use about 1 tablespoon of table salt per quart of water. Soak for ½ hour.

Some cooks prefer to use cornmeal to clean them. If you use cornmeal, use a finely milled grade. Try each method and see which you prefer. After soaking, scrub the clams with a stiff brush and rinse with cold water several times. Discard any shellfish that are open. Drain and set aside in the refrigerator.

54

Clams Cataplana
Amêijoas na Cataplana
Serves 4 to 6

There are many versions of the mouth-watering clams cataplana. *This dish originated on the southern coast of Portugal, the Algarve. It is fairly simple to prepare, yet flavorful. Mussels and other shellfish can be prepared the same way.*
This dish is traditionally made in a cataplana, *a deep bowl-shaped pan of copper or aluminum with a hinged lid that makes it resemble a clam shell. The copper* cataplanas *are usually lined with tin. The lid has clamps to keep it closed tightly. Until recently, the pans were not imported to the United States. If you don't have one of these traditional pans, a deep pot with a tight lid will work well. (Cataplana pans are available through some kitchen specialty stores and catalogs.) Chilled* vinho verde *goes extremely well with this dish.*

2 tablespoons olive oil
1 large onion, thinly sliced (about 1½ cups)
1 bay leaf
3 cloves garlic, mashed
1 tablespoon paprika
hefty pinch dry crushed red pepper
¼ cup finely chopped fresh cilantro
½ ounce *presunto* ham (page 10), or Parma
   prosciutto, coarsely chopped (about ¼ cup)
¼ to ½ pound *chouriço* (page 12), sliced in ½-
   inch rounds
2 quarts cockles or littleneck clams, well scrubbed
   and rinsed (page 54)
1 cup white wine
¼ cup butter
lemon wedges for garnish

1. Heat the oil in a medium-sized skillet over medium-high heat and sauté the onion until a light golden color, about 10 to 15 minutes.
2. Add the bay leaf, garlic, paprika, crushed red pepper, and one-half of the cilantro. Cover and simmer for an additional minute or two.
3. In a *cataplana* pan or deep pot with a lid, combine the onion mixture with the meats and shellfish. Gently turn to distribute the ingredients. Pour the wine over the top.

4. Cover tightly and cook over medium-high heat until clams open, about 10 to 12 minutes (up to 20 to 25 minutes for littlenecks). Check after 8 minutes to be sure that the clams don't overcook. With slotted spoon lift the opened clams onto a serving dish and cover.
5. Over medium-high heat, reduce liquid by half, then remove from the heat. Let the broth cool for 1 minute and finish by whisking in soft butter. (If the broth is too hot when the butter is added, it will not emulsify with the broth.) Pour over the clams or serve on the side as a dipping sauce. Discard any unopened clams. Garnish with lemon wedges and remaining cilantro and serve immediately.

Note: The addition of *presunto* and *chouriço* can make the dish somewhat salty. Adjust the amount you add to your taste.

Variations: Add ½ cup of finely chopped tomatoes along with the garlic and paprika. Cover and cook until the tomatoes are soft and partially dissolved, about 15 minutes, before continuing with the recipe. Mussels can be used in place of the clams.

55

Clams with Potatoes and Chouriço

Amêijoas com Batatas e Chouriço

Serves 6

There are times when I wonder who is the host and who is the guest. Whenever we invite our cousins Tony, Noelia, Evelyn, and Manuel to join us for the day at our home in Maine, they insist on bringing food, since we provide the location. They come bearing covered pots and dishes that emit enticing aromas. It is what I call Portuguese cooperative hospitality. Tony brings his passion for cooking good food and enjoying it to the fullest with family and friends by savoring every bite to the accompaniment of much conversation. His infectious enthusiasm overflows into my kitchen in a way that makes me happy to step aside and watch him create. This recipe of Tony's makes a wonderful appetizer or first course to a seafood dinner—it makes an easy light meal as well. Purge the clams in advance according to the instructions on page 54.

4 quarts soft-shell clams

1 pound (2 large) new potatoes, scrubbed, skins intact, sliced into ¼-inch thick rounds

½ pound *chouriço* (page 12), sliced into ½-inch thick rounds

1 small onion, finely chopped (about ½ cup)

2 large cloves garlic, mashed

2 teaspoons wine vinegar

½ teaspoon Hot Pepper Paste (page 167)

½ teaspoon cumin

¼ teaspoon coarse salt

¼ teaspoon black pepper

12 ounces wine or beer or 6 ounces of each

1. Combine all the ingredients, except the wine, in a 5-quart stock pot, and gently mix. Pour the wine (or beer) over the ingredients and cover.

2. Cook over medium-high heat until clams have opened, approximately 12 to 15 minutes. Discard any unopened clams and serve immediately.

56

Clams Bulhão Pato-Style

Amêijoas à Bulhão Pato

Serves 4

Oral history holds that this dish was created in honor of the Portuguese poet Bulhão Pato, who lived in the 1800s. It is extremely simple and flavorful. It makes a great appetizer. Although parsley can be used in this recipe, having a love of cilantro, I prefer to use it instead. Cilantro can be an acquired taste. Either way, this dish does indeed please the palate. Purge the clams in advance according to the instructions on page 54.

¼ cup Portuguese or extra-virgin olive oil

3 cloves of garlic, finely chopped

1 cup finely chopped cilantro or parsley, more or less, to taste

1 cup *vinho verde* or other light white wine

1 teaspoon Hot Pepper Paste (page 167)

1 teaspoon coarse salt

¼ teaspoon white pepper

24 littleneck clams (about 1 quart)

1. In the bottom of a deep 4-quart pot with a tight lid, heat the oil and lightly cook the garlic, just until it becomes aromatic. Toss in the parsley or cilantro and stir in the wine, Hot Pepper Paste, salt, and pepper.

2. Add the clams, gently turn to coat, and cover tightly. Cook over medium-high heat until the clams have opened, about 15 to 20 minutes depending on the size of the clams. Discard any unopened clams. To serve, ladle the clams with some broth into soup plates. Serve with plenty of crusty bread to soak up the juices.

Note: For those who prefer not to use alcohol, use ½ cup of water and the juice of 1 lemon in place of the wine.

Tip: The cooking time varies depending on the size of the clams. Soft-shell clams or mussels can be subtstituted for the littlenecks in this recipe.

Baked Stuffed Littlenecks

Amêijoas Recheados no Forno

Serves 4

These are wonderful as an appetizer. They can be made up the morning ahead, chilled, and then brought to room temperature 15 minutes before baking. Purge the clams in advance according to the instructions on page 54.

24 large littleneck clams
4 tablespoons butter
4 tablespoons olive oil
1 small onion, finely chopped (about ½ cup)
4 garlic cloves, finely chopped
2 ounces *linguiça* (page 12), coarsely chopped (about ¼ cup)
2 tablespoons finely chopped cilantro
½ teaspoon hot pepper sauce (optional)
¼ teaspoon white pepper
3 cups soft bread crumbs, crusts removed
½ cup water
paprika for sprinkling on top

Preheat the oven to 375 degrees F.

1. Fresh clams, littlenecks especially, can be difficult to open when they're raw. Placing them in a pan of slightly hot water or cooking them just enough to make the shells open a crack, makes the job easier. Carefully shuck the little necks using a clam knife. Watch for tiny chips of shell that may break off during the shucking. Reserve 12 of the shells. Transfer the clam meat to a cutting board and chop coarsely, reserving any juices. Set aside chopped clams and reserved juice.

2. Heat the butter and oil in a small skillet over medium-high heat, until hot but not smoking. Add and sauté the onion until lightly golden. Mix in the garlic, chopped sausage, cilantro, hot pepper sauce, and white pepper. Cook, letting the sausage and garlic sweat with the onions for two minutes. Then remove the pan from the heat.

3. In a medium bowl, combine the onion and sausage mixture with the chopped clams and clam juice.

4. Moisten the bread with water. Do not soak it. Gently squeeze the bread to remove any excess water. Using your hands, crumble the bread into the bowl. Mix everything together.

5. Place a heaping tablespoon of filling firmly onto a clam shell half and sprinkle with paprika. Set the stuffed shells on a sheet pan. Bake in a 375-degree oven, until they turn a rich golden color on top, about 15 to 20 minutes, depending on amount of stuffing in the shells. Serve hot.

Note: Preshucked clams can be purchased from fishmongers. Scallop shells, sometimes sold in fish markets and kitchen specialty stores, work well for stuffing.

Tip: Use an ice-cream scoop to fill the shells. The spring-tension kind come in different sizes. They are perfect for filling these shells. They are also a great time saver for filling muffin tins, stuffing shrimp, and making drop cookies of uniform size.

Poached Cod with Vegetables
Bacalhau de Consoada
Serves 4

This traditional dish is served most anytime, but particularly on Christmas Eve. My grandmother Teresa made this dish in her big white enamel pot. Her version includes green beans, potatoes, and cauliflower, and it was the only way I would eat cauliflower when I was young. Some recipes use kale, cabbage, and carrots instead of green beans. Whatever vegetables you choose, simply adjust cooking times to suit. Leafy greens (mustard greens, broccoli rabe, and spinach) take 5 minutes to cook while kale or cabbage take 10 to 15 minutes.

4 medium boiling potatoes, whole with skins intact (about 2 pounds)
4 medium carrots, peeled and left whole (about ½ pound) (optional)
water
1 pound of either kale, green beans, mustard greens, broccoli rabe, spinach, or a small head of cabbage, rinsed, trimmed, and quartered
1 pound salt cod, soaked in several changes of cold water, 24 to 36 hours, refrigerated*
hard-boiled eggs, peeled, 1 or more per person (page 6)

Dressing:
wine vinegar or cider vinegar to drizzle as needed
extra-virgin olive oil to drizzle as needed
coarse salt and fresh cracked pepper to taste
8 large cloves garlic, coarsely chopped
2 tablespoons finely chopped parsley

*See salt cod instructions on page 11.

1. In an 8-quart pot, place the potatoes, carrots, and kale (if using) with enough water to cover by 2 inches. Cover and bring to a boil, reduce the heat, and simmer gently for 15 minutes.
2. Drain the cod from the soaking water, rinse, and add to the pot. (Potatoes will absorb excess salt and gain flavor from the cod.) Cover and return the ingredients to a boil. Reduce the heat to medium-low, and simmer for about 15 minutes (depending on the thickness of the fish), until tender. Fish should be opaque and just starting to flake. If you are using the more delicate leafy greens like spinach, broccoli rabe or mustard greens, add them after the cod has been cooking for 5 minutes. Simmer the greens for 5 to 10 minutes. Vegetables should be tender.
3. Remove the fish and vegetables from the pot as they become done. Peel the potatoes and arrange on a serving platter with the fish, the other vegetables, and the hard-boiled eggs. Drizzle with oil and vinegar to taste and sprinkle with parsley.
4. Provide decanters of additional extra-virgin olive oil and cider vinegar in addition to salt, pepper, and lots of chopped garlic. Serve with Portuguese or other crusty bread or rolls and olives.

59

Salt Cod Stew

Bacalhau Estufado

Serves 4 to 6

This aromatic broth complements salt cod wonderfully well. We eat this family favorite year round. The presoaked salt cod is gently cooked in a cilantro-infused tomato-and-onion-based broth with rice and potatoes creating a flavorful one-pot meal.

½ pound salt cod, soaked in several changes of
    cold water, 15 to 24 hours, refrigerated*

⅓ cup Portuguese or extra-virgin olive oil

1 medium onion, coarsely chopped (about 1 cup)

1 bay leaf

½ teaspoon paprika

3 large very ripe tomatoes, peeled and coarsely
    chopped (about 2½ cups)

2 cloves garlic, coarsely chopped

¼ cup white wine (optional)

2 medium potatoes cut into 1-inch cubes
    (about 2 cups)

1½ quarts water (6 cups)

¾ cup medium-grain rice

1 to 2 tablespoons finely chopped cilantro
    or parsley

½ teaspoon coarse salt or to taste

¼ teaspoon pepper

*See salt cod instructions on page 11.

1. Taste the fish for salt and let it soak a little longer in fresh water if it is still too salty. Drain, rinse, and cut the fish into medium-sized pieces (2 to 3 inches). Set aside.

2. Heat the olive oil in a 5-quart pot over medium-high heat. Add and sauté the onion until soft and translucent, about 5 minutes. Stir in the bay leaf and paprika. Add the tomatoes and garlic. Reduce the heat to medium-low, cover, and cook the tomatoes until partially dissolved into the onions, about 15 minutes. Pour in the wine, if using, and simmer 1 minute.

3. Add the potatoes and water. Cover and bring to a boil. Toss in the rice and reduce the heat. Simmer until the potatoes and rice are almost done, about 15 to 20 minutes.

4. Add the cilantro or parsley and the salt cod. Continue to simmer until the fish is opaque and the potatoes are cooked, about 10 to 15 minutes more. Ladle the stew into soup bowls and serve with plenty of bread to dip in the fragrant broth.

Variation: Combine cod with scallops, shrimp, or even lobster. To make sure the seafood cooks evenly, add the lobster and cod first. After about 5 minutes add ½ cup scallops, and after a few minutes more add ½ cup shrimp, being careful not to overcook. The shrimp will be done in about 3 minutes.

60

Codfish Cakes
Bolinhos de Bacalhau
Makes about 40 cakes

This easy continental-style recipe for salt cod can be used as an appetizer for a party, as a snack, or as part of a simple meal when combined with rice and greens. It is a recipe served frequently throughout the year and always on Christmas Eve. As a young girl, I enjoyed learning how to form the cakes into their somewhat flattened egg shape.
To form the cakes, use two teaspoons: with one hand, take a spoonful of the mixture, and with the other hand and a rotating motion, insert the bowl of the second spoon behind the mixture, scooping it out of the first spoon. Repeat several times, back and forth, to obtain an oval shape and smooth finish. This technique does take a little practice!

1 pound salt cod, preferably boneless, soaked in
  several changes of cold water, 24 to 36 hours,
  refrigerated*
3 to 4 medium potatoes, whole, skins intact
  (about 1 pound)
3 large eggs, lightly beaten
¼ cup finely chopped onion (optional)
¼ cup finely chopped parsley
½ teaspoon hot pepper sauce (optional)
¼ teaspoon white pepper
coarse salt to taste, if needed
olive oil for deep frying

*See salt cod instructions on page 11.

1. Taste a piece of fish to make sure enough of salt has been soaked away; if not, change the water and soak longer. When the fish is ready, drain the cod from the soaking water and rinse. Place the fish in a 5-quart pot with the potatoes and enough water to cover ingredients completely. Cover and bring to a boil. Reduce the heat to medium-low and simmer 15 minutes.

2. Using a slotted spoon remove the cod to a dish, leaving the potatoes in the pot. When the fish is cool enough to handle, remove any bones and skin and set aside.

3. Continue to cook the potatoes until easily pierced with a fork. Drain the potatoes and peel when they are cool enough to handle.

4. Using a meat grinder, process the cooked codfish, the optional onion, and potatoes. (If you do not have a grinder, shred cod by hand and mash potatoes with masher or fork. Do not use a food processor.) Place the mixture of fish and potatoes in a bowl with the eggs. Mix in the parsley, the optional pepper sauce, and white pepper. Mixture should be fairly thick, but not stiff and dry. Add an extra egg if the mixture seems dry and isn't binding together.

5. Heat 5 to 6 inches of the oil in a 2½-quart saucepan until it is very hot, but not smoking. Cook a small amount of the mixture to test for salt.

6. Shape codfish mixture into slightly flattened egg-shaped cakes. Try to keep them uniform in size. Fry the codfish cakes a few at a time so as not to lower temperature of the oil. Fry until the outside is medium golden and center is hot. They should not be heavy, but fairly light and puffy. Drain on paper towels. Transfer to a platter and garnish with parsley.

Note: The mixture can also be made up ahead, shaped and refrigerated, then deep-fried just before serving.

Variation: For a lighter, fluffy interior, some Portuguese cooks separate the eggs and beat the egg whites to soft peaks before adding them with the yolks to the mixture. Either way, they're like eating potato chips—you can't stop with just one.

Terre Nostre Park, São Miguel, Azores

Salt Cod with Cream

Bacalhau com Nata

Serves 6 to 8

On one of our visits to Portugal, we had the pleasure of dining with family friends in their flat in the older section of Lisbon. Ismailde, who is a wonderful cook, prepared a codfish dish for us while Jose poured his homemade wine. Our son isn't a big eater but considers this his favorite dish. Ismailde thought he didn't care for the meal since he ate only a small amount. In Portuguese, she said to him, "Passarinho, passarinho, quando eu for tua casa, eu não vou comer também." I translated for him: "Little bird, little bird, when I go to your house, I won't eat either." He then surprised us all by replying in Portuguese, with perfect timing, "Mais fica," literally "more stays," meaning "more for me," which set everyone laughing. In this dish, cod is first poached in water, then milk, before it is combined with sautéed vegetables and a rich cream sauce giving a silky mouth feel. The sauce can also be made using the broth from poaching the fish. This dish takes approximately two hours to prepare and uses a number of pans, but it is so luscious that it is really worth the extra effort. Read the recipe through carefully and plan ahead.

Prepare the fish:

1½ pounds boneless salt cod, soaked in several changes of cold water, 24 to 36 hours, refrigerated*

2 quarts water

1 quart hot milk

1. After soaking, taste a piece of the fish to make sure enough of salt has been removed. Soak a bit longer, if needed, changing the water. Pour 2 quarts of water into a large pan and bring to a boil over high heat. Turn off the heat. Remove the codfish from the soaking water, rinse, and add to the pan, making sure that the fish is completely covered with the hot water. Add more boiling water if needed. Cover the pan and poach the fish for 15 minutes or a little longer if the pieces are very thick (more than 1 inch).

2. Drain the fish and reserve the broth if you are using it in the sauce (see below). In a large bowl, hand-shred the fish, removing any bones or pieces of skin. Pour the hot milk over the fish, cover, and let stand for 30 minutes to 1 hour.

*See salt cod instructions on page 11.

Prepare the vegetable mixture:

2 cups olive oil

1 large onion, thinly sliced (about 1½ cups)

1 bay leaf

1 large carrot, shredded or sliced into fine julienne (about 1 cup)

1 clove garlic, finely chopped

1 tablespoon finely chopped parsley

scant ½ teaspoon coarse salt

3 large potatoes, peeled and cut into thin julienne (about 3½ cups)

1. While the fish is poaching in the milk, heat 3 tablespoons of the oil in a large, deep-sided frying pan over medium-high heat. Add and sauté the onion with the bay leaf until the onion is soft and translucent. Stir in the carrots and garlic, and sauté for one minute. Toss in the parsley, season with salt, and set aside.

2. In another deep pan, deep-fry the potatoes in the remaining olive oil until golden. Drain on paper towels and reserve.

63

Make the sauce:

2½ ounces butter

2½ ounces flour (¼ cup plus 1 tablespoon)

1¾ cups milk

1¾ cups heavy cream (for a lighter sauce, use light cream or the codfish cooking broth)

¼ teaspoon white pepper or to taste

¼ teaspoon nutmeg

2 egg yolks, lightly beaten

juice of ¼ lemon

scant teaspoon coarse salt

1. Melt the butter in a medium saucepan over medium-low heat. Stir in the flour, stirring constantly to make a roux. Let it cook on low heat for 2 to 3 minutes to cook the starch.

2. Pour the cool milk slowly into the hot roux, stirring constantly to avoid lumps.

3. Stirring, add the cream or fish stock. Bring to a low simmer, then remove from heat and add pepper and nutmeg.

4. In a medium bowl, stir a small amount of sauce into the egg yolks, to temper them. Then transfer the egg mixture into the cream sauce, stirring constantly. (If you add the eggs to the sauce without tempering them first, they will not blend with the sauce.) Whisk in the lemon juice and any additional salt. Simmer an additional minute, stirring. Set aside.

Assemble:

½ cup fresh bread crumbs for topping

Preheat the oven to 350 degrees F.

1. Drain the codfish from the milk and transfer to a large bowl. Add the onion and carrot mixture and potatoes. Toss lightly to mix the ingredients thoroughly. Fold half of the cream sauce into the mixture and gently blend.

2. Transfer mixture to a baking dish measuring approximately 9 x 13 inches. Spread the mixture gently and evenly. Pour remaining sauce over the top and sprinkle with bread crumbs.

3. Bake at 350 degrees for about 20 minutes or until the top is lightly golden and bubbly. The ingredients should be heated through. Garnish with parsley and a fine julienne of carrot sticks.

Tip: The carrot-onion mixture and the potatoes can be made early in the day, combined, refrigerated, then assembled with the fish and sauce later.

64

Salt Cod Gomes de Sá-Style

Bacalhau à Gomes de Sá

Serves 6 to 8

This popular traditional dish is extremely simple to prepare, beginning a day ahead with the soaking of the salt cod. After poaching the cod in water, soaking it in hot milk keeps it tender. If you are lactose intolerant, you can omit this step. The recipe was created by Gomes de Sá, of Oporto's famous Restaurante Lisbonense. There are different versions of it; which is the original is a subject of debate. This version is the one I learned as the youngest cook in the family.

1 pound thick salt cod pieces, soaked in several changes of cold water, 24 to 36 hours, refrigerated*

1½ to 2 quarts water

about 1 quart hot milk

3 large or 4 medium boiling potatoes, scrubbed, skins intact (about 1½ pounds)

½ cup olive oil

2 large onions, peeled and thinly sliced

3 cloves garlic, finely chopped

¼ cup finely chopped parsley

3 hard boiled eggs, shelled

1 teaspoon coarse salt or to taste

*See salt cod instructions on page 11.

1. Pour the water into a 4-quart pot and bring to a boil. Turn off the heat.

2. Remove the fish from the soaking water, rinse, and add to the boiling water, making sure the fish is completely covered. Cover the pot and let the fish poach 15 to 20 minutes, until the fish is opaque and almost starts to flake.

3. Remove the fish to a bowl and break it into medium-sized pieces, discarding any bones or skin. Pour the hot milk over the fish and let stand for 30 minutes.

4. Meanwhile, boil the potatoes in their skins until they are tender. Cool, peel, and slice the potatoes ½- inch thick. Preheat the oven to 350 degrees F.

5. Heat 2 tablespoons of the oil in a large frying pan. Add and sauté the onions over medium-high heat until golden, about 10 to 15 minutes. Add the remaining oil and garlic. Heat through.

6. Drain the milk from the cod and arrange the cod in a 9 x 13-inch baking dish, alternating layers with the potatoes and onion sauce, ending with the sauce. Season with salt only if needed. Bake in a preheated oven for about 20 minutes.

7. Rinse any residue of shell from the eggs and slice into rounds. Garnish the top of the cooked casserole with a row of egg slices in the middle, a sprinkling of parsley, and black olives along the edges. Serve with a simple green salad.

65

Salt Cod Gomes de Sá-Style, page 65

PORTUGUESE HOMESTYLE COOKING

Salt Cod Bras-Style
Bacalhau à Brás
Serves 4

If there were leftovers from Bacalhau à Gomes de Sá, *my father-in-law would make a quick version* of bacalhau à brás. *In the traditional method, potatoes are cut into fine julienne and fried, then combined with presoaked salt cod, then sautéed with garlic. The mixture was then "embraced" or coated with lightly beaten eggs. My father-in-law's shortcut is a great way to use leftover* Bacalhau à Gomes de Sá.

2 tablespoons olive oil
2 cups leftover *Bacalhau à Gomes de Sá*
4 eggs, lightly beaten
½ teaspoon coarse salt or to taste
¼ teaspoon ground black pepper or to taste
2 tablespoons finely chopped parsley

1. Heat the oil in a medium skillet over medium-high heat. Add and thoroughly heat the leftover cod mixture in the olive oil for about 5 minutes.
2. Add the beaten eggs. Season with salt and pepper, if needed, and cook until eggs are done, stirring occasionally, as if cooking scrambled eggs. Garnish with parsley and serve immediately.

67

Cod Baked with Onion Sauce

Bacalhau no Forno com Cebolada

Serves 4

The rule of thumb for this tasty dish is one onion per person. If you have onions lovers in the family, use large onions. This is adapted from a recipe that is particularly popular in Portugal, especially for wedding feasts, and has made its way to the United States. It is typically made with salt cod that has the skins and bones intact, which can usually be found in Portuguese or Italian markets. In the original recipe the fish is placed skin side up and coated with mayonnaise. I prefer using the boneless and skinless fish for this dish, especially if I am serving it to guests. A drizzling of olive oil replaces the mayonnaise. The following recipe is modified using skinned and boneless salt cod.

½ cup olive oil

4 large onions (one per person), thinly sliced
   (about 6 cups)

2 cloves garlic coarsely chopped

1 bay leaf

1 large very ripe tomato, peeled, seeded, and
   coarsely chopped (about 1 cup)

1 teaspoon hot pepper sauce

1 cup white wine

3 sprigs of parsley

¼ teaspoon white pepper

1 pound salt cod, thick center cut, soaked in
   several changes of cold water, 24 to 36 hours,
   refrigerated*

2 eggs, lightly beaten

1 cup plain bread crumbs

¼ cup olive oil

Preheat the oven to 350 degrees F.

*See salt cod instructions on page 11.

1. In a large skillet, heat the olive oil over medium-high heat. Add and sauté the onions until golden, about 10 to 15 minutes.

2. Reduce the heat to medium-low, add the garlic with the bay leaf, and cook until the garlic is aromatic and lightly colored.

3. Mix the chopped tomatoes into the hot sauce. Cover and simmer until the tomatoes become soft and partially dissolved into the onions, about 15 minutes. Pour in the wine and add the parsley and white pepper. Simmer until the liquid is reduced by half. The sauce should have the consistency of oatmeal. Remove from the heat, discard the bay leaf and the sprigs of parsley, then transfer the sauce into a 9 x 12-inch baking dish.

4. Remove the cod from the soaking water and rinse. Cut into 4 serving pieces.

5. Dip the fish into the beaten eggs and then into the bread crumbs, coating all sides. Place the pieces of fish on top of the onion sauce.

6. Drizzle a small amount of olive oil on the top of the fish. Bake in a 350-degree oven for 35 minutes or until the breadcrumbs are a light golden color. Garnish with fresh parsley and serve with Punched Potatoes (page 139).

Baked Scrod

Pescada no Forno

Serves 4 to 6

My aunt Ana makes this simple dish of baked fish with pre-boiled potatoes.

2 pounds fresh scrod fillets or other white fish
6 tablespoons olive oil
1 teaspoon paprika
¼ teaspoon white pepper
2 cloves garlic, finely chopped
2 tablespoons butter, softened
2 tablespoons lemon juice
8 small Red Bliss potatoes, peeled, halved, and parboiled
2 teaspoons coarse salt or to taste

Preheat the oven to 350 degrees F.

1. Drain the fish and pat dry. Brush the fish with 1 tablespoon of the olive oil, then season with paprika, pepper, and half of the garlic. Place the fish skin side down in the baking pan and dot top with butter. Sprinkle with lemon juice.
2. Combine potatoes in a bowl with the remaining olive oil, garlic, and 1 teaspoon of the salt. Toss well and arrange around the fish in pan. Sprinkle the remaining salt over the fish.
3. Cover and bake at 350 degrees for 20 to 25 minutes or until fish is opaque and the potatoes are heated through.

69

Broiled Salmon
Salmão Grelhado
Serves 4

Many good cooks have come to America from the island of Faial in the Azores. Among them is Leonia Clarimundo, whose method for preparing salmon is utterly simple. The butter and lemon become one with the flavor of cilantro, creating a stimulating aroma that is very special. Second only to the people from the Alentejo region, the people of Faial are great lovers of fresh cilantro. This may be explained by the fact that many of the early settlers of Faial came from the Alentejo and Algarve regions of the mainland.

4 salmon steaks, ¾-inch-thick, skins intact
1 tablespoon coarse salt or to taste
1 stick butter
juice of ½ lemon or to taste
4 cloves garlic, finely chopped
¼ teaspoon fresh ground pepper
¼ cup finely chopped cilantro or parsley

1. Season the fish steaks on both sides with salt. Broil or grill over a hot fire, 4 to 5 minutes on each side until opaque or to desired doneness. Remove to a serving dish, cover, and set aside.
2. Meanwhile, in a 1-quart saucepan over medium-low heat, melt the butter then add the lemon juice, garlic, and pepper. Cook briefly, just until the garlic becomes aromatic. Toss in the cilantro and heat through for two minutes. Drizzle over the salmon and serve immediately.

70

Salmon Baked in a Clay Tile, page 71

Salmon Baked in a Clay Tile
Salmão Assado na Telha
Serves 4 to 6

The Portuguese are known for making multiple uses of most anything, including clay roof tiles. Of course, in cooking, the curved clay tiles are not taken from a roof, but are created in the same curved shape—about 7 inches long and 4 inches wide—except with closed ends. This recipe is almost guaranteed to win over any who are not fond of salmon. Although in Portugal this dish is cooked in an unglazed clay "roof tile," which makes a great presentation, the tiles are difficult to obtain in the United States. The flavor is not as scrumptious when it is prepared in a metal, glass, or glazed dish. I recommend using an unglazed clay baker or deep-dish pizza stone, about 2-inches deep, like those sold at kitchen specialty stores. Follow directions for using the clay baker so that it doesn't crack.

Rich Nunes adapted this recipe from one he enjoyed in the Azores. He substitutes salmon for lidio, a fish found in Portuguese waters and not available in American markets. The method is unusual, but the result is a very tasty fish that is not greasy. Ask your fishmonger to remove the thin rib bones from the fish or do it yourself using needle-nose pliers to pull them out.

20 cloves garlic, finely chopped
½ cup olive oil as needed
2 salmon steaks, 1-inch-thick, (about 1 pound),
    halved lengthwise with center bone removed
4 thin crosscut slices onion
2 strips lean bacon or thinly sliced prosciutto,
    cut in half, crosswise
½ pound *chouriço* (page 12), cut into ¼-inch slices
coarse salt as needed
freshly ground black pepper

Preheat the oven to 350 degrees F.

1. Scatter the garlic over the bottom of the clay baker in an even layer, making a bed. Pour the olive oil over the garlic. It should barely cover the garlic. Add more if needed.
2. Remove any tiny bones from the salmon. Place each steak half skin side up on top of the bed of garlic in the baker, without crowding (1½ inches apart).
3. Place one half-strip of bacon against and slightly pressing into one side of each piece of salmon. Because the fish steaks are upright, not flat, the bacon flavor is imparted to the salmon while the bacon fat drips to the bottom of the pan. Press one slice of onion against the opposite side of each piece of fish. There will be bacon on one side and onion on the other side of each steak.
4. Scatter slices of the sausage around the outside edge of the baker. Sprinkle the fish skins with coarse salt and season all with ground pepper.
5. Bake for 25 to 30 minutes or to desired doneness. Garnish with finely chopped parsley. Serve with Punched Potatoes (page 139).

Note: Instead of salmon, use an equally flavorful type of fish; a mild tasting fish does not work well in this recipe.

Placing salmon fillets instead of steaks skin side down in the baking dish, with the other ingredients on top results in a more oily taste.

Tips: If you happen to know a potter, perhaps you can have "tiles" made for individual servings. They should be about 7 inches long by 4 inches across, like a hollowed log split down the middle.

Place unglazed clay dish on a sheet pan before placing in the oven to keep clean-up to a minimum.

71

Fish Stew with Shellfish
Caldeirada com Mariscos
Serves 8

Typically, a caldeirada *contains only fish, usually more than one kind, in its aromatic broth. Fishermen used whatever fish they caught, even conger eels. Some* caldeiradas *are made with a bottom layer of bread instead of potatoes. This Continental version is enriched with clams and shrimp. A multitude of flavors commingle in this dish to delight seafood enthusiasts. It is perfect for casual summer entertaining. This recipe is prepared in the traditional method. All the ingredients are assembled raw in a single pot and are not stirred during the cooking process. Instead, the pot is moved back and forth across the burner, shaking the ingredients, "stirring" them without disturbing the layers. With only a single cup of white wine and no additional water, a delicious broth comes from the ingredients themselves. The secret is slow cooking over medium-low heat and a tight cover. To complete this meal, simply serve chunks of crusty bread to soak up the broth, flavorful black olives, and plenty of* vinho verde *or other crisp white wine.*

½ cup olive oil

3 large onions, thinly sliced (about 4½ cups)

2 large Red Bliss potatoes, scrubbed, skins intact, cut into ½-inch slices (about 2½ cups)

3 large meaty very ripe tomatoes, peeled and chopped (about 4 cups, divided)

4 cloves garlic, coarsely chopped (divided)

2 bay leaves, torn in half (divided)

1½ sweet green peppers, thinly sliced (divided) (about 1 cup)

¼ cup finely chopped cilantro (divided)

½ teaspoon dry crushed red pepper (divided)

2 tablespoons sweet paprika for sprinkling (divided)

1 teaspoon coarse salt

½ teaspoon fresh ground black or white pepper (divided)

24 small littleneck clams

2 pounds fish, cut into chunks of about 3 inches (halibut, monk, scrod, eel, or a combination)

½ pound medium shrimp, peeled and deveined

1 medium pinch saffron (about 1 teaspoon)

1 cup white wine

1. Pour the olive oil into a thick bottomed 8- or 10-quart pot. Add the onion slices forming a thick single layer followed by a layer of potatoes, overlapping the slices as necessary.

2. Scatter one third of the tomatoes, garlic, bay leaves, sweet peppers, cilantro, and crushed red pepper over the potatoes, followed by a sprinkling of paprika, salt, and ground pepper.

3. Add the littlenecks, followed by the fish. Repeat step 2.

4. Top with a single layer of shrimp and sweet green peppers and repeat step 2 again.

5. Dissolve the saffron in 1 tablespoon of warm water and let sit for 15 minutes. Mix with the wine and pour over the layered ingredients. Cover tightly and place over medium-high heat for 5 minutes or until you hear the wine start to boil. Quickly reduce the heat to medium-low.

6. Simmer gently, without uncovering, for about 30 to 45 minutes. Occasionally shake the pan gently back and forth. Check for doneness and adjust seasoning. The shrimp on top should be opaque and tender and the peppers cooked. Cook an additional 5 minutes if needed.

7. Place pot in center of table and serve, making sure to scoop up some of each layer. Ladle over slices of dry or toasted country bread placed in individual soup plates.

Clockwise from lower left: Clams Cataplana (page 55), Salmon Baked in a Clay Tile (page 71), Fisherman's Stew of Graciosa (page 74), Salt Cod Gomes de Sá-Style (page 65).

73

Fishermen's Stew of Graciosa
Caldeirada à Moda do Pescador da Graciosa
Serves 8 to 10

With limited kitchen equipment on board ship, fishermen still managed to create fish stews with magnificently seasoned broth. Each member of the crew took part in preparing the ingredients, using some of the fish from their catch. A stew could contain anywhere from one to three or four kinds of fish, including sardines and eels. The recipe prepared here is that of the Azorean Portuguese fishermen and their descendants. It is associated with the island of Graciosa (meaning "gracious"), one of the nine islands in the Azores. In this version, the fish is poached rather than stewed. Spices and seasonings are added to the poaching liquid, creating a spicy broth that is ladled over the fish.

Stew:

4 pounds dressed cusk, cut into 1-inch-thick steaks (or thick fillets cut into serving pieces; see Note below)

1 quart water or enough to barely cover the fish

3 sprigs parsley

2 medium onions, thinly sliced (about 2 cups)

3 bay leaves

1½ tablespoons coarse salt

1 tablespoon olive oil

1. In the bottom of an 8-quart pot, place the fish in layers. Pour in enough cold water to barely cover the fish. Add the parsley, onions, bay leaves, salt, and olive oil.

2. Cover tightly, place over medium-high heat, and bring to a boil. Reduce the heat and simmer gently until the fish is opaque, about 20 minutes.

Seasoning paste:

7 cloves garlic, coarsely chopped

2 teaspoons coarse salt

1½ teaspoons cumin seed or ½ teaspoon cumin powder

1½ tablespoons finely chopped parsley

2 pickled chili peppers, each about 1 inch long, finely chopped (page 4)

1 teaspoon ground safflower (page 13) (use paprika if safflower is unavailable)

3 tablespoons tomato paste

1 tablespoon sugar

¼ teaspoon ground nutmeg

½ cup olive oil

¼ cup wine vinegar

1. Using a large mortar and pestle, mash the garlic with the salt, forming a paste.

2. Mash in the cumin, parsley, chili peppers, and safflower. Stir in the tomato paste, sugar, and nutmeg. Drizzle in the olive oil followed by the vinegar. (If you do not have a mortar and pestle or yours is not large enough, make the paste in a medium bowl using the back of a spoon or a fork.) Stir to blend the ingredients well.

To serve:

1. With a slotted spoon, transfer the cooked fish to a serving dish. Cover and keep warm.

2. Whisk the seasoning paste into the fish broth, making sure it is well dispersed. Simmer for about 5 minutes over medium-low heat.

3. Ladle some of the seasoned broth over the fish and serve remaining broth on the side. Or place generous pieces of fish in individual soup plates and spoon the broth over it. Serve with plenty of bread to dip in the broth, or give the soup a continental touch with a slice of toasted bread placed on the bottom of each plate.

Note: When cusk is cut into steaks it yields a gelatinous substance that gives the broth a rich body that is lacking when skinned and boneless fillets are used.

74

Periiwinkles with Garlic

Caracois/Caramujos com Alho

Serves 2 to 4

Warm summer nights bring back memories of sitting outside with my father and some of his friends, sharing a bowl of periwinkles delicately flavored with garlic, onion, herbs, and spice. Equipped with pins or toothpicks, we carefully pried the periwinkles from their shells, savoring every bite. Anyone who enjoys escargot should try this recipe! It makes for an interesting appetizer or snack.

4 pounds saltwater periwinkles (about 5 cups)
¼ cup finely chopped parsley or coriander
1 small onion (3-inch diameter), peeled, left whole
1 scant tablespoon coarse salt
3 cloves garlic, peeled and smashed
1 tablespoon hot pepper sauce
1 tablespoon finely ground black pepper
1 bay leaf
2 cups cold water as needed

Day ahead:
1. Rinse the periwinkles and soak for 1 hour with 1 tablespoon salt in sufficient water to cover. Drain, rinse, and chill overnight.

Next day:
2. Rinse the periwinkles in several changes of water. Combine the remaining ingredients with the periwinkles in a 3-quart pan with sufficient cold water to just cover.
3. Cover the pan and bring to a boil over medium-high heat. Once the water begins to boil, reduce the heat and simmer for 20 minutes. Drain the water from the pot and transfer the periwinkles to a serving bowl.
4. Serve hot with toothpicks or pins to pick out the periwinkles. To eat, insert pins or toothpicks into the shell, discard thin round flap and remove curly meat of the periwinkle.

Note: The disk-like flaps at the opening of the the periwinkles will separate easily when the periwinkles are done.

75

Boiled Lobster
Lagosta Fervida
Serves 4

Fresh lobsters absorb the aromatic and flavorful seasoning, making melted butter unnecessary. The succulent and sweet soft-shell lobsters of the early summer are a favorite. Vinho verde, Portuguese "green" wine, and lobster are well matched.

10 large cloves garlic, coarsely chopped
1 tablespoon coarse salt
2 teaspoons Hot Pepper Paste (page 167)
½ teaspoon cumin seed
1 bay leaf
3 sprigs parsley, coarsely chopped
1 small onion, coarsely chopped (about ½ cup)
4 chicken lobsters, (about 1¼ pounds each)

1. Using a mortar and pestle, mash the garlic with the salt, forming a paste. Add the remaining ingredients—except for the onions and lobsters—mashing well after each addition, to open up the essence of the spices.

2. Fill a 12-quart stockpot three-fourths full of water (about 10 quarts). Add the seasoning paste and the onion, cover, and bring to a boil over medium-high heat.

3. Add the lobsters, re-cover, and bring to a second boil. From this point, cook the lobsters for 10 to 12 minutes. Remove from the pot and serve immediately. Serve with or without melted butter.

Tip: For a spicy alternative, use a mixture of hot pepper sauce and olive oil for dipping instead of melted butter.

76

Curried Shrimp
Camarões de Caril
Serves 4 to 6

This recipe is adapted from a dish I enjoyed at a Portuguese function many years ago. It is one of my favorite dishes to prepare, especially for guests. The shrimp are gently sautéed in a spicy tomato- and onion-based curry sauce, then served over plain boiled rice.

1½ pounds large shrimp, peeled and deveined, shells reserved

4 cups water

1 cup white wine

1 small onion, finely chopped (about ½ cup, divided)

1 bay leaf

1½ cups long-grain or converted rice

1 teaspoon salt

1 tablespoon butter

1 tablespoon olive oil

1 large very ripe tomato, peeled, seeded, and finely chopped (about 1 cup)

1 clove garlic, finely chopped

1 teaspoon hot pepper sauce

½ teaspoon paprika

1 tablespoon sweet or hot curry powder dissolved in ¼ cup warm milk

½ cup heavy cream

1 teaspoon coarse salt or to taste

1. In a 2½-quart saucepan place shrimp shells, water, wine, half of the onion, and the bay leaf. Cover and bring to a boil over high heat. Reduce the heat to medium-low and simmer for 15 minutes. Strain and reserve the broth. Discard the shells.

2. In a separate medium saucepan, bring 3⅓ cups of the shrimp broth to a boil. Add the rice and salt. Reduce the heat, cover, and simmer until rice is tender and liquid is absorbed, about 20 to 25 minutes. Keep warm.

3. Meanwhile, in a medium-sized skillet, heat the butter and oil over medium-high heat. Add the shrimp and sauté for 2 minutes. Transfer the shrimp to a dish and cover.

4. Add the remaining onion to the same skillet and sauté until lightly golden, about 10 minutes. Mix in the tomatoes, garlic, hot pepper sauce, and paprika. Reduce the heat, cover, and simmer until the tomato has broken down and is partially dissolved, about 15 minutes.

5. Stir in the curry mixture, blending well, and continue cooking for another minute.

6. Pour in the remaining broth, stir, then quickly reduce by half. Pull the pan off the heat and whisk in the cream. Return to medium-low heat and, without boiling, simmer until slightly thickened. Return the shrimp to the pan to heat through for 1 minute.

7. Fluff up the rice with a fork and arrange on a serving platter. Arrange the shrimp on top and spoon some of the curry sauce over it. Serve any extra sauce on the side.

77

Peel-and-Eat Shrimp Portuguese-Style
Camarões à Portuguesa
Serves 4 to 6

I still can see my father standing at the stove preparing this shrimp-lover's delight. Besides being a perfect light lunch, this dish makes a great appetizer. Sometimes my father would add coarsely chopped sweet green peppers to the pot. He never puréed the broth, but I occasionally do. Serve the broth, puréed or not, on the side as a dip for the shrimp.

¼ cup olive oil

1 small onion, thinly sliced (about ½ cup)

1 large very ripe tomato, peeled, seeded and
    coarsely chopped (about 1 cup)

1 bay leaf

3 cloves garlic crushed

¼ teaspoon crushed dried red pepper

½ cup *vinho verde* or other white wine

1 tablespoon finely chopped fresh cilantro

2 pounds fresh shrimp, rinsed, in their shells

½ teaspoon coarse salt or to taste

2 tablespoons butter

1. Heat the olive oil in a 3-quart saucepan, over medium-high heat Add and sauté the onion until lightly golden.

2. Stir in the tomato, bay leaf, garlic, and crushed red pepper. Cover and cook over medium-low heat until mixture is soft and tomatoes are partially dissolved, about 15 minutes.

3. Pour in the wine, stir, re-cover, and bring to a boil over medium-high heat. Reduce the heat to medium-low, add the cilantro, shrimp, and salt. Lightly mix and cover tightly. Simmer for 3 minutes or until the shrimp are tender. Be careful not to overcook or the shrimp will be tough.

4. Using a slotted spoon, transfer the shrimp to a serving dish and cover. Melt the butter into the broth, then strain or, using a hand-held blender, purée the broth. Serve on the side as a dip for the peeled shrimp.

78

Shrimp Rissoles

Rissóis de Camarão

Makes about 3½ dozen

These delectable savories can be served as a single course, as a snack, or as an appetizer. Although they are most often made with shrimp, a filling of chicken is tasty as well. They can even be made with shredded poached salt cod. This is adapted from a recipe from my friend Isaura, who uses olive oil to fry the onions and corn oil to fry the assembled turnover. Cornstarch is used to bind the filling. These rissoles can be made ahead and frozen before frying (see Note following recipe). When you have unexpected guests, just pop as many as you need from the freezer and fry them up. Make them small or make them a bit larger, but make them. Serve with your favorite wine.

Pastry:
2 cups milk
4 tablespoons butter
1 teaspoon salt
2 cups flour

1. In a 2-quart saucepan, place the milk, butter, and salt. Warm over medium-high heat until the milk is scalded, not boiling. Reduce the heat to medium-low.
2. Using a wooden spoon, vigorously stir the flour into the milk. Keep stirring over medium-low heat until it forms a dough. When the dough pulls away from the sides of the pan and forms a ball, remove the pan from the stove.
3. Turn the dough out onto a lightly floured work space. Using a plastic dough scraper or wooden spoon, turn the warm dough to knead briefly until smooth and the dough slightly springs back when pressed with your finger. (Don't overwork the dough.) Divide the dough in half, forming two balls, and cover with an inverted bowl. Set aside to cool to nearly room temperature.

Filling:
2 tablespoons butter
¼ cup finely chopped onion
1 cup milk
½ tablespoon finely chopped cilantro or parsley

1 to 2 teaspoons hot pepper sauce, to taste
½ teaspoon coarse salt or to taste
½ teaspoon freshly ground white pepper
¼ teaspoon nutmeg
2 tablespoons cornstarch or flour
2 tablespoons water
½ pound shrimp, peeled, deveined, cooked, well
    drained, and coarsely chopped (about 1½ cups)

1. Melt the butter in a 1-quart saucepan. Add and sauté the onion over medium-high heat until a light golden color, about 10 minutes.
2. Reduce the heat to medium-low, pour in the milk, and heat to scalding, not boiling. Stir in the cilantro or parsley, hot pepper sauce, salt, pepper, and nutmeg.
3. Combine the cornstarch or flour with the water. Stir into the milk and simmer over medium-low heat, stirring constantly, until it thickens, about 1 to 2 minutes. (Don't over cook or the cornstarch will break down and the mixture will loosen.) Stir in the chopped shrimp, heat through for 1 minute, and remove from heat. Set aside to cool completely.

Assemble:
1. Take half the dough and roll out to ⅛-inch thickness. Using a cutter that is 3½ to 4 inches in diameter (smaller if making appetizers for a party), cut disks of dough.

79

2. Place 1 teaspoon of filling in the middle of a circle. Fold the dough over to form a half circle, pressing the edges together. Set aside on a sheet pan or tray lined with plastic wrap. Repeat until all the filling is used.

Fry:
egg wash (3 large eggs beaten with ¼ cup water)
fine plain bread crumbs
olive oil or corn oil for frying

1. Dip the pastries in beaten egg, then quickly into the bread crumbs, shaking off any excess bread crumbs. Set aside. In a deep skillet, fry the rissoles, two or three at a time, in hot oil until golden brown. Serve hot or at room temperature.

Note: To freeze: Line a sheet pan with plastic wrap and set the pastries down in a single layer without overlapping. Cover well with plastic wrap, smoothing out as much air as possible. Freeze. They will keep for at least a month, but you most likely will use them before that time.

Variation: Substitute 1½ cups finely chopped cooked chicken, rabbit, or shredded poached salt cod for the shrimp. Stir briefly, add 1 tablespoon finely chopped celery, stir, and assemble.

80

Shrimp Rissoles

Grilled Shrimp with Garlic and Cilantro
Camarão com Alho e Coentros Grelhados
Serves 4

One of the best ways to eat shrimp is when it is simply grilled. The lemony tang of cilantro works so well with shrimp—they are truly a well-matched pair. If you use wooden skewers, be sure to soak them in warm water for about ½ hour before grilling.

8 cloves garlic, finely chopped
½ teaspoon coarse salt or to taste
½ cup finely chopped cilantro
1 teaspoon hot pepper sauce
½ cup white wine or lemon juice
16 jumbo shrimp, peeled, deveined, tail on skewers, preferably wooden

1. Using a mortar and pestle, mash the garlic with the salt, forming a thick paste. Blend in the cilantro and hot pepper sauce. Transfer to a medium bowl, then stir in the wine. Add the shrimp, turning gently to coat. Cover and refrigerate for ½ hour.
2. Remove the shrimp from the marinade and thread on presoaked skewers.
3. Grill the shrimp over hot charcoal for 1½ to 2 minutes, on each side.
4. Serve with a salad and Tomato Rice (page 147). Portuguese *vinho verde* is perfect with shrimp. *Piripiri* sauce (page 5) for dipping adds a zesty touch.

81

Tuna Madeira-Style

Atum á Moda da Madeira

Serves 4

Working in a jacket factory after school was a culinary learning experience as well as a manufacturing one. New England Sportswear, where I worked, was a melting pot of cultures. At lunch breaks, food was always one of the topics of conversation. It seems that when the canneries were built in Portugal, they enabled rural inland areas to add some fish to their diets—canned sardines and canned tuna. Canned tuna was eaten only on the mainland, however. On the island of Madeira, fresh tuna steaks are the standard. A coworker from the island of Madeira, Adelaide Figueira, taught me her method for preparing fresh tuna. I take liberty with this dish and use cilantro instead of parsley. Because cilantro is a taste that some have yet to acquire, the choice is up to you. To my taste, the cilantro complements the flavor of the tuna especially well.

2 cloves garlic, coarsely chopped
1 tablespoon coarse salt
1 teaspoon Hot Pepper Paste (page 167)
4 fresh tuna steaks, ½ inch thick, rinsed well in ice-cold water
1 cup red wine vinegar (more if needed)
1 cup water (more if needed)
olive oil as needed
1 tablespoon finely chopped cilantro or parsley

1. Using a mortar and pestle, mash the garlic with the salt, forming a paste. Blend in the Hot Pepper Paste. Coat both sides of the tuna steaks. Transfer the fish to a baking dish large enough to accommodate the fish in a single layer.

2. Into a medium bowl or large measuring cup, pour equal amounts of vinegar and water. Blend well and pour over the fish, making sure there is enough marinade to cover the fish completely. (The amount varies according to the size of the dish you use.) Cover and marinate in the refrigerator for several hours or overnight.

3. Reserving the marinade, transfer the fish to a platter and blot the fish with paper towels.

4. Pour enough oil to cover the bottom of a medium skillet (about ¼ cup) and heat over medium-high until it is very hot, but not smoking. Fry the slices of tuna briefly, about 3 minutes on each side and remove to a serving platter.

5. Pour the reserved marinade into the same skillet, bring to a boil, reduce the heat to medium-low and simmer for 2 minutes, stirring occasionally. Add the cilantro or parsley and heat through. Pour the sauce over the fish and serve with boiled potatoes. You'll want to serve this with crusty bread to soak up every drop of sauce.

82

Marketplace in Lisbon

CHAPTER 3 • SEAFOOD

Stuffed Pork Loin, page 104

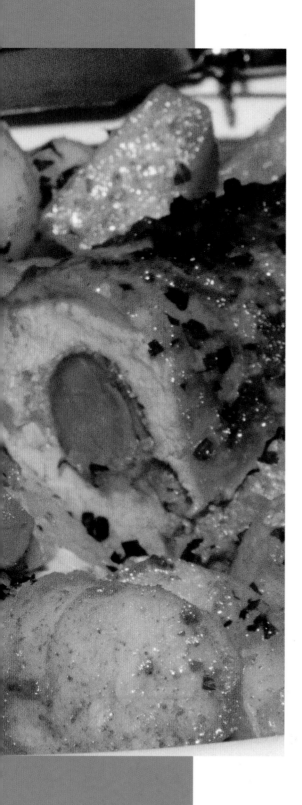

4

POULTRY & MEAT

Aves e Carne

In the past, only the wealthy Portuguese could enjoy meat every day, the poor of the country made their soups hearty, to fill and sustain themselves between meat meals. Portuguese immigrants, who brought these habits with them, have been known to live off soups all week long, scrimping and saving to make a better life in their new homeland. As families fared better, traditional meat dishes became increasingly visible.

When the nights get chilly, signaling the coming of fall and Old Man Winter, I look forward to the heartier meals of my heritage. Though fish is always on the table during the colder months, there is something that is soul-comforting and heartwarming about stews and braises of chicken, rabbit, beef, and pork. Poultry and meat are quite often steeped in a wine-and-garlic marinade overnight before they are stewed or braised. Lamb and liver are not left out, you can be sure. A simple dinner that includes meat, *Cozido à Portuguesa* (page 117), almost mirrors the New England boiled dinner. Depending on what meats are available, this boiled dinner can be very simple or very extravagant. Preparation for some of the dishes begin a day or two ahead; plan accordingly.

Walter the Chicken Man

Growing up in an ethnic neighborhood, we were used to seeing chickens running around fenced-in backyards. Although less common today, with the convenience of supermarkets, it still occurs. We never bought a chicken in a supermarket. Instead, we went to see Walter the chicken man, who received live chickens in cages from poultry farms. When we had selected our chicken, he broke its neck and hung it by its feet over a barrel. After cutting its throat, he drained the blood and dipped the chicken into hot water, then brought it to a machine where a rotating belt pulled out the feathers. Walter's wife gutted and washed our future dinner in the sink. She even trimmed the toenails. The chicken was then packaged up, gizzards, feet, and all.

My younger brothers and sisters were not old enough to have seen the chicken man in action, but they were not spared other chicken experiences. One year my father decided to raise chickens. Naturally my sisters quickly gave them names and treated them as pets. When my sisters discovered that one of their pets was our Sunday dinner, they were understandably very upset, and my mother quickly declared that there would be no more edible pets in our house. After that, we returned to Walter the chicken man and used his services until he retired. That same flock of chickens yielded a greater-than-average number of roosters. While this did not please some of our neighbors, those who came from Portugal and Poland loved the roosters, whose predawn crowing reminded them of the old country. Somehow, the eggs and chickens in markets today never taste quite as good as those fresh from the chicken coop.

Although turkeys were raised on our cousin Margaret's farm in Portugal, they seldom were here in America. Before the turkeys in Portugal were slaughtered, they were fed brandy until they were drunk, in hopes of tenderizing the meat. Turkeys were customarily served for dinner on Christmas, Easter, special occasions—and in America, on Thanksgiving. Today, except at Thanksgiving, the focus of festive meals has shifted from turkey to roast beef, lamb, and pork.

Stewed Chicken
Galinha Estufada
Serves 4 to 6

This one-pot meal is tasty enough to serve to guests. When I make it with potatoes instead of rice (see Variation, below), I save any broth left over from the stew to use when I cook shrimp and scallops. The combination of tomatoes cooked with onions and garlic in olive oil is an aromatic marriage that entices the palate.

4 tablespoons olive oil
1 medium onion, coarsely chopped (about 1 cup)
1 large very ripe tomato, peeled, seeded, and
    chopped (about 1 cup)
½ tablespoon paprika
2 cloves garlic, finely chopped
1 bay leaf
½ cup white wine (optional)
1 2½- to 3-pound chicken, cut up, rinsed
3½ cups water
1½ cups converted rice or other long-grain rice
2 teaspoons coarse salt or to taste
¼ teaspoon black pepper to taste
½ cup peas, frozen or fresh, shelled
2 tablespoons finely chopped parsley

1. Heat the oil in a 5-quart Dutch oven over medium-high heat. Add and sauté the onions until a light golden color, about 10 to 15 minutes.
2. Put in the tomatoes, paprika, garlic, and bay leaf. Reduce the heat, cover, and simmer until the tomatoes are soft and partially dissolved, about 15 minutes.
3. Pour in the wine, if using, and simmer for 2 more minutes. Add the chicken and water, adding extra water if needed to just cover the chicken. Re-cover the pot tightly and bring to a boil over medium-high heat. Reduce the heat and simmer the chicken for 15 minutes.
4. Toss in the rice, salt, and pepper. Stir, re-cover, and continue to simmer for another 20 minutes. Stir in the peas and 1 tablespoon of the parsley.

Simmer for 5 minutes more or until the chicken is nearly falling off the bone. Remove the pan from the heat. Let the stew rest for 10 minutes before serving. Garnish with additional parsley. The rice should be tender and the liquid should be absorbed.

Variation: Add 4 medium potatoes, peeled and quartered, instead of the rice and peas. Potatoes are done when easily pierced with a fork.

Tip: Because my children did not like the soft chicken skin, I would transfer the chicken to a baking dish just before adding the rice or potatoes to the pot. The chicken finished cooking in a 350-degree oven, giving it a nice crisp skin. It was then placed on a platter surrounded by the rice or potatoes.

The cutting techniques I learned from my father require skill, good eye-hand coordination, and much practice. To finely chop an onion, for example, I cut it in half and hold one section, cut side up, in my left hand. Using a sharp paring knife, I make controlled crosshatch cuts half an inch deep as I turn the onion. Then I cut a slice horizontally beneath the cross-hatch cuts, releasing pieces of minced onion. I learned young, and constant practice made this method second nature to me, so I can honestly claim to be accident-free. However, my dear father-in-law was horrified when he first saw me cutting onions this way, and actually scolded me! I will add that a sharp knife and a cutting board yield the same results with greater safety.

Roasted Chicken

Galinha Assada

Serves 8

The secret to this recipe is browning the chicken pieces in a cast iron pan, instructs Senhorina Bettencourt, who has made many gatherings noteworthy by serving her garlic-and-wine-marinated chicken dish. The recipe can easily be doubled for picnics, buffet tables, and especially for Super Bowl parties. It is a guaranteed hit. Chicken wings make flavorful appetizers when prepared this way. Hot pepper sauce may be added to give them extra zing.

8 to 10 chicken legs, halved at joint; or 3 pounds chicken wings, tips removed
2 tablespoons coarse salt or to taste
1 tablespoon white or black pepper or to taste
10 cloves garlic, finely chopped
1 large onion, thinly sliced (about 1½ cups)

Marinade:
1 cup red wine
3 tablespoons tomato paste
1 cup water
3 cloves garlic, mashed
1 tablespoon Hot Pepper Paste (page 167) (optional)
½ cup olive oil

1. Using a sharp knife, remove excess fat from each piece of chicken, including any under the skin. Rinse the chicken and blot with a clean towel. Season each piece with salt, pepper, and chopped garlic, seasoning all sides and under the skin. Place the chicken in a glass or ceramic bowl and top with the onion slices.

2. Prepare the marinade in a separate bowl, mixing the red wine with the tomato paste. Slowly stir in the water, mashed garlic cloves, and Hot Pepper Paste if using. Mix well and pour over chicken. Marinate in the refrigerator for several hours or overnight.

3. About 1½ hours before serving, remove the chicken to a separate dish to drain, reserving the marinade. Preheat the oven to 350 degrees F.

4. In a black cast-iron skillet, heat the oil so that it is very hot, but not smoking. Brown the chicken, a few pieces at a time in the olive oil over medium-high heat. Turn the chicken to brown on all sides.

5. Remove and place the chicken in a covered roasting pan, preferably of dark enamel. Basting frequently with the marinade, roast at 350 degrees for 1 hour or until the chicken is nearly falling off the bone. Remove the cover during the last 15 minutes of roasting.

Tip: When possible, use a cast-iron skillet for browning the chicken before roasting. It improves both flavor and color.

Stewed Chicken, page 87

Roasted Chicken with Garlic

Galinha Assada com Alho

Serves 4 to 6

On Sundays, roasted chicken was almost sure to follow chicken soup. Back then, my brother Rudy (Rufino Jr.) and I would compete for the crisp and spicy chicken skin. There was never enough skin to satisfy us.

6 cloves garlic, coarsely chopped
2 teaspoons coarse salt or to taste
2 tablespoons paprika
1 tablespoon finely chopped parsley or cilantro
1 bay leaf, crumbled
½ teaspoon white pepper
2 tablespoons olive oil
1 3- to 4-pound roasting chicken, rinsed, patted dry

Preheat the oven to 350 degrees F.

1. Using a mortar and pestle, mash the garlic with the salt, forming a paste. Mix in the paprika, parsley, bay leaf, and pepper, blending well. Slowly drizzle the olive oil into the paste as you stir it.

2. Rub this mixture all over the chicken and under the skin.

3. Place breast side up in an enamel roasting pan. Roast at 350 degrees for 20 minutes per pound. The chicken is done when thigh juices run clear and a thermometer reads 165 degrees.

Variation: For an added touch, just before placing the chicken in the oven, drape 4 to 6 slices of smoked bacon over the top. Baste the chicken occasionally during the cooking period.

90

Chicken Pies
Empadas de Galinha
Makes about 2 dozen 2½-inch pies

Edite Biscaia, who comes from the Alentejo region where these little pies are commonly made, shared her recipe with me. She lines small tart or muffin pans with a circles of dough, adds the filling and a top crust, creating little individual pies. I prefer the more flavorful dark meat of chicken legs and thighs for this recipe. These little pies are great as appetizers, snacks, and at tailgate picnics. The filling can be made the day ahead.

Filling:

2½ to 3 pounds of chicken pieces cut up, preferably legs and thighs

2 cloves garlic, peeled

2 large sprigs of parsley

1 bay leaf

1 cup white wine or ½ cup wine vinegar and ½ cup white wine

4 cups water or as needed

2 tablespoons olive oil

4 slices lean bacon

1 small onion, coarsely chopped (about ½ cup)

¼ pound (4 ounces) *chouriço* or *linguiça* (page 12), casing removed and coarsely chopped (about ½ cup)

2 teaspoons coarse salt or to taste

1 teaspoon ground marjoram

½ teaspoon ground white pepper

2 egg yolks, lightly beaten

1. In a 4-quart soup pot, place the chicken, garlic, parsley, and bay leaf. Pour in the wine or vinegar then just enough water to cover the top of the chicken. Cover and bring to a boil over medium-high heat. Reduce the heat and simmer until the chicken is nearly falling off the bone, about 50 minutes.

2. Remove the chicken, reserving the broth. When the chicken is cool, remove the meat from the bones. Coarsely chop or hand-shred the chicken meat, transfer to a medium bowl, and set aside. You should have about 2 cups chopped chicken.

3. Heat the oil with the bacon in a small skillet until hot, but not smoking. Sauté the bacon until the fat is rendered. Remove the solid pieces and set aside. Add and sauté the onion until nearly golden, about 8 minutes. Mix in the sausage, salt, marjoram, and pepper. Cook for 2 to 3 minutes or until the sausage lightly browns and releases some of its juices. Transfer to the bowl containing the chicken. Crumble the crisp bacon and mix into the chicken filling.

4. Strain the broth. Mix a small amount of the broth (about 2 to 4 tablespoons) with the egg yolks, whisking it in quickly to emulsify.

5. Pour a small amount of egg sauce over the chicken mixture. Mix well. Filling should come together almost in a ball, like loose meatballs. Add more broth if needed. You should have about 3 cups of filling.

Shortcut: Replace steps 1–3 with the following: With the exception of the yolks , combine all the filling ingredients in the pot, leaving the sausage whole, and cook until the chicken is very tender. Remove the meats. Cut the sausage into small pieces, bone the chicken and hand-shred the meat. Continue with step 4.

continued on next page

91

Pastry:

1½ cups all-purpose flour
½ cup cake flour
1 teaspoon table salt
4 tablespoons cold butter, firm but pliable, cut
  in pieces
2 egg yolks, lightly beaten
½ cup cold water or milk

1. Sift the flours and salt together and place in a bowl with the butter. Using a fork or pastry cutter, cut the butter into the flour until coarse lumps of butter and flour appear throughout.
2. Pile the flour and butter mixture onto a work surface. Make a well in the center. Pour the beaten yolks into the well with 1 tablespoon of the water or milk. Using a fork, blend the eggs with the water or milk, gradually pulling in more of the flour. Slowly add the remaining liquid to the middle while simultaneously mixing in more flour. When the mixture is too thick to mix with the fork, turn it with your hand until it starts to come together as a dough. Lightly dust with flour and gently knead the dough so that it is pliable but not sticky. Be careful not to overwork the dough.
3. Dust lightly with additional flour, cover, and let the dough rest for 15 minutes.

Assembly:
Preheat the oven to 400 degrees F.

1. Divide the dough in half. Roll out one half to about ⅛-inch thick and cut 3½-inch circles. Repeat with the second half of the dough. Line small tart tins or mini-muffin pans with the circles of dough.
2. Place 1 tablespoon of filling in center of the bottom circle. Place a second circle on top and press edges together and turn upward to seal. Repeat until all the filling is used.
3. Bake at 400 degrees for 25 minutes, until golden. Serve hot or room temperature.

Note: You may find it easier and quicker to do all of one operation at a time: first line all the individual tins with a circle of dough, fill each one, and then top each one with a second circle of dough.

Variation: I find that the following method is easy, especially if I am in a hurry. I use a ravioli mold that has open round pockets. Assemble the pies as you would ravioli. After sealing the filling with the top crust, separate the individual "pies," placing the flat side down and pinching up the edges. Bake on a parchment-lined sheet pan. The mold makes 12 pastries at a time. The shape, of course, is not traditional, but it works well if you are pressed for time. Another speedy method, also not traditional, is to cut rolled out sheets of dough into squares, place a small amount of filling in the middle, and fold the dough over into triangles.

In his eagerness to teach his children the ways of our culture, my father's methods sometimes backfired. During one "lesson," Dad was demonstrating to my older brother Joe how to prepare a live rabbit for dinner. With some reluctance, Joe quietly watched my father kill and skin a rabbit, and followed him into the kitchen where my father prepared his tasty dish. After adding the last of the seasoning to the pot, my father turned to Joe and asked whether he would like to try some. Pensively, without much hesitation, Joe replied, "I, uh, don't think so." My father couldn't comprehend his reluctance. The rest of the family had no trouble enjoying the meal.

Rabbit Hunter-Style
Coelho à Caçador
Serves 4 to 6

Hunters, like fishermen, did not carry much cooking equipment with them. Of all the rabbit stews, this one, my favorite, could not be simpler. Everything is added at once, and like the one-pot fishermen's stew (Caldeirada com Mariscos, page 73), it is cooked very slowly. Potatoes are traditionally served with this dish, as is red wine.

1 4-pound rabbit, cut into serving pieces
1 large onion, coarsely chopped (about 1½ cups)
1 large very ripe tomato, peeled, seeded, coarsely chopped (about 1 cup)
2 slices bacon, coarsely chopped
4 tablespoons olive oil
¼ cup finely chopped parsley
4 cloves garlic, coarsely chopped
1 tablespoon coarse salt or to taste
1 teaspoon paprika
1 teaspoon Hot Pepper Paste (page 167)
¼ teaspoon black pepper
1 bay leaf
1 cup red wine

1. Except for the wine, combine all the ingredients in a heavy-bottomed, 4-quart pot. Turn the ingredients to mix thoroughly.
2. Pour the wine over the top, cover tightly, and place over medium-high heat.
3. Listen carefully for the sound of boiling. Immediately reduce the heat to medium-low, then simmer, covered, for about 1 hour or until the rabbit is tender, and easily pierced with a fork. Serve with boiled potatoes.

Note: If you are using an electric stove, remove the pot when the ingredients start to boil, until the heat of the burner has cooled down a bit.

Tip: To cut the rabbit in serving pieces, sever behind the front legs and in front of the back legs, cutting straight across. Separate the upper pieces in half, along the backbone. The middle can be cut crosswise in two, if it is large enough.

93

When I was a child, our multicultural neighborhood contained French, Polish, Portuguese, Irish, and Mexican families. There was much visiting back and forth, and so there were many opportunities to sample distinctive dishes from other countries. One neighbor, however, who visited our house often, was not enthusiastic about cooking. Having just finished preparing supper as she arrived one evening, my father asked her whether she had ever eaten Spanish chicken. When she answered that she had not, he gave her a dish of his chicken to take home. The next day our neighbor returned the empty plate with compliments to the cook, only to learn that the "chicken" was really rabbit!

It is best to use fresh rabbit whenever possible, and one weighing not more than 3 to 4 pounds.

Baked Rabbit with Onion Sauce
Coelho com Cebolada
Serves 4 to 6

Freshly killed rabbits, at one time, were readily available from friends or neighbors. Now there are not as many people raising rabbits in their backyards, but rabbit is more often available in supermarkets. This recipe has origins in my father's home town of Galveias. The flavor of the onion sauce is absorbed by the meat, resulting in a flavor worth savoring. It surprises many that rabbit prepared in the Portuguese manner does not have a gamey taste. It is customary to use rendered pork fat in this recipe, but I prefer butter.

Day ahead:

1 3½- to 4-pound rabbit, cut into serving pieces, rinsed

4 cloves garlic, finely chopped

¼ cup finely chopped parsley

1 teaspoon coarse salt or to taste

½ teaspoon black pepper

½ teaspoon Hot Pepper Paste or crushed red pepper (page 167)

1 bay leaf

2 cups white wine

1. In a large bowl, combine the rabbit with the garlic, parsley, salt, black pepper, Hot Red Pepper Paste, and bay leaf. Turn to mix.
2. Add the wine, adding more if needed, to just cover the rabbit. Cover and refrigerate overnight.

Next day:

4 tablespoons butter or olive oil

3 large onions, thinly sliced (about 4½ cups)

1 medium tomato, peeled and coarsely chopped (about ½ cup), or 1 tablespoon tomato paste

Preheat the oven to 350 degrees F.

1. Reserving the marinade, transfer the rabbit to a separate dish.
2. Melt the butter in a large skillet over medium-high heat until it starts to sizzle. Add the rabbit and lightly brown on all sides. Transfer the rabbit to a 9 x 13-inch baking dish.
3. Add the onion to the same skillet and sauté until light golden in color, about 10 to 15 minutes.
4. Reserving the liquid, strain the garlic and bay leaf from the marinade and add to the pot with chopped tomato or tomato paste. Reduce the heat, cover, and simmer until the tomatoes have become soft and partially dissolved, about 15 minutes.
5. Pour the reserved marinade into the onion and tomato mixture and stir. Let it simmer for about 5 minutes until slightly thickened. Ladle the onion sauce over the rabbit. Place in a 350-degree oven and bake until tender, about 1 hour. Garnish with sprigs of parsley and serve with boiled potatoes.

Variation: This—and any of the rabbit recipes—can be easily prepared with chicken.

94

Grilled Rabbit

Coelho Grelhado

Serves 4 to 6

This recipe takes outdoor grilling beyond the everyday burgers and hot dogs. Poultry, rabbit, sausages, lamb, or seafood are more likely to appear on my grill—to the delight of eager eaters.

2 cloves garlic, finely chopped

1 teaspoon coarse salt or to taste

2 tablespoons finely chopped parsley

1 tablespoon paprika

¼ teaspoon white pepper

1 small onion, finely chopped (about ½ cup)

2 cups dry white wine

¼ cup olive oil

1 3- to 4-pound rabbit, cut into serving pieces

1. Using a mortar and pestle, mash the garlic with the salt, forming a paste. Blend in the parsley, paprika, and pepper. Transfer to a small bowl and add the onion. Stir in the wine. Pouring slowly, whisk in the olive oil.

2. Place the rabbit in a bowl or deep dish. Pour the marinade over rabbit meat, cover, and refrigerate overnight.

3. The next day, reserving the marinade, transfer the rabbit to a bowl. Grill or broil the rabbit, basting with the marinade, until tender. Serve hot.

95

On our son's seventh birthday, while he and his friends were playing in another room, a freshly killed skinned rabbit was brought to me by a friend. I immediately placed the rabbit in a colander in the kitchen sink to rinse and drain. There the rabbit sat, upright in the colander, until our daughter noticed it and ran to tell her brother and his friends. What a commotion followed! Before I knew it, ten children were crowded around my kitchen sink, staring at the rabbit, which stared silently back at them! Some of the parents, hearing this story, called to tease me about what else I might be cooking up.

I usually saved the head of the rabbit for my father who, like many Portuguese, considered rabbit brains a delicacy. Unless you can find freshly killed rabbit, most rabbits you will find in supermarkets are headless which, I must admit, pleases me.

Recording recipes for this book, I found myself asking silly questions like, "How much rabbit blood do you use for the rice?" I shook my head and chuckled as soon as I asked the question because I knew the obvious response from my friend Isaura would be "whatever blood is in the rabbit."

Braised Rabbit with Rice

Coelho com Arroz de Cabidela

Serves 4

When Fernanda Simões came to this country, she arrived in New Jersey. She met her husband when she made a return visit to Portugal and eventually found her way to Massachusetts. She told me that this dish is older than she is, older than her mother before her. It traditionally includes the liver, kidneys, and blood of the rabbit. The trick to using rabbit blood from a freshly killed rabbit is to mix it immediately with vinegar to prevent coagulation. The same holds true for chicken and pig blood. I usually don't include the liver and kidneys when I make this dish. When I cannot get a freshly killed rabbit, I use frozen rabbit, which of course does not include the blood. The flavor of the stew is slightly different but still delicious. The rice in this dish should not have absorbed all the liquid, leaving it somewhat wet.

Day ahead:

3 cloves garlic, coarsely chopped
1 teaspoon salt
1 teaspoon paprika
1 teaspoon hot pepper sauce
½ cup white wine
¼ cup olive oil
1 4-pound rabbit, cut into serving pieces, rinsed

1. Using a mortar and pestle, mash the garlic with the salt, forming a paste. Mix in the paprika, hot pepper sauce, and wine. Transfer to a ceramic or glass dish, whisk in the oil and add the rabbit, turning to coat all sides. Cover and marinate overnight.

Next day:

¼ cup olive oil
1 medium onion, finely chopped (about 1 cup)
1 small very ripe tomato, peeled, seeded, and
    coarsely chopped
1 bay leaf
2 tablespoons finely chopped parsley
2 cups boiled water
1 cup converted rice or other long-grain rice
rabbit's blood (if using)

1. Heat the olive oil in a 5-quart stock pot over medium-high heat, until it is very hot, but not smoking. Add and sauté the onion until light golden in color, about 10 to 15 minutes. Put in the tomatoes or tomato paste with the bay leaf and stir to blend. Reduce the heat to medium-low, cover, and simmer until the tomatoes are soft and partially dissolved, about 15 minutes.

2. Transfer the rabbit with the marinade to the pot. Toss in the parsley, stir, and cover tightly. Bring to a boil over medium-high heat, then reduce the heat and gently simmer for 30 minutes.

3. Pour in the hot water, re-cover, and continue to simmer for another 30 minutes, until the rabbit meat is nearly falling off the bone.

4. Stir in the rice. If you are using rabbit blood, add it with the rice. Cover and simmer for 20 minutes or until the rice is done. The liquid will not be totally absorbed. Transfer to a serving platter and garnish with additional parsley.

Oven-Braised Rabbit

Coelho Assado

Serves 4 to 6

This is an Azorean-style oven-braised rabbit. Like many other Azorean stews and braises, it has a hot-spicy flavor and uses nutmeg as an interesting counterpoint. Rabbit is a very good, high-protein alternative to poultry, for those who do not eat red meat and are looking for something different. The braising sauce is so flavorful, one might ask for a spoon. See the recipe for alcatra *(page 115) for details about braising in a clay cooker.*

Day ahead:

1 4-pound whole rabbit (or have butcher remove head)

4 cloves garlic, coarsely chopped

2 teaspoons coarse salt or to taste

½ teaspoon white pepper or to taste

1 medium onion, coarsely chopped (about 1 cup)

1 cup water

½ cup white wine

¼ cup olive oil

1 tablespoon tomato paste

1 teaspoon Hot Pepper Paste (page 167)

½ teaspoon nutmeg

1 bay leaf

4 to 6 large Red Bliss potatoes, peeled and halved

1. Season the rabbit with the garlic, salt, and pepper and place in a shallow dish. Except for the potatoes, mix the remaining ingredients in a medium bowl and pour over the rabbit. Cover tightly and chill overnight.

Next day:

1. Preheat the oven to 350 degrees F. Reserving the marinade, transfer the rabbit to another dish.

2. Using a large skillet, preferably cast-iron, heat the oil over medium-high heat and brown the rabbit all over. Place the rabbit in a casserole or prepared clay pot. Add reserved marinade and potatoes.

3. Cover and braise in a 350-degree oven for 1 hour, until the potatoes are easily pierced with a fork and the rabbit is very tender.

When Portuguese cooks get together for a social event, it is more than just preparing a meal for a lot of people. While the potatoes are being peeled or clams scrubbed, levity is in abundance. Perhaps it is the Portuguese sense of humor, but I find jokes and wisecracks funnier when told in Portuguese. Everyone is part of a big kitchen machine, each picking a task, knowing what needs to be done, and helping someone else when needed without waiting for someone else to pick up the slack. Fernanda Simões is always dubbed "the Boss" or "Bossa." This little 70-plus-year-old woman is as cute and delightful as she is petite, gentle, and unpretentious. I guess we are so fond of her because she takes ribbing so well. We even offer her a kitchen stool to sit on while she works. She keeps an "eye" on the crew from the boss's chair as she shakes her 2-foot wooden spoon in a comical gesture. Someone responds with a remark that cracks everyone up.

We don't skimp on our lunch breaks at these gatherings. Someone always prepares a noontime meal that is a feast in itself—a sit-down meal of grilled fish, pork, or steak, boiled rice or perhaps fried or boiled potatoes, vinegar sauce, crusty bread, olives, and of course, wine. We usually end the break with an *expresso com cheirinho,* an espresso with a tiny drop of brandy. The well-fed crew now is fortified for the remaining 8 or 9 hours of cooking, serving, and cleanup.

97

Pork with Clams Alentejo-Style

Carne de Porco à Alentejana

Serves 6

The name of this popular dish implies an origin in the province of Alentejo. According to some, however, its origin lies in the Algarve region. It is traditionally made with tiny sweet cockles, which are difficult to obtain here. Instead, I use the smallest littleneck clams that I can find (no bigger than 2 to 3 inches) or steamer clams, if that is all I can get. The pork is traditionally browned in lard or bacon fat, but to reduce the cholesterol, olive oil can be used instead. It will have a slightly different flavor, but still definitely Portuguese. A lean pork tenderloin is what I prefer to use, but less expensive pork butt can be used alone or in combination with more expensive cuts of pork, especially if you're cooking for a large crowd. Keep in mind that pork tenderloin takes less time to cook than the butt end. The boiled potatoes traditionally served with this dish have given way to the popular fried potatoes.

Day ahead:

1½ pounds pork tenderloin, trimmed of the
    silvery tendon or sinew
1 pound pork butt, trimmed of visible fat, gristle,
    and sinew
8 cloves garlic, coarsely chopped (adjust amount
    to your taste)
1 tablespoon paprika
¼ teaspoon black pepper
1 bay leaf, crumbled
¼ cup finely chopped cilantro
1 tablespoon Sweet Red Pepper Paste (page 166)
2 teaspoons hot pepper sauce
2 cups white wine
3 pounds small littleneck clams, 2- to 3- inches in
    diameter, about 6 per person

1. Cut the pork into cubes not greater than 1½-inches. Place in a chilled ceramic or glass bowl.
2. Using a mortar and pestle, mash the garlic. Blend in the paprika, black pepper, and crumbled bay leaf, forming a paste. Mix in the cilantro, Sweet Red Pepper Paste, and hot pepper sauce, blending well.
3. Blot the cubes of pork with a paper towel to absorb any excess moisture. Using clean hands, rub the garlic mixture onto the pork, coating the pieces thoroughly.

4. Pour 1 cup of the wine over the pork. Mix gently, cover, and marinate 24 hours in the refrigerator, turning the meat occasionally.
5. Purge the clams, following instructions on page 54.

Next day:

½ cup olive oil
1 medium onion, finely chopped (about 1 cup)
1 large very ripe tomato, peeled, seeded, coarsely
    chopped (about 1 cup)
1 tablespoon tomato paste (optional)
3 large sprigs of parsley
reserved marinade

1. About ½ hour before cooking, remove the pork from the marinade and transfer to a separate bowl, reserving the marinade. Allow the meat to drain well.
2. Heat ¼ cup olive oil in a 2-quart saucepan over medium-high heat until very hot, but not smoking. Add the onion and sauté until golden, about 15 minutes.
3. Reduce the heat to medium-low and stir in the tomatoes. Cover, and simmer until the tomatoes are soft and partially dissolved, about 15 minutes. Strain the reserved marinade, then add to the tomato mixture. Blend in the tomato paste, if using. Stirring occasionally, continue to simmer gently,

uncovered, for 30 minutes or until mixture is reduced by a third. Set aside.

4. Heat remaining ¼ cup olive oil in a large heavy skillet over medium-high heat until very hot, but not smoking. In small batches, without crowding, gently brown the drained pork until golden, about 10 minutes per batch. (Crowding and excessively damp meat will prevent proper browning.) Remove the browned meat with slotted spoon to a separate pan, cover, and keep warm.

5. Pour off any excess fat from the skillet. Add the tomato and onion sauce with remaining wine to the same skillet. Bring to a simmer on medium-low heat and cook for 2 to 3 minutes, scraping up caramelized drippings from the bottom of the pan, and stirring to blend well. Return the pork to the pan and continue to simmer gently for 15 minutes. Do not boil.

6. Place the clams on top of the meat and cover the pan. Continue to simmer until the pork is fork tender and the clams are opened, 10 to 15 minutes more, depending on the size and type of shellfish used. Discard any unopened clams. Transfer to a serving platter, garnish with remaining chopped cilantro, and a fine julienne of red pepper. Surround with small boiled potatoes or top with fried potato cubes.

Tips: You can make the sauce earlier in the day and refrigerate until needed: remove the pork from the marinade, transfer to another bowl, cover, and refrigerate until ½ hour before cooking. Make the onion and tomato sauce as directed and refrigerate until needed.

If deep-red flavorful tomatoes are not available, substitute good-quality canned tomatoes or add a tablespoon of tomato paste to the sauce with the chopped tomatoes.

When we cook for a huge crowd, we steam the clams separately and incorporate some of the clam

juice into the onion-and-tomato sauce, to which the browned meat is eventually added.

Variations: Friends who are originally from northern Portugal use paprika and salt instead of sweet red pepper paste; others marinate with lemon juice instead of wine. I have even seen some Portuguese cooks add a small amount of coarsely chopped *linquiça* or *chouriço* sausage and a tablespoon or two of butter to the sauce, leaving traditionalists shaking their heads.

Grilled Pork Cutlets

Febras de Porco Grelhadas

Serves 6

Backyard chefs enjoy grilling these tasty cutlets. Easy to prepare, they are perfect for a light meal.

2 cloves garlic, finely chopped
½ tablespoon Sweet Red Pepper Paste (page 166)
2 tablespoons olive oil
6 lean boneless pork cutlets, ½-inch thick

1. Using a mortar and pestle, mash the garlic and blend well with the Sweet Red Pepper Paste.
Mix the oil and paste, then spread over the cutlets and turn to coat evenly.
2. Grill the cutlets over a hot fire, about 3 minutes each side. Be careful not to overcook.
3. Serve in a crusty roll with soup and a salad to make a light meal. These are also great topped with sautéed onions and Roasted Sweet Peppers (page 155).

Terre Nostre Park, São Miguel, Azores

Sautéed Medallions of Marinated Pork

Bifanas de Porco

Serves 6

Bifanas are medallions of either pork or beef that are marinated with wine and garlic and then pan-fried. Served with caramelized onions in crusty rolls called papo-secos *(page 180), these are perfect sandwiches whatever the occasion.*

Day ahead:

3 cloves garlic, coarsely chopped
1 teaspoon coarse salt
1 teaspoon Hot Pepper Paste (page 167), or to taste
3 teaspoons paprika, divided
2 cups white wine
12 medallions of pork loin, evenly cut ¼-inch thick

1. Using a mortar and pestle, mash the garlic with the salt, forming a paste. Blend in the hot pepper paste and 1 teaspoon of the paprika.
2. Coat the medallions evenly with the paste and place in a shallow dish.
3. Pour the wine over, adding more if necessary, just covering the meat. Marinate the medallions in the refrigerator overnight.

Next day:

olive oil for frying as needed
3 large onions, thinly sliced (about 5 cups)

1. Remove the medallions from the marinade and drain, reserving marinade. Heat ½ cup of oil in a medium skillet over medium-high heat. Add the onions and sauté until nearly golden, about 7 minutes. Add the remaining paprika and cook for 3 minutes more. Cover and set aside, keeping warm.
2. Pour enough oil into a large skillet to cover the bottom by ½ inch. Heat the oil over medium-high heat until very hot, but not smoking. Brown the medallions in small batches without crowding. Fry quickly, about 1 minute each side. Serve in crusty rolls with the onions and an ice cold beer.

101

Roast Pork with Sweet Red Pepper Paste

Lombo de Porco Assada com Massa de Pimentão

Serves 4 to 6

This was—and still is—a popular dish in our home, especially with potatoes roasted with traditional seasonings (Batatas Assadas, page 140). This style is of the Alentejo.

2 large cloves garlic, finely chopped
1 bay leaf, crumbled
1 teaspoon paprika
1 tablespoon Sweet Red Pepper Paste (page 166)
2 tablespoons olive oil
1 3-pound pork loin

Preheat the oven to 350 degrees F.

1. Using a mortar and pestle, mash the garlic, bay leaf, and paprika. Blend in the Sweet Red Pepper Paste. Slowly drizzle in the olive oil and mix.
2. Cut crosshatches on the surface of the roast. Rub the paste all over the roast, pushing some of the paste into the crosshatches. Place meat in a lightly oiled roasting pan.
3. Roast at 350 degrees for about 1 hour or until pork reaches an internal temperature of 150 degrees. Let the roast stand for 10 to 15 minutes before carving. The roast will continue to cook during the standing time. Slice and transfer to a serving platter.

Tip: If you are planning to serve roasted potatoes with this dish, you can roast them in the same pan as the pork.

Roasted Pork Loin Beira Alta-Style
Lombo de Porco à Moda da Beira Alta
Serves 4 to 6

Teresa Cunha Mendonça, originally from the Beira Alta region, demonstrates her use of citrus juices to marinate pork in this recipe. The orange and lemon juices marry nicely with the white wine to give the pork an extraordinary flavor.

2 cloves garlic
1½ tablespoons coarse salt
½ teaspoon white pepper
1 3-pound pork loin roast
juice of 1 lemon (about ¼ cup)
juice of 1 orange (about ½ cup)
1 cup white wine
1 medium-sized very ripe tomato, peeled, seeded, finely chopped (about ½ cup)
1 tablespoon red wine vinegar
4 tablespoons butter, cut in pieces
1 orange, cut into thin wedges
1 lemon, cut into thin wedges

1. Using a mortar and pestle, mash the garlic with the salt and pepper, forming a paste. Wipe excess moisture from the meat. Rub the paste all over the roast, pushing into any crevices and coating all sides.
2. Place the pork in a roasting pan and pour the citrus juices over it. Add the wine, tomatoes, and vinegar to the pan. Marinate for 1 to 2 hours in the refrigerator, turning occasionally.
3. Preheat the oven to 350 degrees F. Remove the pan from the refrigerator and dot the roast with the butter, distributing the pieces evenly over the top. Roast, basting occasionally with the pan juices, until the meat thermometer indicates an internal temperature of 150 degrees. Let the roast rest for 10 to 15 minutes before carving. Slice and arrange pork on a serving platter and garnish with the orange and lemon wedges.

103

Stuffed Pork Loin
Lombo de Porco Recheado
Serves 8 to 10

The chouriço *sausages and caramelized onions make a perfect stuffing without overpowering the pork. Have the butcher butterfly the loin or cut it yourself so it will lie open to be stuffed. I do not recommend a roast made from two loins tied together, simply because the slices do not hold together well during carving. The length of the roast determines the amount of sausage used. For instance, if the roast is 8 inches long, I cut a link of sausage the same length. If the sausage is left whole and surrounded by the onions, the carved servings have a charming bull's-eye effect. Not only is this recipe easily adaptable for larger roasts, but the simplicity and flavor of this dish makes it perfect for entertaining.*

½ cup olive oil, divided

2 large onions, finely chopped (about 3 cups)

1½ links (about 10 ounces) *chouriço*, casings removed, coarsely chopped or left whole

1½ cups shredded St. George cheese (page 4) or other semisoft cheese, such as Havarti

4 tablespoons finely chopped parsley, divided

1 4-pound pork loin, butterflied

3 cloves garlic, coarsely chopped

2 teaspoons coarse salt

2 teaspoons paprika

¼ teaspoon pepper

1 bay leaf crumbed

Preheat the oven to 350 degrees F.

1. Heat ¼ cup of the oil in a medium-sized skillet over medium-high heat until it is hot, but not smoking. Add the onions and sauté until quite golden. Add the chopped sausage and cook briefly, about 3 minutes. Transfer onions and sausage to a medium bowl. Set aside to cool for about 15 minutes.

2. Combine the shredded cheese and 1½ tablespoons of the parsley with the onions and sausage, mixing well.

3. Open the roast flat on a work surface and spread the sausage mixture over the meat, leaving a 1-inch border around the edges. Roll the meat up, like a jelly roll, and tie securely with butcher's twine, enclosing the ends. (If you are leaving the sausage whole, first spread the cooked onions and cheese over the meat, then place a link of the sausage, casing removed, the length of the roast, centered on top of the onions and cheese, close the roast around the sausage core, and tie with butcher's twine.)

4. Using a mortar and pestle, mash the garlic with the salt, paprika, and pepper. Mix in 1 tablespoon of the parsley, the crumbled bay leaf, and 2 tablespoons of the olive oil. Rub the paste over all sides of the meat and into crevices. Place the roast in a lightly oiled roasting pan.

5. Roast for about 1 hour at 350 degrees, or until the internal temperature is 150 degrees. Let roast rest for 10 to 15 minutes before carving. Serve with rice or potatoes.

Variations: Add 1 to 1½ cups lightly cooked spinach with the stuffing. Use *presunto* or prosciutto in place of the sausage, or use fillet of beef in place of pork.

Tripe

Dobrada

Serves 4 to 6

Although dobrada originated in Oporto, north of Lisbon, this version is adapted from a dish that graces the dinner table of Isaura Nogueira, who is originally from the province of Beira Alta. This adventuresome dish is made by cooking tripe, beans, and meat separately, then bringing them together in a lightly spiced sauce. In continental Portugal, this stew is traditionally made with lima beans. In the Azores, however, white kidney beans were historically more plentiful, so Azoreans tend to use them in this stew still. The sauce of this Continental version is paler than the red Azorean version. In this interpretation, the juice of oranges is used in place of the more common lemon juice. Simple preparations begin two days ahead, so plan accordingly.
The tripe available in markets today is of good quality, white and clean. Nonetheless, I suggest the additional cleaning procedure that follows.

One to two days ahead:
2 medium meaty pig's hocks
5 tablespoons coarse salt or as needed

1. Rinse the hocks and pat dry. Heavily salt the hocks on all sides, place in a shallow dish, cover, and refrigerate for up to 2 days.

Day ahead:
1 pound dried lima or white kidney beans

1. Place the beans in a large bowl and rinse with water. Pick through the beans, removing any stones and shriveled, deformed, or floating beans. Drain and rinse again. Soak the beans overnight in 8 cups of water or enough to cover by 2 inches.

Cleaning the tripe:
2½ pounds tripe
1½ cups coarse salt as needed
½ cup white vinegar
1 large orange

1. Purify the tripe: Using a sharp paring knife, remove any excess fat from the side opposite the honeycomb; the fat is whiter than the creamy color of the tripe.

2. Rub the coarse salt completely and thoroughly over the tripe and into the crevices on both sides, as if you are scrubbing it. Rinse several times with water. Place in a dish and pour the vinegar over it, coating both sides. Let stand for 30 minutes, then rinse well.

3. Place the tripe in a medium bowl and pour orange juice over it, tossing in the peel. Turn the tripe in the juice to make sure it is coated all over. Cover. Let stand for minimum of 6 hours. You can also cover the bowl and leave it overnight, refrigerated.

Next day:
4 quarts water or as needed
¼ cup white wine
½ of a small onion (about ¼ cup)
3 cloves garlic
1 bay leaf

1. Cook the tripe: Discard the orange peel and rinse the tripe. Put it in a 4-quart saucepan with enough water to barely cover. Cover tightly and bring to a boil over medium-high heat. Reduce the heat and gently simmer the tripe until very tender, about 3 hours. (Some Portuguese like the tripe very well cooked while others like it to be tender but not mushy.)

2. Cook the hocks: While the tripe is cooking, rinse the hocks of the salt and place in a 2-quart saucepan with the onion, wine, garlic, bay leaf, and enough water to cover completely. Cover and place over medium-high heat and bring to a boil. Reduce the heat and simmer until the meat is falling away from the bone, about 1 hour. Reserving the liquid, remove the hocks and set aside to cool. Remove the meat along with the fat and skin from the bone. Cut into 1-inch cubes. Discard just the bone. Refrigerate with broth until needed.

3. Cook the beans: Once the hocks are cooking, drain and rinse the beans. Place them in a 4-quart pot with enough fresh water, about 6 to 8 cups, to cover them by about 2 inches. Cover and bring to a boil. Reduce the heat and simmer, stirring the beans occasionally, for 45 minutes to 1 hour until tender but not mushy. Transfer the cooking water and the beans into separate containers and chill until needed.

4. Drain the tripe well, discarding the cooking water. Cut into 1-inch pieces. Cover and refrigerate until needed.

Sauce:

3 tablespoons olive oil
2 ounces slab bacon, cut into ½-inch cubes
½ pound *chouriço* (page 12), cut into ¼-inch rounds
1 large onion, finely chopped (about 1½ cups)
3 cloves garlic, coarsely chopped
1 small very ripe tomato, peeled, seeded, finely chopped (about ¼ cup) or 2 tablespoons tomato paste
½ cup white wine
1 tablespoon hot pepper sauce
1 bay leaf

1. Heat the oil in a 4-quart saucepan over medium-high heat. Add and sauté the bacon, cooking until the fat has been rendered. Remove the solid pieces and reserve. Toss in the *chouriço* and briefly sauté until lightly browned, then remove to a dish. Add the onions to the pan drippings and sauté until golden.

2. Add the garlic and cook until it becomes aromatic. Reduce the heat to medium-low and stir in the tomato. Cover and simmer until the tomato is partially dissolved, about 15 minutes. Pour in the wine, hot pepper sauce, and bay leaf. Simmer for 2 minutes.

3. Add the drained beans, the hock meat, tripe, sausage, and bacon, stirring to mix. Pour in equal amounts, starting with 1 cup each, of the cooking liquids from the beans and the hocks. The stew should be slightly thicker than a soup but not as thick as chili. Simmer for 10 minutes. If the stew is too thick, thin it with additional broth. Serve in deep bowls with bread on the side or spoon over hot boiled white rice.

Spicy Tripe
Dobrada Picante
Serves 4 to 6

John Silva, originally from Graciosa, the quiet bartender at the Portuguese Veterans Post #1 in Peabody, Massachusetts, is known for his recipe for tripe. Though he says he is not a cook, his tripe says otherwise.
The basic preparations are essentially the same as in the preceding recipe, except the bacon and chouriço are boiled whole with the hocks instead of fried separately. When the hocks are done, the broth is reserved, the bacon is cut into ½-inch cubes, and the sausage sliced in ¼-inch rounds. The hocks are boned and the meat and fat are chopped into ½-inch cubes. For his sauce, John uses lard to fry the onions, but he says you can use olive oil. It is his Azorean touch that creates a spicier sauce—one that attracts customers on Saturdays at noon. Here is his secret recipe that he was generous enough to share. It is scaled down in size for 2½ pounds of tripe. Read through the previous recipe for tripe, and plan ahead.

Sauce:

1½ tablespoons olive oil or lard

¾ cup finely chopped onion

8 cloves garlic, coarsely chopped

3¾ ounces canned tomato sauce, (about ½ cup) (see page 165 for homemade *Tomatada*)

3¾ ounces hot pepper sauce (about 6½ tablespoons)

3¾ ounces water

3 ounces tomato paste (about 5 tablespoons)

1 teaspoon paprika

scant ½ teaspoon ground cumin

1. Using the same measurements, follow the instructions for the tripe, beans, and hocks in the tripe recipe, on pages 105–106, except add the bacon and sausage whole to the pot with the hocks instead of frying them.

2. Heat the olive oil or lard in a 5-quart saucepan over medium-high heat. Add and sauté the onion until translucent. Toss in the garlic and sauté until it is aromatic. Stir in the tomato sauce, hot sauce, water, tomato paste, and paprika. Reduce the heat and simmer until the paste is dissolved, then assemble by adding the cooked tripe, boiled sausage, bacon, and hock meat.

3. The beans in this version are drained from the cooking liquid first, then added to the pot. Pour in just enough of the broth from cooking the hocks (about 2 quarts) so that the stew is the right consistency: not as thick as chili, but not as thin as vegetable soup. Sprinkle the ground cumin over the top, stir, then simmer for about 10 minutes. Serve with bread or boiled hot rice.

107

Pig's Feet Alentejo-Style
Pés de Porco à Alentejana
Serves 4

Elvira Covil came from the same area as my father—the Alentejo—where pork recipes are plentiful. The pig's feet can be used alone in this recipe or combined with hocks, which have more meat. My father would use his pocket knife, scraping the bones, to get every last bit of meat. Elvira cooked the meat with the sauce, but I suggest that you cook the meat separately to eliminate much of the gelatin and strong flavor.

Day ahead:

1 pound lima or white kidney beans
4 small pig's feet or hocks
coarse salt, about ½ cup

1. Soak beans overnight in enough water to cover by 2 inches.
2. Coat the pig's feet (or hocks) with salt and refrigerate overnight.

Next day:

3 quarts water or as needed
1 small onion, peeled, left whole
4 tablespoons olive oil
2 large onions, thinly sliced (about 1½ cups)
2 cloves garlic, coarsely chopped
1 scant tablespoon paprika
2 teaspoons coarse salt or to taste
¼ teaspoon pepper or to taste
1 bay leaf
1 large very ripe tomato, peeled, and coarsely chopped (about 1 cup)
½ cup white wine
½ tablespoon apple cider vinegar
1 tablespoon finely chopped cilantro or parsley

1. Rinse the salt from the pig's feet or hocks, then place them in a 4-quart pot. Add the whole onion and enough water to cover. Cover tightly and bring the ingredients to a boil over medium-high heat. Reduce the heat to medium-low and simmer until the meat is nearly falling off the bone, about 1½ hours. Depending upon the age of the pig and size of the feet, cooking may take longer. When the feet or hocks are done, drain off the cooking water and set the feet or hocks aside.

2. Meanwhile, drain the beans from the soaking water and rinse. Place the beans in a separate 3-quart saucepan and add enough water to cover by 2 inches, about 6 to 8 cups. Cover and bring to a boil. Reduce the heat and simmer until the beans are tender, about 45 minutes.

3. Heat the olive oil in another 4-quart saucepan over medium-high heat. Add and sauté the onions until a light golden color. Stir in the garlic, paprika, salt, pepper, and bay leaf, cooking 1 minute, until the garlic is aromatic. Mix in the tomatoes and cover. Reduce the heat and simmer until they become soft and partially dissolved, about 15 minutes.

4. Pour in the wine and apple cider vinegar. Stir in the beans and cilantro. Simmer for two minutes. Put in the pig's feet, turn to coat with the sauce, heat through, and serve.

Grilled Pork Ribs

Costelas de Porco Grelhada

Serves 4 to 6

These ribs can be made spicy or not—the essence of hot red peppers gives these ribs a characteristic Azorean flavor either way. Baby back ribs can be used as well; just adjust the cooking time.

6 cloves garlic, coarsely chopped
1 tablespoon coarse salt
juice of 1 whole lemon
1 tablespoon Hot Pepper Paste (page 167),
    or to taste
1 cup white or rosé wine
5 pounds meaty pork spare ribs, about 12 ribs

1. Using a mortar and pestle, mash the garlic with the salt, forming a paste. Add the lemon juice and hot pepper paste, stirring to blend.

2. Place ribs in a large dish or bowl and coat evenly with seasoning mixture. Pour the wine over the ribs, adding more wine as necessary to coat all sides. Marinate for 1 hour in the refrigerator.

3. Reserving the marinade, place the ribs over medium-hot, not blazing, coals. Grill, turning often and basting with the marinade, until the meat is rich brown and tender, about 1¼ hours or 40 minutes each side. If the ribs cook over too hot a fire, they will burn before cooking completely. You can partially cook the ribs in a 350-degree oven for about 1 hour, then finish on the grill. Slice in between the bones and arrange on a platter to serve.

109

Oven-Braised Short Ribs

Costelas no Forno

Serves 4 to 6

It would be an understatement to say my father was a rib man. Savoring every bite, he would pick the bones clean.

2 tablespoons olive oil
2 cloves garlic, coarsely chopped
2 medium onions, thinly sliced (about 2 cups)
1 tablespoon paprika
2 tablespoons Sweet Red Pepper Paste (page 166)
½ cup red wine
½ cup water
5 pounds meaty beef or pork short ribs
¼ cup olive oil

Preheat the oven to 300 degrees F.

1. In a bowl, combine olive oil, garlic, onions, paprika, and Sweet Red Pepper Paste, blending well. Stir in the wine and water.
2. Place the ribs in a roasting pan and pour the seasoned braising liquid over them. Cover and place in a 300-degree oven. Cook for 2 to 2½ hours or until the meat is nearly falling off the bone. Remove the ribs from the pan, slice between the bones and set aside.
3. Heat the oil in a large skillet over medium-high heat until hot, but not smoking. Add the ribs and cook to just brown the meat a bit, caramelizing the juices on the meat. Alternatively, place the ribs under a broiler to brown and crisp the skin. Arrange the ribs on a platter and serve with boiled potatoes and pan juices.

Variation: If you want spicier ribs, top with some hot pepper sauce to taste.

Rations

Rancho

Serves 6 to 8

This soul-warming stew comes from northern Portugal. It's ideal for the chilly days of winter. Definitely a meal in itself, this dish lies somewhere between a soup and a stew. It most likely received its name during times when it was doled out to soldiers as their food ration. My friend Isaura Nogueira, who is originally from the region of Beira Alta in northern Portugal, shared this recipe with me. She suggests using tomato paste rather than fresh tomatoes for a more intense flavor. This dish takes slightly more than 2 hours to prepare, so plan ahead.

1 pound (2¼ cups) dried chickpeas, soaked overnight in enough water to cover by 2 inches

¼ cup olive oil

1 pound stew beef, cut into 1½- to 2-inch pieces, wiped dry (excess moisture will prevent the beef from browning properly)

½ ounce chopped salt pork or 2 strips bacon, coarsely chopped

1 medium onion, thinly sliced (about 1 cup)

3 cloves garlic, finely chopped

1 teaspoon tomato paste

1 teaspoon hot pepper sauce, Portuguese or Tabasco

8–10 cups water

1 pound chicken pieces (thighs, legs)

4 medium Red Bliss or new potatoes, peeled, cut into ½-inch cubes (about 4 cups)

1 pound *chouriço* or *linguiça* (page 127), cut into chunks

1 medium head (6-inch diameter) Savoy cabbage, cored and cut into several wedges

½ cup elbow macaroni or other small pasta

1 teaspoon coarse salt or to taste

1. Drain and rinse the chickpeas. Set aside.

2. Heat the oil in a 5-quart stockpot over medium-high heat until it is very hot, but not smoking. Add the stew beef in small batches, without crowding, and brown the pieces on all sides. Remove the beef, cover, and reserve.

3. Add the salt pork to the same pan, brown until crisp, rendering the fat. Then remove the solid pieces and reduce the heat to medium. Add the onion to the rendered fat and sauté until a light golden color, about 15 to 20 minutes.

4. Mix in the garlic, tomato paste, and hot pepper sauce. Cook until the tomato paste is blended thoroughly, about 3 to 5 minutes.

5. Return the stew beef to the cooking pot. Add 8 cups of the water and chickpeas. Cover and bring to a boil over high heat. Reduce the heat and simmer for about 30 minutes.

6. Add the chicken, with additional 1–2 cups of water if needed to cover and continue to simmer for another 20 to 30 minutes or until all the meats are tender.

7. Remove meats from the pot. Trim the chicken of any bones, skin, and gristle. Cut the chicken meat into pieces and reserve, covered, with the beef.

8. Add the potatoes to the pot and return the soup to a boil. Reduce the heat again and simmer for 15 minutes. Toss in the sausage, cabbage, pasta, and salt, cooking for 12 minutes or until pasta is cooked and cabbage is tender but not mushy.

9. Return the meats to the pot and heat through. Ladle stew into bowls and serve with plenty of crusty bread to dip into the flavorful broth.

Health Tip: Replace the salt pork with 2 tablespoons of olive oil. One day before you plan to serve it, prepare the soup through step 6. Chill the broth overnight. Skim the congealed fat off the surface and continue with the remaining steps.

Beef Portuguese-Style

Carne Guisada

Serves 6

This is a stove-top braise my father often served on Sundays. He didn't marinate the meat overnight, but feel free to do so. It is an easy one-pot meal.

3 cloves garlic, finely chopped

1 tablespoon Sweet Red Pepper Paste (page 166)

1 tablespoon finely chopped parsley

2 teaspoons paprika

2 bay leaves, crumbled

2 tablespoons olive oil

1 3½-pound chuck roast, bone-in, or bottom
    round roast

2 medium onions, thinly sliced (about 2 cups)

¼ teaspoon crushed red pepper (page 4)
    (optional)

1 cup red wine

1 to 2 cups water, as needed

2 large, very ripe tomatoes, peeled, seeded, and
    coarsely chopped (about 2 cups)

2 tablespoons finely chopped parsley

6 large new potatoes, peeled and quartered

3 large carrots, peeled and cut into large chunks

1. Using a pestle, mash the garlic in the bowl of a mortar. Add the pepper paste, parsley, paprika, and bay leaves, mashing well after each addition. While mixing, drizzle in the olive oil. Rub this mixture over the meat and place the meat in a Dutch oven with the onions and the crushed red pepper, if using.

2. Mix the wine with the water and pour into the pan, adding more wine and water, if needed, in equal amounts so that it comes a third of the way up the side of the roast. (If you wish to marinate this roast, simply cover at this point and set in the refrigerator several hours or overnight, occasionally turning the meat in the marinade.)

3. In the same pan, place the tomatoes and 1 tablespoon of the parsley around the meat. Cover tightly and place the pan over medium-high heat. When the liquid starts to boil, reduce the heat and simmer until almost tender, about 1½ hours. Add the potatoes and carrots.

4. Continue to simmer, covered, until beef is tender and vegetables are done (about 30 minutes more).

5. Remove the beef and vegetables to a serving platter and cover. Reduce the braising liquid by half and pour over the beef and vegetables. Garnish with fresh chopped parsley.

112

Pot Roast Azorean-Style

Carne Assada Açorean

Serves 6 to 8

This is very similar to my father's stewed beef (see Beef Portuguese-Style, page 112), but Noelia Ortins marinates the meat with an Azorean variation on the seasonings and cooks her roast in the oven. Although this dish is called carne assada—which means "roast beef"—technically this dish is oven-braised.

Day ahead:

1 4-pound bottom round roast or bone-in chuck
    roast
4 cloves garlic, coarsely chopped
1 tablespoon coarse salt or to taste
1 tablespoon tomato paste
1 tablespoon Hot Pepper Paste (page 167)
1 teaspoon black pepper
1 teaspoon ground nutmeg
1 bay leaf
1 medium onion, thinly sliced (about 1 cup)
1½ cups rosé wine

1. Place the meat in a enamel or other nonreactive roasting pan. Using a mortar and pestle, mash the garlic with the salt, forming a paste.
2. Transfer the paste to a small bowl and mix in the tomato paste, Hot Pepper Paste, black pepper, nutmeg, bay leaf, and onion. Stir in the wine. Pour seasoned wine over the roast, then turn the meat in the marinade to coat all sides. Marinate overnight in the refrigerator, turning the meat occasionally.

Next day:

1 cup water or as needed
8 Red Bliss potatoes, peeled and left whole or
    halved if large
2 tablespoons water
2 tablespoons cornstarch
1 tablespoon sugar

Preheat the oven to 350 degrees F.

1. Remove the roast from the refrigerator and add enough water to the pan so that the liquid comes a third of the way up the side of the roast. Cover the roasting pan and place in the oven. Cook the roast for 1¾ hours, basting frequently.
2. Add the potatoes, placing them around the meat. Mix the water, cornstarch, and sugar and add to the roasting pan. Cover and continue to cook for 35 to 45 minutes more, until the meat is tender and the potatoes are done. Remove the meat, slice, and arrange on a platter with the potatoes. Ladle some the sauce over the meat. Serve any extra sauce on the side.

113

Braised Beef Terceira-Style

Bife Guisada à Moda da Terceira

Serves 8 to 10

Lucia Rebelo, who was born in Terceira, taught me to make this tender braised beef dish. With this method, introduced to the Portuguese by the Arabs centuries ago, there is one unusual step: the roast is browned after it is cooked. In this recipe the braising liquid is puréed into a rich sauce.

Day ahead:

1 5-pound bottom round roast
1½ teaspoons coarse salt
3 cloves garlic, left whole
1 pound bacon, three slices left whole; the rest
    coarsely chopped
2 tablespoon Sweet Red Pepper Paste (page 166)

1. Make three cuts about 1 inch deep, evenly spaced on one side of the roast. Into each cut, place ½ teaspoon salt, 1 clove of garlic, and 1 strip of bacon.
2. Rub the roast all over with Sweet Red Pepper Paste. Cover and chill overnight.

Next day:

½ pound butter
4 large onions, sliced (about 6 cups)
3 cups white wine (approximately)
¼ cup olive oil

1. In a Dutch oven, melt the butter. Add the onions with the remaining bacon and sauté until the onions are translucent.
2. Place the roast on top of the onions and bacon. Add enough wine to immerse the roast about one third of the way up the side.
3. Cover the pot and bring to a boil. Reduce the heat to the lowest setting and simmer for about 3 hours, until tender. Reserving the liquid, remove the meat to a platter.
4. Heat olive oil in a large cast-iron skillet over medium-high heat until hot, but not smoking. Add the roast and brown the meat on all sides. Remove the meat to a warm platter, cover, and set aside.
5. Purée the pan juices and return to the pot. Bring the juices to a boil and reduce by half. Return the roast to the pan, reduce the heat, cover, and simmer for 2 minutes to heat through. Turn off the heat and let rest for 10 minutes. Slice just before serving. Arrange slices on a platter and ladle the sauce over them.

Beef Rump

Alcatra

Serves 6 to 8

The Azorean Portuguese from the island of Terceira are famous for this unique dish. Simply seasoned with allspice, pepper, salt, and bay leaf, it is traditionally served on the Feast of the Holy Ghost, but can be served on other occasions, as well. Cooked in red wine, the meat takes on a deep mahogany color. Other Azorean islands have versions of this popular meal. Some cooks use white wine for a lighter color. Served with rice as a separate course after the Soup of the Holy Ghost (page 40), it is prepared in a clay pot. The traditional pot is somewhat like an inverted lampshade in shape. Similar deep, unglazed clay bakers may be found at kitchen specialty shops (or see the Resource Guide at the end of the book). New clay pots must be seasoned; see the Note following the recipe. Unglazed clay pots must be soaked before each use and placed in a cold oven to prevent cracking.

1 presoaked unglazed 4-quart red-clay pot
1 stick soft butter
3 large onions, thinly sliced
½ pound slab bacon, cut into 1-inch pieces
6 cloves garlic, mashed
2 bay leaves
1 5-pound rump or chuck roast, bone-in, cut into 4-inch pieces
1 pound shin bone (if using rump roast)
½ teaspoon whole allspice (Jamaican is best)
½ teaspoon black peppercorns
1 teaspoon coarse salt
4 tablespoons firm butter, cut into pieces
1 cup water
4 to 6 cups medium-bodied red or white wine

1. Generously grease the interior of the pot with soft butter.

2. Place half of the onions in the bottom of the pot followed by half of the bacon, garlic, and 1 bay leaf. Add the meat, including the bone from the roast or shin bone, followed by the second bay leaf, the garlic, and remaining bacon. End with the remaining onions. Scatter the allspice and peppercorns over the top along with the salt. Dot the top with the pieces of cold butter.

3. Mix the water with 1 cup of the wine. Pour over the ingredients followed by enough additional wine to cover everything by 1 inch.

4. Place the pot in a cold oven. Set the temperature to 400 degrees F. When the liquid begins to boil, reduce the temperature to 300 degrees. Cover the pot with foil and cook, without turning the ingredients, until tender, about 3 to 3½ hours more.

5. Turn off the heat. Uncover the pot and remove some of the broth for cooking the rice. Leave the uncovered pot in the oven just until the oven heat has dissipated. The top will brown a little. Serve meat with rice cooked in broth.

continued on next page

Notes: Lucia Costa, who learned to prepare this dish as a young girl in Terceira, says long slow cooking is necessary to this dish.

A new unglazed clay pot needs to be seasoned to avoid passing an earthy flavor to food. To season, fill the pot with water and add several cabbage or collard leaves and some onion peelings. Then place the pot on a flame-proof diffuser over medium heat. Bring to a boil then reduce to a simmer. Simmer for about 2 hours and then drain.

When you want to cook in the pot, immerse it in water and soak for about 24 hours. Then proceed with the recipe by generously greasing the interior with butter.

Beef Rump

Boiled Dinner Portuguese-Style
Cozido á Portuguesa
Serves 6 to 8

Since the Portuguese are not wasteful, the traditional boiled dinner can encompass a large variety of ingredients, which most often includes pig's ears, feet, and snouts. Other characteristic ingredients in this dish are beef, a variety of sausages, and vegetables. It is usually served with rice cooked in some of the broth. Here in the United States, the above-named pig parts are not always included, especially in my parents' house, because my brothers and sisters did not relish the idea of eating pig's ears, feet, or snouts. My father occasionally included only a piece or two for himself. Personal preferences and what is available determine the quantity and range of variety. This recipe shows a sampling of a broad range of ingredients; however it can be pared down to simply the brisket, one or two types of sausages, potatoes, carrots, cabbage, and rice.

Day ahead:
2 pounds beef brisket
1 pound pork ribs (optional)
coarse salt as needed

1. Coat the brisket—and ribs, if using—with coarse salt, place in a bowl or dish, and cover. Place in the refrigerator overnight.

Next day:
2 tablespoons olive oil
½ teaspoon black peppercorns
1 bay leaf
2 cloves garlic, whole
2½ quarts water or as needed
1½ pounds chicken, cut into serving pieces (optional)
1 *salpicão* (page 127) (optional)
½ pound *chouriço* (page 127) (optional)
1 *farinheira* (page 127) (optional)
½ pound *morcela* (page 127) (optional)
2 large onions, peeled, left whole
2 white turnips or small rutabaga, peeled and cut into medium chunks (about 1½ cups)
3 large carrots, peeled and cut into large chunks
3 large waxy potatoes, peeled and halved or quartered depending on size
1 medium head (about 6-inch diameter) Savoy cabbage, quartered
2 cups long-grain or converted rice

117

continued on next page

1. Wipe off the excess salt from the ribs and brisket. Place the brisket in a 10-quart stockpot. Add the olive oil, peppercorns, bay leaf, and garlic with just enough water to cover completely. Cover tightly and bring to a boil over medium-high heat. Reduce the heat and simmer for 30 minutes, skimming the surface occasionally.

2. Add the ribs, if using, and continue to simmer for an additional 1½ hours.

3. When the meats are almost tender, add the chicken, if using, and simmer for 20 minutes, then add the sausages, continuing to simmer for another 15 minutes until the meats are tender; cooking time will depend on ingredients used. Remove the meats as they become done, cover, set aside, and keep warm. If you use *salpicão,* remove the casing at this time.

4. Remove 2¼ cups of broth to a medium saucepan and reserve.

5. Taste the remaining broth for salt and add if needed. Add the onions, turnip, carrots, and potatoes to the same large pot. Place the cabbage on top. (Although all the vegetables may not be submerged in the broth, they will steam.) Cover tightly and bring to a boil over medium-high heat. Reduce the heat and simmer over medium-low for about 20 to 25 minutes.

6. While the vegetables are cooking, prepare the rice. Taste the reserved broth for salt. Bring the broth in the saucepan to a boil, adding salt if needed. Add the rice and stir, reduce the heat to medium-low. Cover and cook until rice is done, about 25 minutes.

7. Remove the vegetables with a slotted spoon as they become done. Cover and set aside. Slice the meats and arrange on a serving platter with vegetables. Serve hot with rice on the side. Black Portuguese olives, cruets of olive oil and vinegar for drizzling over the vegetables, and dense country-style bread are typical accompaniments to this dish.

Note: Reserved leftover broth makes a delicious soup base. Simply strain, chill, and remove any solidified fat.

Marinated Beefsteaks
Bife em Vinha d'Alhos
Serves 4

Teresa Mendonça recommends white wine instead of red for her marinated steak. Try this flavorful marinade with beef tips. Skewer and grill them over a hot charcoal fire. The sauce can be made in a separate pan without the caramelized juices or skipped completely.

4 sirloin or rib eye steaks, ½-inch thick
8 cloves garlic, coarsely chopped
1 tablespoon coarse salt or to taste
½ teaspoon ground black pepper
1 tablespoon finely chopped parsley
1 bay leaf, crumbled
1 cup white wine
2 tablespoons butter
2 tablespoons olive oil
½ cup heavy cream
4 eggs (optional)

1. Trim any excess fat from along the outside edges of the steaks. Using a mortar and pestle, mash the garlic with the salt. Mix in the pepper, then the parsley and bay leaf, forming a paste. Season the steaks on both sides with the paste. Place in a deep-sided dish.

2. Slowly pour the wine over the steaks and marinate for 2 hours in the refrigerator. Reserving the marinade, remove the steaks to a separate dish.

3. Heat the butter with the oil in a large skillet over medium-high heat. Fry the steaks quickly, 3 minutes each side. Remove to a platter and cover.

4. Strain the marinade, add to the pan, and deglaze the caramelized juices, scraping up any brown bits. Remove the pan the from heat, whisk in the cream, and place over medium-low heat. Return the steaks to the pan and cook for 2 minutes. Sauce should be slightly thickened.

5. While the steak is simmering in the sauce, quickly fry the eggs in a separate pan. Transfer steaks to individual dishes and top each with an egg. Pool some of the sauce around the steak and serve immediately with fried potatoes.

Portuguese Beefsteak
Bife á Portuguesa
Serves 2 to 4

Cream or butter is used to enhance the pan juices of this savory garlic-infused steak. While my brothers enjoy this mouth-watering dish with Buttered Rice (page 145), I love it with Portuguese-Style Potato Fries (page 139). When we were kids, our Aunt Ana would pack up freshly cooked steaks for us to take for picnic lunches at a nearby beach. Thinly sliced rump steak is perfectly suited for this family favorite.

1 pound rump steak, ¼-inch thick slices trimmed of any visible fat

2 to 3 cloves garlic, thinly sliced

6 tablespoons butter, divided

1 tablespoon finely chopped parsley, divided

½ teaspoon coarse salt or to taste

¼ teaspoon black pepper

For the sauce:

4 tablespoons softened butter or ¼ cup cream (light or heavy)

1. Place the steaks on your cutting board or work surface. Lay slices of garlic on each side of the steaks (about 4 on each side). Using a tenderizing mallet, pound the garlic into the meat. Repeat on the reverse side of the steaks.

2. Melt 2 tablespoons of the butter in a skillet over medium-high heat. Add and sauté the steaks in batches, for 2 to 3 minutes on each side. Remove to a warm, covered plate.

3. Remove the pan from the heat and stir in 4 tablespoons soft butter, moving it around the edges to melt slowly into the pan juices. Blend well to emulsify. Alternatively, add cream and parsley to the pan juices, stir, and heat without boiling until liquid is reduced slightly.

4. Return the steaks to the pan, season with salt and pepper, and heat through. Garnish with additional parsley and serve with rice or potatoes.

Broiled Garlic Steak
Bife Grelhadao com Alho
Serves 4

Shared by my friend Fatima, this recipe is simple, fast, and so perfect when you're craving garlic. Azoreans are not inhibited when it comes to using garlic. Make sure the steaks are wiped of moisture so that the seasoning will stick.

24 cloves garlic, coarsely chopped (6 cloves per steak, 3 per side)
1 tablespoon coarse salt
¼ teaspoon freshly ground black pepper to taste
juice of 2 whole lemons
4 tablespoons butter, softened
4 rib-eye steaks, ¾-inch thick, blotted dry
2 tablespoons olive oil as needed

1. Using a large mortar and pestle, mash the garlic with the salt and pepper, forming a paste. Stir in the lemon juice. Mix in the softened butter, blending thoroughly.

2. Divide the garlic butter in half. Using one half of the garlic butter, coat one side of each steak. Place the steaks with the uncoated sides up, in a single layer on a sheet pan that has been drizzled with 1 tablespoon of the oil. Evenly coat the top side of the steaks with the remaining garlic butter. Drizzle the remaining oil over the top of the steaks.

3. Broil each side 3 to 4 inches from the source of heat, about 5 minutes per side, or until desired doneness. Serve with rice or potatoes.

121

Grilled Lamb Chops

Costeletas de Cordeiro Grelhado

Serves 6 to 8

My cousin Evelyn adds just the right amount of seasoning and lemon juice to balance the somewhat strong flavor associated with lamb. The real secret, Evelyn says, is to remove all visible fat. Grill so that the meat stays a bit pink in the middle for a tasty-to-the-last-bite result.

18 lamb shoulder chops or desired cut, ¾-inch thick
2 tablespoons coarse salt
6 cloves garlic, finely chopped
1 teaspoon oregano
1 teaspoon ground black pepper
juice of 1 lemon (about 4 tablespoons)
olive oil to drizzle (about 2 tablespoons)

1. Trim each chop of all visible fat and gristle, even in between sections of the meat. Set aside. Using a mortar and pestle, mash the garlic with the salt, forming a paste. Grind in the oregano and pepper, releasing their essences. Rub the mixture over the chops, coating evenly. Drizzle with the lemon juice and olive oil. Toss gently and marinate for several hours, or overnight in the refrigerator, turning occasionally.

2. Grill over a hot charcoal fire for the best flavor, 3 to 5 minutes each side or to desired doneness.

Liver Marinated in Wine and Garlic
Iscas em Vinha d'Albos
Serves 4

My father always removed the thin membrane from the outside of liver. "If it isn't removed before cooking," he instructed, "the slices of liver will curl." The marinade is a great counterpoint for the rich flavor of liver. The liver should be slightly pink in the middle when done; otherwise it will be dry. Marinating the liver first makes this the ultimate liver-and-onion classic.

1 pound pork or calves liver, ¼-inch thick, membrane removed
4 cloves garlic, finely chopped
1 bay leaf
1 cup dry white wine
1 tablespoon lemon juice
2 tablespoons finely chopped parsley
6 slices fairly lean bacon
2 medium onions, thinly sliced (about 2 cups)
½ teaspoon coarse salt or to taste
⅛ teaspoon freshly ground black pepper or to taste

1. Place the liver in a medium glass bowl. In a separate bowl, whisk the garlic, bay leaf, wine, lemon juice, and half of the parsley. Pour over the liver, cover, and marinate in the refrigerator for 2 hours.
2. Reserving the marinade, drain the liver well.
3. Fry the bacon in a large skillet over medium-high heat, until crisp. Remove solid pieces from the rendered fat with a slotted spoon and reserve.
4. Add and sauté the onions in the bacon fat until golden, about 10 minutes. Using a slotted spoon, transfer the onions to a serving platter and cover. Pan-fry the liver quickly in the pan drippings—a minute or two on each side. Remove the liver to the platter holding the onions, cover, and set aside.
5. Strain the marinade, add to the pan drippings, and cook over medium-high heat until the liquid is reduced by half. Pour the sauce over the liver and garnish with the remaining parsley. Serve with boiled potatoes and a crisp green salad.

Note: Red wine vinegar or a mixture of ½ cup dry white wine and ¼ cup white wine vinegar may be substituted for the white wine and lemon juice. Some cooks use wine vinegar or water to stretch the use of wine in marinades.

Tip: The thin membrane is easier to remove if the liver is partially frozen; if the liver is fresh, freeze it just long enough to make it stiff. Use a sharp knife to cut the liver into ¼-inch slices, or ask the butcher to slice it for you. Sometimes it can be purchased presliced. Use the point of a sharp paring knife to separate the membrane from the liver.

Linguiça Morcela, Salpicão, and Chouriço

5

SAUSAGES

Salsichas

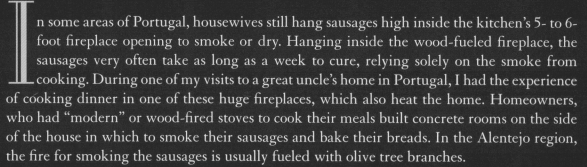

In some areas of Portugal, housewives still hang sausages high inside the kitchen's 5- to 6-foot fireplace opening to smoke or dry. Hanging inside the wood-fueled fireplace, the sausages very often take as long as a week to cure, relying solely on the smoke from cooking. During one of my visits to a great uncle's home in Portugal, I had the experience of cooking dinner in one of these huge fireplaces, which also heat the home. Homeowners, who had "modern" or wood-fired stoves to cook their meals built concrete rooms on the side of the house in which to smoke their sausages and bake their breads. In the Alentejo region, the fire for smoking the sausages is usually fueled with olive tree branches.

Here in the United States smokehouses of varying sizes, made of brick, cinder block, poured concrete, or metal, dot the backyards of Portuguese immigrants. These are used to smoke fresh pork marinated in wine, seasoned with spices, and stuffed in natural casings.

Sausage is a keynote ingredient that is added to soups, stews, and seafood dishes. It is often grilled, or simply sliced, and eaten with a torn piece of bread. Sausages vary regionally, but the most well known are *linguiça* and *chouriço*.

Today, it is less common for Portuguese families to raise pigs for slaughter, so the sausages made by Portuguese immigrants and their offspring are usually the *linguiças* and *chouriços,* made with pork meat purchased at the supermarket. If a whole, live pig is bought at a farm today, it is usually for a big celebration feast. After it is slaughtered, the meat, tripe, blood, and intestinal casings are brought home to be used in main dishes and in many types of sausages, including blood sausages.

SOME COMMON PORTUGUESE SAUSAGES

Chouriço (shor-EE-soo) Similar to the Spanish *chorizo,* a pork sausage seasoned with garlic, paprika, spices, and wine; used in soups and stews. It is thicker and spicer than the *linguiça.*

Farinheira (far-ren-YEH-rra) A flour-and-pork sausage, seasoned with garlic, paprika, and sometimes the juice of oranges, it is commonly pan-fried, grilled, or used in boiled dinners.

Linguiça (leeng-QUEE-sah) This sausage is similar to *chouriço* but made with different cuts of pork. Milder in taste, *linguiça* is usually seasoned with garlic, wine, paprika, or sweet red pepper paste, depending on the region. It is usually grilled or sautéed.

Morcelas (mor-SELL-las) A spiced pork-blood sausage that is commonly used in boiled dinners. It is a combination of pork, fat, pork blood, and spices.

Salpicão (sal-pee-COWN) This sausage has a diameter of 2½ to 3 inches and is similar to a rolled ham but more heavily flavored with garlic and paprika. It is used for soups, stews, and braises. The casing is usually removed before serving. *Chouriço* can be used in its place.

A combination of *morcela, farinheira,* and *chouriço* is usually included in Portuguese boiled dinner. *Salpicão* and *chouriço* are used in soups, although those who prefer a less spicy sausage usually use *linguiça* in soups or stews, and also cook it with dry-heat methods.

MAKING SAUSAGE

Pigs were customarily slaughtered just before winter, so sausages were made then and preserved. Even today, many old-timers, though they have refrigerators, are still reluctant to make sausages in the warmer months.

Methods for preparing sausages as well as other Portuguese foods depend on the availability of equipment. My father cleverly improvised some of the items he needed for preparing sausages. His homemade funnel consisted of a muffin cup with a hole punched through the bottom. Another piece of metal was attached to the base of the cup, forming the funnel through which the ground meat was forced into sausage casings. Also needed were a large bowl and many willing hands, whose thumbs and fingers substituted for the short wooden dowels we eventually used to press the meat through the funnel.

The procedure my father used was always the same, whatever type of sausage he was making. On the first day, he mixed all the ingredients and let the mixture stand overnight (24 hours). The next day, he called us all to the kitchen and gave us our assignments. Some would attach the readied casings to the funnel end of the muffin cup. Others would tie off the end of the casing or with needles at hand, be ready to prick any air bubbles. The rest of us, holding the casing securely to the funnel, stuffed the sausage mix into the funnel, forcing the meat down with our fingers and gently squeezing the mixture to the end of the casing, packing firmly. The ends were then tied and the sausages were hung to air-dry the exterior of excess moisture. The sausages were then smoked and hung again for the color to darken, called the "bloom."

Old methods die hard. While hand-cranked mechanical stuffers speed up the process, many traditionalists still stuff the casings by hand. They maintain that the mechanical method alters the meat texture and flavor and pushes the flavorful marinade from the chilled meat as it is cranked through to the casings.

Many Portuguese cooks continue to smoke their sausages the old way, too, using smokehouses in their backyards. These vented smokehouses stand between 5 and 7 feet tall and 40 to 60 inches square. After a blazing wood fire set inside the smokehouse dies to smoldering embers, and the heavy dark smoke is gone, the sausages are hung high inside—no closer than 3 to 4 feet above the embers. The door is left open about two inches until any remaining excess moisture or condensation has evaporated. The door is then closed and the sausages are smoked for about 12 hours. Sausages are sometimes smoked for two shorter time periods. At the end of the smoking the exterior of the casings is somewhat firm. The door of the smoker is opened, and the sausages eventually develop a bloom. The texture becomes even firmer as the sausages cool. Here in North America we store the finished sausages in the refrigerator, but in Portugal it is not unusual to store them covered in lard or oil until needed.

Hand-stuffing the sausage casings

The sausages are pricked with needles to release air pockets

Sausages air drying before smoking

Typical smokehouse filled with sausages ready for smoking

Door left slightly ajar at the start of smoking, allowing excess moisture to escape

Some finished sausages

POINTS TO REMEMBER IN SAUSAGE-MAKING

When making sausages, be especially careful to observe good sanitation. If there is one thing that was emphasized by my teacher, Ernest Vieira, when I studied culinary sanitation practice, it was the importance of keeping ingredients chilled and working in small batches. All equipment should be clean and sanitary; pre-chill equipment *and* ingredients. This is especially important when using meat that is ground or cut into small pieces. As with any recipe, having all things ready before you begin enables you to prepare the recipe quickly, efficiently, and without compromising food safety.

• Prepare the casings by soaking them in cool water for 15 minutes. Then rinse them under cold running water. To rinse casings, open one end and allow water to flow into and through to the opposite end. Store casings in the refrigerator, covered with cold water, until ready to use.

• When processing the meat, work in small batches and keep unused meat refrigerated. Have all ingredients ready and work quickly, removing the meat from the refrigerator last. (When I am trimming and cutting the meat, I keep it in a bowl placed in a larger bowl that is filled with ice.)

• Generally, salt should be added last, just before the casings are stuffed, because salt will draw juices from the meat. The exception is when Sweet Red Pepper Paste, *massa de pimentão* (page 166), which contains salt, is part of the sausage recipe.

• For best results, always follow the instructions of your particular smoker. Before placing the sausages in the smoker, be sure that the casings are dry and free of grease. The exterior should have an almost papery feel to it. The sausages should be nearly room temperature to prevent condensation from forming on them. Do not overpack your smoker. Leave sufficient space between sausages to allow air to circulate properly. Condensation will prevent the proper color and finish to form on the casings. This stage should not be rushed. Patience is important for the entire process.

• Maintaining temperature in the smoker is also important. Generally, modern electric smokers have a probe that is inserted into the sausage. The temperature can then be read on an external dial, without decreasing the temperature inside the smoker by opening it.

• At temperatures between 40 and 140 degrees Farenheit, botulism can develop. In commercial and large-scale home production, safety is ensured by the addition of Prague Powder, a preservative that contains sodium nitrate. The following recipes have been tested successfully with an electric smoker without using Prague Powder. Strict sanitation procedures, the quantity of salt and acidic wine, thorough mixing, and proper smoking are the factors that ensure success. Both wine and salt act as preservatives.

A variety of marinades are used in sausage-making. Generally, trimmed, cubed pork meat is marinated in white or red wine, or a mixture of the two. If red wine is used alone, the result is a dark sausage that becomes even darker during the smoking process. The wine is sometimes diluted with water. Additional seasoning comes from garlic, salt, hot sauce, or Sweet Red Pepper Paste, plus whatever else the cook desires. The meat is marinated for 24 to 48 hours and turned occasionally during that period.

The two recipes for *linguiça* that follow are family favorites. The first is my father's and represents the Alentejo region of his birth. The second recipe—one he guarded carefully—comes from my father-in-law, Arthur Ortins. He sold his popular sausage in his grocery store for many years, and I acquired his secret recipe only recently. Both recipes use pork butt.

Linguiça Alentejo-Style
Linguiça à Alentejana
Makes about 10 pounds

This recipe is different from sausages of other regions in that it doesn't contain any wine. The size of the cut meat must be small enough to fit through a stuffing funnel. Remember to follow the directions of your smoker. Typically, the casing is filled in one long continuous length, which is then wrapped around the hanging rod. I like to cut them in shorter lengths, which makes them easier to handle and I can give some away in tied loops.

10 pounds pork butt, boned and trimmed, about 20 percent fat to 80 percent lean

2 heads garlic (about 20 large cloves), finely chopped

1½ cups Sweet Red Pepper Paste (page 166)

8 ounces salt-packed pork intestines, size 34 mm, cut into 24-inch lengths, prepared for stuffing (page 130)

Equipment:

an accurate meat thermometer

a manual or electric meat grinder, prechilled, and large grind plate

a large stainless-steel bowl, thoroughly cleaned and prechilled

an extra-large stainless-steel bowl, thoroughly clean

large quantity of ice

Day ahead:

1. Fill the extra-large bowl three quarters of the way with ice and set the large bowl inside it. In small batches, quickly cut the pork into ½- to 1-inch cubes. (You can have your butcher precut the meat using extra-large grind on a machine.) Remove any sinew or gristle. Remove the gland as well, if possible, because it is bitter. The ratio should be about 20 percent fat to 80 percent meat.

2. Once all the meat has been processed, mix in the garlic and Sweet Red Pepper Paste, blending well. Chill for 24 hours, turning the meat occasionally to remix.

Next day:

1. Just before stuffing the casings, remove a small amount of meat and fry in a skillet. Taste for seasoning and add more pepper paste if necessary.

2. Stuff by hand using a funnel that has a wide exit end or use the sausage attachment on a meat grinder without the cutting blade. Apply the readied casings, wetting the attachment nozzle with extra water so the casings slide easily on the attachment.

3. Tie off the bottom end of the casing, leaving an 8-inch length of string.

4. Stuff, feeding the meat through the prechilled grinder. Gently squeeze the meat to the end of the casings, but do not overstuff. With a sterilized needle, prick any air bubbles that are created. The sausages should feel firm, but have a slight give to

131

allow for shrinkage of the casings during smoking.

5. Using the string at the end of the casing, tie off the opposite end, leaving a 2-inch gap of string, forming a loop. The gap of string will rest on the hanging rod. Continue with remaining meat.

6. Hang the sausage loops on a rod to let casings air dry in a cool room about 12 to 15 hours. Casings will darken somewhat as they dry.

To smoke:

The smoking instructions, adapted from Rytek Kutas' book *Great Sausage Recipes and Meat Curing,* are for use with an electric or gas smoker. (See Resource Guide for more information.) Keep in mind that directions for your smoker may differ.

1. Preheat the smoker to 100 to 110 degrees F.

2. Add the sausages and maintain this temperature for about 1 hour or more with damper open and door slightly ajar, until casings are dry to the touch. Close the smoker door, then increase the temperature setting to 130 degrees, building the temperature slowly. If the exterior is still moist, and if the heat is too hot too soon, or if the process is rushed, the sausages will not smoke properly. They are more likely to steam. Slow smoking makes a more tender sausage.

3. When the internal temperature of the sausage reaches 100 degrees, increase temperature setting to 150 degrees, then close the damper to halfway.

4. After the casings are brown, add a pan of dampened (not soaking) sawdust; close the damper so it is only one quarter of the way open.

5. When the amount of smoke from the damper decreases, add another pan of moistened sawdust. Repeat 2 or 3 times more, or a total of 4 or 5 times. Remove pan completely when sausage color is dark.

6. If the sausages have not reached an internal temperature of 125 degrees at this point, adjust temperature setting of the smoker to 160 to 165 degrees and continue to smoke the sausages until they reach an internal temperature of 125 degrees.

7. Continue to smoke the sausages until an internal temperature of 152 degrees is reached. To reach the final internal temperature of the sausages, it may be necessary to fill the empty sawdust pan with boiling water and place in smoker.

8. Remove sausages from the smoker. Rinse with cool water, reducing the internal temperature to 100 degrees. Hang sausages on wooden dowels to dry for 20 to 25 minutes; sausages will darken—or bloom—as they dry. When completely cooled, refrigerate, covered with wax paper.

Old-fashioned sausage-making was not without its taboos. Mixing the meat with seasoning was most often done with one's hands, and it was, and is still, believed by some Portuguese that women should not be allowed to handle the pork meat during the time of their monthly cycle for fear of spoiling the meat.

Arthur Ortins' Linguiça

Linguiça de Etur Ortins

Makes about 12 pounds

This recipe is unusual because of the spices my father-in-law included. Follow the food safety procedures outlined at the beginning of this chapter; be sure to use an accurate thermometer to check the internal temperature of the meat and to pre-chill and sanitize your equipment.

2 heads garlic, peeled, finely chopped
1 tablespoon black pepper
1-2 tablespoons paprika
1½ teaspoons ground allspice
¼ cup onion, finely chopped
12 pounds boneless pork butt, about 20 percent
    fat to 80 percent lean
3½ cups red wine or as needed
3½ cups water or as needed
5 to 6 tablespoons coarse salt or to taste
34-mm pork casings, cut to 18-inch lengths,
    prepared, rinsed well, and refrigerated
butcher's twine
large quantity of ice

Day ahead:

1. Mix the first five ingredients together and set aside.
2. Fill an extra-large bowl three quarters of the way with ice and set a large stainless-steel bowl inside it.
3. In small batches, quickly cut the pork into ½- to 1-inch cubes. You can use a meat grinder with a coarse blade. (You can also have your butcher precut the meat using extra-large grind on a machine.) Remove any sinew or gristle. Remove the gland as well, if possible, because it is bitter. The ratio should be about 20 percent fat to 80 percent meat.
4. Add equal amounts of wine and water to the seasoning and blend. Pour over the meat, stirring.

Add more wine and water in equal parts so that the meat is wet but not swimming in liquid. Mix thoroughly and marinate 24 hours in the refrigerator, turning occasionally.

Next day:

1. Add salt and mix well. Cook a piece of the marinated meat and taste for seasoning. Adjust if needed.
2. Using a pre-chilled sausage stuffer, attach one end of the casing to the funnel and tie off the other end with butcher's twine.
3. Process the mixture through the grinder with the sausage attachment (the cutting blade should be removed), stuffing the casing firmly but gently until filled. Pour a small amount of the marinade into the attachment from time to time to facilitate moving the meat along the casing. Prick any air pockets with a sterilized needle. (A needle that is threaded doesn't get lost as easily.) Give the sausage a very gentle squeeze to close up the space where there was an air pocket.
4. Leaving a 2-inch gap of string, tie the ends of the sausage together to form a loop. Rinse the sausages, wipe with a clean towel and hang on dowels to air-dry.

To smoke:

1. Place sausages in a preheated smoker and proceed as on the previous page.

133

Chouriço

Chouriço

Makes about 5 pounds

Follow the food safety procedures described at the beginning of this chapter. Read through the recipe for Linguiça Alentejo-Style (page 131–32) for detailed instructions that apply to this recipe as well.

5 pounds pork butt cut into ½- to 1-inch cubes (or have your butcher to cut the meat with large grind plate)
1 head garlic, peeled and finely chopped
4 ounces paprika
1¼ cups red table wine as needed
1¼ cups white table wine as needed
1 tablespoon Hot Pepper Paste (page 167)
3 tablespoons coarse salt
34-mm pork casings, prepared, rinsed well

Day ahead:
1. Combine the ingredients, except for the salt, adding equal amount of white and red wine to just cover the meat. Marinate in the refrigerator for 24 hours, stirring occasionally.

Next day:
1. Before stuffing the casings, add 2 tablespoons of the salt, mix well, and cook a piece of meat to taste for seasoning. Add more salt as needed.
2. Stuff the casings, tying off every 18 inches.
3. Place the sausages in a preheated smoker and follow the smoking directions on page 132.

Grilled Linguiça

Linguiça Grelhada

Serves 4

As a light lunch, with soup, or as an appetizer, grilled linguiça *is hard to beat. The aroma of sausage grilling is irresistible. This charming story captures the essence of its appeal. A man was eating plain bread, surrounded by enticing gusts of* linguiça *drifting from a neighbor's barbecue. When the man's wife asked him what he was eating, he replied, chewing wistfully on his humble bread, "Comer pão cheira de linguiça"—"Eating bread with the smell of linguiça!"*

1 pound *linguiça,* cut into 4- or 5-inch lengths

1. Grill over hot coals or broil until the skin is a rich brown color and blistered.
2. Place in crusty rolls or serve with bread.

Variations: Grilled sausage can be sliced into rounds and served with toast points as an appetizer. Tossing caramelized onions and/or roasted peppers in a roll with the sausage makes for an immensely flavorful sandwich.

Linguiça and *chouriço* can be cut into small cubes, lightly sautéed, combined with chopped onion and shredded soft cheese, then used as a stuffing for meats, or for stuffing clams, prebaked tartlet shells, or even mushrooms, which can then be placed under a broiler to melt the cheese and lightly brown the tops. Serve as an appetizer or snack.

134

Fireman's Linguiça

Linguiça à Bombeiro

Serves 2 to 4

This aptly named appetizer is commonly served in Portuguese restaurants. It is prepared tableside in a clay vessel that looks like a rowboat. (These vessels may be purchased from Portuguese specialty shops; see Resource Guide.) Clay slats sit crosswise like seats in the boat and hold sausages above alcohol, which is poured into the floor of the vessel. Aguardente—sometimes called "Bang Bang" in the United States—is a distilled liquor made from the grape skins after they have been removed from the wine press. This liquor is similar to Italian grappa, but any brandy, even Cognac, can be substituted. With an outdoor grill—for safety—and a little improvising, it can be prepared pretty easily at home. (The grill is not turned on, nor are hot coals used.) The object is to suspend the sausage slightly above the liquor, which is then ignited to sear the meat. Please use care when preparing this dish.

1 pound *linguiça,* cut into 5-inch lengths, nearly room temperature
1 cup brandy, as needed

1. Position a shallow pan securely on the flat surface of your grill, outdoors. Place a small cooking rack in the pan, and arrange sausage on top of it.
2. Pour the brandy over the sausage into the pan. There should be a depth of about a ½ inch of liquor.
3. Carefully ignite the brandy. Use long-handled barbecue tongs to turn the sausage until it is golden brown and heated through. Remove from the heat. Serve with crusty bread and olives, or with a green salad for a light lunch.

135

Chickpea Salad with Salt Cod, page 150

6

VEGETABLES & GRAINS
Vegetais e Grão

Usually a Portuguese family will find a sunny spot in which to plant a vegetable garden, sometimes giving up the entire backyard to the cultivation of fresh produce. Seeds for many of their familiar favorites are unavailable in the United States, so many immigrants brought seeds with them from the old country, cultivated them, and saved the seeds from their first American harvest to plant the following spring. These seeds were shared among relatives and friends and newcomers from Portugal or the Azores—a practice that continues today. While there is not a large repertoire of vegetable dishes in Portuguese cooking, the benefits of fresh vegetables come primarily from our soups, which more often than not contain the nutritious greens and other treasures harvested from our gardens.

Harvesting freshly ripened vegetables and herbs from the garden was and still is an enjoyable task. Sharing our abundance with friends and neighbors makes it even more so. When I was young, my father planted a huge garden in which he grew parsley, garlic, onions, corn, kale, carrots, peppers, turnips, potatoes, tomatoes, broad beans, strawberries, and of course, cilantro. Planning a meal based on what was ripe in the garden was not uncommon. When all the vegetables had been harvested, we would begin to prepare the garden for the coming winter. One of the important tasks was to collect those plants—cilantro was one of many—that had been allowed to go to seed. We would gather the branches, heavy with seeds, and place them in a large metal box. My father would set this box in a south window in our cellar. The seeds would dry in the warm sunlight and fall from the branches. In the spring the seeds would be re-sown with seed potatoes for the new year's crop.

When the first Portuguese ate a potato, it was the start of a love affair—an affair that recrossed the ocean with the Portuguese immigrants who arrived in America. Punched, roasted, fried, or boiled—potatoes are an irresistible starch, entwined in the fabric of Portuguese cooking.

Rice and legumes, which provide starch and have a long shelf life, are equally favored. Short-grain rice is most commonly used for soup and pudding, while medium- and long-grain rice are used in braises, stews, and individual rice dishes. Converted rice, because of its nonsticky texture, has become popular with some Portuguese cooks in this country; others continue to use unprocessed long-grain rice. Fiber- and protein-rich legumes are used in soups, stews, and salads (such as Friar's Beans, page 148). They even turn up as beer nuts—cooked, salted lupini beans, called *tremoços,* are often served with a brew. You eat them by nipping off one end of the shell and squeezing the bean into your mouth. Chickpeas, or kidney, roman, lima, and fava beans are all used in hearty proportions.

Special occasions are not a prerequisite for enjoying cooking and eating *al fresco.* I remember a particular summer when we were putting cedar shingles on the house. Several of my father's friends came over to help. At the day's end, my father showed his appreciation in typical Portuguese manner by feeding his helpers. To the strains of Portuguese music playing on his Motorola, he grilled fresh sardines and an assortment of meats. The feast was rounded out with sautéed spinach, bread, boiled potatoes, delicious fresh corn from the garden, wine, cheese and pears picked fresh from our tree. A day of shared work ends in a day of shared feasting.

Portuguese Potato Fries

Batatas Fritas à Portuguesa

Serves 4

These fried potatoes are a great favorite in our family. I always make extra because half of the potatoes are eaten before they ever reach the table! Fried in olive oil, they are terrific with steak, seafood, and especially Carne de Porco à Alentejana (page 98), which was traditionally eaten with boiled potatoes in my father's town. Unlike American fries, these potatoes are tender rather than crisp. Although Portuguese fries are not meant to be crisp, presoaking the potatoes in cold water, then blotting dry, removes excess starch that absorbs oil and prevents the potatoes from crisping on the outside.

6 large potatoes (preferably russets) (allow 1½ per person)
olive oil (approximately 1½ quarts or enough to give a minimum depth of 5 inches for deep frying)
coarse salt as needed

1. Peel the potatoes and slice into ¼-inch rounds.
2. Heat the oil over medium-high heat until it quivers. Fry the potatoes in small batches until golden. Remove the potatoes with a slotted utensil to drain on paper toweling or brown paper. Salt to desired taste.

Note: Frying in small batches allows movement of the potatoes and keeps the temperature of the oil more constant, so the potatoes brown quickly. If you use vegetable oil, the flavor will be different from that of the traditional olive oil.

Punched Potatoes

Batatas à Murro

Serves 4

This popular but simple potato preparation can be made on short notice. Red Bliss, Idaho bakers, or new potatoes all work well in this recipe.

8 small or 4 medium-sized potatoes, whole, skins intact, scrubbed
8 cloves garlic, finely chopped
1 tablespoon coarse salt or to taste
olive oil to drizzle
wine vinegar to drizzle (optional)

Preheat the oven to 400 degrees F.

1. Pierce the potatoes all over with a fork and place in a shallow baking dish. Bake the potatoes for 1 hour or until tender.
2. Give each potato a slight punch with the side of your closed fist (hard enough to crack it open a bit, but not hard enough to smash it to smithers). Scatter the chopped garlic in the opening of each potato.
3. Season with coarse salt and drizzle each with olive oil. Add a dash of vinegar to taste if desired. Serve immediately.

Roasted Potatoes

Batatas Assadas

Serves 4

You can surround a turkey or roast of beef or pork with these potatoes, basting them with savory pan juices. The seasonings create a heady fragrance that stimulates the taste buds.

6 large new potatoes, peeled and cut into ¾-inch wedges
4 cloves garlic, finely chopped
1 tablespoon paprika
½ tablespoon coarse salt or to taste
1 teaspoon black pepper
¼ cup olive oil
1½ tablespoons parsley, finely chopped

Preheat the oven to 350 degrees F.

1. In a large bowl combine the potatoes with the garlic, paprika, salt, and pepper. Gently mix, evenly coating the potatoes. Drizzle with the olive oil and sprinkle with the parsley; mix to coat evenly.
2. Place in a roasting pan (or add to a pan of roasting meat) and roast at 350 degrees, turning occasionally, for about 45 minutes to 1 hour, or until tender.

Potatoes with Wine and Tomato

Batatas com Vinho e Tomate

Serves 6

Wine and tomatoes take roasted potatoes to a new level—one that has more than eye-appeal.

4 tablespoons butter, melted
4 tablespoons olive oil
2 teaspoons paprika
3 cloves garlic, finely chopped
½ tablespoon finely chopped parsley
2 teaspoons coarse salt
1 teaspoon hot pepper sauce
½ teaspoon black pepper
6 large Red Bliss or new potatoes, peeled and quartered
1 medium very ripe tomato, peeled, seeded, and finely chopped (about ½ cup) or 1 tablespoon tomato paste
½ cup white wine

Preheat oven to 350 degrees F.

1. In a large bowl, combine the butter, olive oil, paprika, and garlic.
2. Stir in the parsley, salt, hot pepper sauce, and ground pepper.
3. Add the potatoes and the tomatoes, gently mixing. Transfer ingredients to a roasting pan. Slowly pour in the wine. Put the pan in the preheated oven and roast until the potatoes are tender, about 50 to 60 minutes.

140

Rice with Salt Cod

Arroz de Bacalhau

Serves 4 to 6

It is remarkable how a simple dish can be so satisfying. Accompanied with a salad, bread, olives, and wine, this rice dish makes a tasty meal.

½ pound salt cod, soaked in several changes of cold water, 16 to 24 hours, refrigerated*
4 cups water, or as needed
¼ cup olive oil
1 small onion, finely chopped (about ½ cup)
1 small ripe tomato, peeled, seeded, and coarsely chopped (about ¼ cup) or 2 teaspoons tomato paste
1 bay leaf
1 clove garlic, coarsely chopped
¼ teaspoon paprika
⅛ teaspoon black pepper
1 cup long-grain rice
1 teaspoon coarse salt or to taste
1 tablespoon finely chopped cilantro or parsley

*See salt cod instructions on page 11.

1. Remove the fish from the soaking water and rinse. Cut the fish into 2-inch pieces and place in a 2½-quart saucepan. Add 2 cups of fresh water or enough to cover the fish completely. Cover and bring to a boil over medium-high heat. Reduce the heat to medium-low and simmer for 10 minutes. Drain the fish and set aside.
2. Heat the oil in a 4-quart saucepan over medium-high heat. Add the onion and sauté until golden. Add the tomato or tomato paste, bay leaf, garlic, paprika, and black pepper. Cover, reduce the heat, and simmer until the tomato is very soft and partially dissolved, about 15 minutes.
3. Pour in the remaining 2 cups of water and re-cover. Bring to a boil, stir in the rice, salt, and one half of the parsley or cilantro. Re-cover, reduce the heat, and simmer for 25 minutes, until the rice is done and the liquid is absorbed. Combine with the cooked fish, gently tossing and transfer to a serving platter. Garnish with extra parsley or cilantro.

Health Note: Rice dishes, both savory and dessert, are susceptible to Bacillus Cereus intoxication when not handled properly. Hot dishes, fresh or leftover, should be served at temperatures above 140 degrees F. Reheat leftover savory rice dishes to 165 degrees. Dishes to be served cold should be held at a temperature of 40 degrees or below and served well chilled.

141

Seafood Rice

Arroz de Marisco

Serves 6 to 8

Sometimes rice is prepared on the stove top then finished in the oven to dry any extra moisture. This rice dish with seafood, adapted from Isaura Noguiera's recipe, is a perfect example. For special occasions, pour the rice into a ring mold. After removing it from the oven, invert it onto a serving platter, remove the mold, and place a garnish of cilantro sprigs in the middle. Served with a salad of mixed greens, it makes a perfect lunch or separate course in a larger meal.

1 1¼-pound boiled lobster

½ pound medium shrimp, peeled and deveined, shells reserved

3½ cups water

¼ cup olive oil

1 small onion, finely chopped (about ½ cup)

1 large very ripe tomato, peeled, seeded, and coarsely chopped (about 1 cup)

1½ tablespoons tomato paste

1 clove garlic, finely chopped

2 teaspoons coarse salt

1 cup long-grain or converted rice

2 tablespoons finely chopped cilantro or parsley

1 teaspoon hot pepper sauce

¼ teaspoon saffron crushed and soaked in a tiny bit of water for 15 minutes

½ teaspoon turmeric

2 ounces white button mushrooms, cleaned and thinly sliced (about ½ cup)

½ pound small bay scallops

½ cup baby peas (fresh shelled or frozen)

1 tablespoon butter, softened

Preheat the oven to 350 degrees F.

1. Shell the lobster, reserving as much of the juice as possible. Coarsely chop the meat and set aside with reserved juice.

2. Place shrimp shells and the water in a saucepan. Cover, and bring to a boil over medium-high heat. Reduce the heat to medium-low and simmer for 15 minutes. Reserve the cooking water and discard the shells.

3. Heat the oil in a 4-quart pot over medium-high heat. Add and sauté the onion until lightly golden. Add the tomatoes, tomato paste, and garlic. Cover and simmer until the tomatoes are very soft and partially dissolved, about 15 minutes.

4. Measure the amount of lobster juice and add enough shrimp broth to make 3½ cups of liquid. Pour into the onions and tomatoes. Add the salt and bring to a boil. Stir in the rice with the cilantro, hot pepper sauce, saffron-water, and turmeric. Reduce the heat, re-cover, and simmer the rice for 15 minutes.

5. Add the mushrooms and continue to simmer until liquid is almost absorbed and the rice is tender, about 5 to 10 more minutes. Mix in the scallops and shrimp. Stir in the peas and the lobster meat. Simmer 1 more minute. Remove from heat. Butter a 9 x 13-inch glass baking dish or mold. Transfer the rice to the baking dish. Bake at 350 degrees for 20 minutes to set and absorb any excess liquid.

Rice with Chicken

Arroz de Frango

Serves 4 to 6

"Use a combination of green, red, and orange bell peppers for a colorful effect," suggests Maria Fernandes Bettencourt. She added that this rice, richly flavored with chicken, can also be served nicely on a buffet table.

3 chicken thighs

3 cups water

2 tablespoons olive oil

1 medium onion, finely chopped (about 1 cup)

1 small very ripe tomato, peeled, seeded, and coarsely chopped (about ¼ cup) or 1 teaspoon tomato paste

1 clove garlic, finely chopped

1 bay leaf

1 teaspoon coarse salt or to taste

¼ teaspoon white pepper

1 cup long-grain or converted rice

1 green, yellow, or red pepper, cored, seeded, and cut into ½-inch pieces

1. Put the chicken in a 2½-quart pot with the water and place over medium-high heat. Cover and bring to a boil, reduce the heat to medium-low and simmer until the chicken is tender, about 30 minutes. Reserving the cooking liquid, remove the chicken. Bone the meat and cut into ½-inch chunks and set aside. Discard the bones.

2. In a separate 2½-quart pan, heat the oil over medium-high heat and sauté the onions until soft and lightly colored.

3. Reduce the heat, then add the tomatoes or tomato paste, garlic, and bay leaf. Cover and simmer until the tomatoes are very soft and partially dissolved, about 15 minutes.

4. Pour in 2 cups of the reserved cooking water, salt and pepper. Stir and cover. Bring to a boil, add the rice, then simmer for 15 minutes. Add the chopped pepper and continue cooking until rice is tender and liquid is absorbed (about 10 minutes more).

143

When we were young, we made frequent Sunday trips to the beach. It was like going on Safari—Portuguese-style. First, Titi (Aunt Ana) made her Buttered Rice (page 145) and pan-fried rump steaks covered in natural juices and enriched with butter (page 120). Then we loaded my uncle's station wagon with the playpen, folding chairs, towels, beach toys, and all kinds of essential gear. Then everyone—grandparents, aunt and uncle, cousins, brothers, and I— piled in. Once there, we would find our favorite spot under a shade tree that bordered the sand. We spread the blanket, opened the playpen, unfolded the chairs for my grandparents, and prepared to eat the wonderful picnic lunch my aunt had made. The rest of the afternoon would be ours to enjoy the sand and water.

Seafood Rice (front, page 142), Rice with Carrots and Peas (back left, page 145), and Tomato Rice (back right, page 147)

Buttered Rice

Arroz de Manteiga

Serves 4

As children, we called this favorite "sticky rice."

2 cups water
3 tablespoons butter, softened, divided
1 teaspoon coarse salt
⅔ cup short-grain rice

1. In a 2½-quart saucepan, combine the water, 1 tablespoon of the butter, and the salt. Cover and bring to a boil. Stir in the rice. Cover and simmer over medium-low until rice is done and water is absorbed, 20 to 25 minutes.
2. Add the remaining butter and mix in thoroughly.

Variation: Add 1 tablespoon of finely chopped cilantro or parsley.

Rice with Carrots and Peas

Arroz de Cenoura e Ervilhas

Serves 6 to 8

Flavored in a most delicate way with peas and carrots, this rice is elegant enough to serve on special occasions.

1 tablespoon oil
1 tablespoon butter
1 small onion, finely chopped (about ½ cup)
4 cups water
1 teaspoon coarse salt
1 bay leaf
2 cups long-grain or converted rice
1 large carrot, peeled and cut into ½-inch cubes
¾ cup peas, fresh or frozen
fresh parsley sprigs for garnish

1. Heat the oil and butter in a 3-quart pot over medium-high heat. Add and sauté the onion until soft and translucent, about 5 minutes.
2. Add the water, salt, and bay leaf. Cover and bring to a boil. Stir in the rice. Re-cover, reduce the heat to medium-low, and simmer for 15 minutes.
3. Add the carrots and peas and continue cooking until carrots are tender and rice is done, about 10 to 15 minutes more.
4. Butter a tube mold and fill with the hot rice, packing the mold firmly. Immediately invert onto a serving platter and garnish with sprigs of fresh parsley.

Variation: Add ½ pound *chouriço* (page 127), cut into ½-inch cubes, to the onions and lightly brown. Continue with the recipe.

145

Rice with Chicken Giblets

Arroz com Moélas de Galinha

Serves 4 to 6

Unearthing this recipe from family archives was worth the digging. When I was thirteen, a distant cousin in Canada whom I was visiting, made a dish similar to this, using elbow pasta. Although I never got the recipe, I never quite forgot it. Then Elena, a very close friend of my father's, invited me to delve through her family recipes. I couldn't believe my find. This version is made with rice and very much like what I ate when I was young. It is tasty with pasta or rice.

2 tablespoons olive oil
1 medium onion, finely chopped (about 1 cup)
2 cloves garlic, finely chopped
1 bay leaf
½ cup finely chopped parsley
1 medium very ripe tomato, peeled, seeded, and finely chopped (about ½ cup) or 1 tablespoon tomato paste
2 cups water
½ pound chicken giblets, trimmed of any fat or gristle, rinsed and coarsely chopped
1 teaspoon coarse salt
1 cup medium- or long-grain rice

1. Heat the oil in a large skillet over medium-high heat. Add the onion and sauté until translucent, about 5 minutes. Reduce the heat to medium-low.
2. Add the garlic, bay leaf, and parsley, cooking until the garlic becomes aromatic, then stir in the tomatoes. Cover, and simmer until the tomatoes are soft and partially dissolved, about 15 minutes. If you are substituting tomato paste, make sure the paste is well blended, about 3 minutes.
3. Pour in the water and add the chopped giblets, hearts, and salt. Cover and bring to a boil over medium-high heat. Reduce the heat and simmer for 25 minutes, then add the chopped liver, if using. Skim the surface of the water of any protein foam. When the giblets are almost tender, add the rice. Stir well, cover, simmer until the rice is tender and excess liquid is absorbed, about 20 minutes.

146

Tomato Rice
Arroz de Tomate

Serves 4 to 6

From the moment I had my first taste of it, as a young girl at prima Marguerida's (cousin Margaret's) farm in Portugal, I was hooked. It would be foolhardy not to take advantage of the ripest and most flavorful tomatoes at harvest time to prepare this rice dish, which is a Portuguese favorite. The tomatoes should be as fresh as possible; the best ones, of course, would come very ripe, straight from your garden. I like to use the Portuguese variety coração de boi/toro (page 14), *but a meaty variety such as beefsteak is a good substitute. This dish is especially good with seafood. Because the growing season for tomatoes is limited in some parts of the United States, in the dead of winter, use good-quality canned tomatoes or tomato paste rather than the pale supermarket tomatoes.*

3 tablespoons olive oil or 2 slices smoked bacon, coarsely chopped

1 medium onion, finely chopped (about 1 cup)

2 large very ripe tomatoes, peeled, seeded, and chopped (about 2 cups) or 1 tablespoon tomato paste

1 clove garlic, finely chopped

2 cups water

1 teaspoon coarse salt

1 cup long-grain rice

1 tablespoon finely chopped parsley

6 small black olives for garnish

1. Heat the oil or bacon in a 2½ quart saucepan over medium-high heat. (If using bacon, remove crisp bits after fat is rendered.) Add and sauté the onion until lightly colored. Reduce the heat to medium-low. Stir in the tomatoes with the garlic. Cover and cook until the tomatoes are soft and partially dissolved, about 15 minutes. If using tomato paste, make sure it is well blended.

2. Add the water. Bring to a boil over medium-high heat and add the salt. Toss in the rice, stir, and cover. Reduce the heat and simmer for about 20 minutes.

3. Stir in the parsley and continue cooking until the rice is tender and the liquid is absorbed, about 5 to 10 minutes more.

4. Fill a custard cup mold with serving portions, packing firmly, and immediately invert onto individual serving plates. Remove the mold, center a black olive on top of the rice, and serve.

147

Beans with Rice

Feijão Guisado com Arroz

Serves 4

This common peasant recipe makes a simple but delicious side dish.

½ cup dried red kidney beans soaked overnight
    in 3½ cups water
4 cups water, divided
3 tablespoons olive oil
1 small onion, finely chopped (about ½ cup)
1 clove of garlic, finely chopped
½ bay leaf
1 teaspoon coarse salt or to taste
1 cup short- or long-grain rice
1 tablespoon wine vinegar
½ teaspoon white pepper

1. Drain the beans from the soaking water and rinse. Place the beans in a 1-quart saucepan with 2 cups of fresh water. Cover and bring to a boil over medium-high heat. Reduce the heat and simmer until very tender (about 45 minutes). Drain and keep warm.
2. Heat the oil in a 2½-quart saucepan over medium-high heat. Add the onion, garlic, and bay leaf and sauté until the onion is translucent, about 5 minutes. Add the remaining 2 cups of water. Cover, bring to a boil, and add the salt. Stir in the rice. Reduce the heat to medium-low.
3. Simmer the rice until tender (20 to 25 minutes) and remove from heat.
4. Add the reserved beans, vinegar, and pepper to the rice and blend well. Remove the bay leaf and serve as a side dish or as a vegetarian main dish.

Friar's Beans

Feijão Frade

Serves 6

Black-eyed peas give this bean salad a healthy and interesting appeal. It is a dish that vegetarians will appreciate. Serve it with fish or alone as a light meal.

½ pound black-eyed peas, soaked several hours in
    sufficient water to cover by 2 inches
1 small red onion, finely chopped (about ½ cup)
3 tablespoons olive oil
1 tablespoon wine vinegar or cider vinegar
1 tablespoon parsley, finely chopped
1 teaspoon coarse salt or to taste
2 hard-boiled eggs, peeled, and chopped or cut in
    wedges for garnish

1. Drain and rinse the beans. Place in a 2-quart saucepan with enough fresh water to cover, about 4 cups. Cover and bring to a boil over medium-high heat. Reduce the heat and simmer until very tender but not mushy, about 40 minutes. Drain well. Place the cooked beans in a medium bowl with the onion.
2. In a separate bowl or measuring cup, whisk the oil with the vinegar and parsley. Season with salt. Pour over the beans and toss gently. Transfer the beans to a serving dish and garnish with the eggs. Serve hot or at room temperature as a side dish with fish or as a main dish for a light meal.

Variation: Add flakes of cooked fresh tuna or well-drained, oil-packed canned tuna.

Bean and Sausage Stew
Feijoada
Serve 4 to 6

Feijoada, a traditional dish in Brazil as well as in Portugal, contains beans, the ears and feet of a pig, and a combination of sausages, stewed meat, and dried beef. The northeast region of Portugal, Trás-os-Montes, is well known for its feijoada, *which includes cabbage. My dear friend Marguerite (whose recipes also appear elsewhere in this book) shared her simple version of* feijoada *with me many years ago. A favorite in my family, it is easy to prepare and very satisfying on a cold night. I do not include the pig's ears and feet. If you wish to use the ears, belly, and hocks of a pig, be sure to scrape the ears well of any hairs, then cook the meat in plain water until quite tender before adding to the pot of beans. Azoreans often use kidney beans for this dish, while Continentals use white lima beans and Brazilian Portuguese use black beans. I encourage you to try different beans—lima, fava, or kidney beans—and substitute or combine other Portuguese sausages for variety.*
Serve with plenty of crusty bread to dip in the broth.

½ pound dry kidney beans, soaked overnight in enough water to cover by 2 inches

4 tablespoons olive oil

1 medium onion, finely chopped (about 1 cup)

1 medium very ripe tomato, peeled, seeded, and coarsely chopped (about 1 cup)

1 tablespoon paprika

1 clove garlic, finely chopped

1 bay leaf

1½ pounds *linguiça* (page 127), sliced into ¼-inch rounds

¼ cup red wine

2 medium potatoes, peeled and cut into 1-inch cubes (about 2 cups)

¾ cup water or as needed

1. Drain the beans from the soaking water and rinse. Place the beans in a 2-quart saucepan with 3 cups of water, or enough to cover the beans by 1 inch. Cover and bring to a boil over medium-high heat. Reduce the heat to medium-low and simmer for 45 minutes until the beans are tender. Set aside.

2. Heat the oil in a 4-quart pot until quite hot. Add and sauté the onion until a light golden color. Toss in the tomatoes, paprika, garlic, and bay leaf and stir. Reduce the heat. Cover and simmer until the tomatoes are soft and almost dissolved, about 15 minutes. Add the *linguiça* and cook, about 2 minutes.

3. Pour in the wine, if using, and simmer 2 minutes. Add the potatoes with just enough cold water to cover them. Cover, bring to a boil over medium-high heat. Reduce the heat and simmer the ingredients until potatoes are almost tender, about 15 minutes.

4. Stir in the beans with enough of their cooking broth to barely cover (about ½ cup). Simmer, uncovered, an additional 15 minutes. Turn off the heat. Allow the stew to stand for about 15 minutes before serving.

Chickpea Salad with Salt Cod
Salada de Grão de Bico com Bacalhau
Serves 4

Accompanied with a simple green salad, olives, crusty bread, and vinho verde, *this dish makes a no-fuss meal. When I am in a hurry or if I get a sudden impulse for this dish, I will use canned chickpeas and canned oil-packed tunafish. I pile this on a bed of lettuce and lunch is ready.*

½ pound dry chickpeas, soaked at least 15 hours in
    3½ cups water
2 quarts water or as needed
½ pound dry salt cod, soaked in several changes of
    cold water, 16 to 24 hours, refrigerated*
1 small sweet onion, finely chopped (about ¼ cup)
1 large clove garlic, finely chopped
3 tablespoons olive oil
1 tablespoon cider vinegar
1½ tablespoons finely chopped parsley or cilantro
1 teaspoon coarse salt or to taste
2 hard-boiled eggs, chopped or cut in wedges for
    garnish
½ teaspoon paprika

*See salt cod instructions on page 11.

1. Drain the chickpeas and rinse. Place in a 3-quart saucepan with enough water to cover by 2 inches, about 4 cups. Cover and bring to a boil over medium-high heat. Reduce the heat and simmer until very tender, but not mushy, about 1½ hours. Drain and set aside.

2. Remove the fish from the soaking water and rinse. In a medium pot, bring the remaining 4 cups of water to a boil. Turn off the heat and add the cod. Cover for 15 to 20 minutes, then drain. Set aside until it is cool enough to handle.

3. Hand-shred the cod, discarding any skin or bones, and place in a serving bowl together with the chickpeas, onion, and garlic.

4. In a small bowl, whisk the oil with the vinegar. Stir in the parsley and with salt, if needed. Pour the dressing over the chickpeas and toss gently.

5. Garnish with the eggs and a sprinkling of paprika. This dish can be served hot, cold, or at room temperature, as a light meal or on the side with fish.

150

Stewed Green Beans

Feijão Verde Guisado

Serves 6

Fresh green beans never had it so good! The vinegar, tomato, and cilantro combine to make ordinary green beans zesty and flavorful. A little touch of cumin—Cousin Evelyn's Azorean influence—goes a long way.

1 pound green beans

1 tablespoon olive oil or 2 ounces salt pork, coarsely chopped

¼ pound *linguiça* (page 127)

1 medium onion, coarsely chopped (about 1 cup)

1 medium very ripe tomato, peeled and finely chopped (about ½ cup) or 1 tablespoon tomato paste

4 cloves garlic, finely chopped

1 bay leaf

½ cup water

¼ cup finely chopped cilantro

1 teaspoon coarse salt or to taste

scant ¼ teaspoon ground cumin

¼ teaspoon white pepper

¼ teaspoon crushed red pepper (page 5) (optional)

¼ cup wine vinegar

toasted pine nuts or sliced almonds for garnish (optional)

1. Snap off and discard the tips of the beans, then rinse. Cut the beans into 2-inch pieces.

2. Heat the oil or render the fat from the salt pork in a large skillet over medium-high heat. Remove any solid pieces of salt pork and discard. Lightly brown the sausage pieces in the oil or rendered fat, then transfer to a dish.

3. Toss in the onions and sauté until a light golden color. Add the tomato, garlic, and bay leaf. Reduce the heat to medium-low and cover. Simmer until the tomato is very soft and partially dissolved, about 15 minutes.

4. Add the water and 2 tablespoons of the cilantro along with the salt, cumin, pepper, and crushed red pepper. Pour in the wine vinegar and stir.

5. Put the beans into the pot, re-cover, and simmer until the beans are just tender with a little bite left, about 10 to 12 minutes. Return the sausage to the pan. Garnish with a sprinkling of the remaining cilantro and pine nuts or almonds.

151

Little Fish of the Garden

Peixinhos da Horta

Serves 4

As a child, I made a special dish with my father called peixinhos da horta, *or "little garden fish." Going into the garden with him was always an adventure. Together we discovered what was ripe, harvested our crop, and decided what we would make with our ingredients. Without doubt, eating the rewards of our labor was the best part of having a garden! I did not particularly like green beans, but when they were prepared this way, I couldn't eat enough. Today, serving these as an appetizer, I find they do not last much longer than when I was a child.*

1 pound flat beans
water as needed
1½ teaspoons coarse salt or to taste
4 eggs, lightly beaten
½ cup all purpose flour
¼ teaspoon white pepper or to taste
1 cup olive oil or as needed for frying

1. Rinse the beans and trim the tips. Place the beans in a medium saucepan with 1 teaspoon of the salt and enough water to cover by 1 inch. Cover and bring to a boil over medium-high heat. Reduce the heat and simmer until almost tender, about 3 minutes. Drain well and blot to remove excess water.

2. Make a batter of the eggs, flour, remaining salt, and pepper.

3. Heat about 1 cup of oil in a small skillet until hot, but not smoking. Working with three beans at a time, dip the beans in the batter forming a group of three.

4. Immediately place the grouped beans in the skillet and pan-fry. The beans should stick together as they fry, although sometimes you may get one or two that separate. When the beans are a light golden color on both sides, remove from the pan with a slotted spoon and drain on paper towels. Serve hot or at room temperature as an appetizer or a side dish.

Little Fish of the Garden

Sautéed Greens

Esparregado

Serves 2 to 4

Usually, young tender greens (grelos) like spinach, mustard greens, and broccoli rabe are simply sautéed in garlic oil and seasoned with salt and pepper, but this traditional preparation of tender spinach is very popular in our home, especially served with pork. It also goes well with beef. Baby mustard greens and spinach are most often used in this recipe, each one possessing a unique flavor when married with the cider vinegar. Frozen spinach can be used; just be sure to cook it and then drain it well.

1 pound fresh spinach, thick ribs removed, rinsed well, coarsely chopped

1 cup water

3 tablespoons olive oil

1 clove garlic, mashed or cut in half

1 bay leaf

2 tablespoons flour

1 tablespoon cider vinegar

1 teaspoon coarse salt or to taste

⅛ teaspoon pepper or to taste

1. Place the spinach in a pot large enough to accommodate it. Add water to just cover and bring to a boil. Reduce the heat and simmer over medium-low until the spinach is barely wilted, about 5 minutes. Drain well and reserve.

2. Heat the oil in a small skillet (a nonstick pan works well) until hot, but not smoking. Lightly brown the garlic and bay leaf in the oil. When the garlic is a light golden color, remove it from the pan with the bay leaf.

3. Reduce the heat to medium-low and add the spinach, turning it in the oil to coat thoroughly. Sprinkle the flour over the spinach and mix.

4. Drizzle the vinegar over the spinach and season with the salt. Turn the greens, almost mashing them onto themselves, until well mixed. Cook until excess moisture evaporates and the greens start to hold together and pull away from the pan surface almost like a mousse. Shake the skillet back and forth so that greens roll into a log shape. Roll out onto a serving plate as you would an omelette.

154

Lemon Carrots

Cenoura com Limão
Serves 4

In Portuguese kitchens vegetables usually appear in soups instead of as side dishes. This dish is a delicious exception, especially if carrots are your passion. This recipe is simple enough to make on short notice. The lemon juice is a perfect counterpoint to the sweetness of carrots.

1 pound carrots, peeled and cut into ¼-inch rounds
1 cup water
2 tablespoons olive oil
3 tablespoons butter
1 clove garlic finely chopped
4 tablespoons fresh lemon juice
1 to 2 tablespoons finely chopped cilantro
1 teaspoon coarse salt or to taste

1. Combine the carrots and water in a 2-quart saucepan. Cover and bring to a boil over medium-high heat, then reduce the heat and simmer for 5 minutes or until the carrots are nearly tender. Drain off the water.
2. Heat the oil with the butter in a medium skillet until they are quite hot. Add the garlic and sauté until it becomes aromatic. Add the lemon juice, 1 tablespoon of the cilantro, and the salt. Simmer for 1 minute.
3. Toss in the carrots, turning them in the pan to coat thoroughly. Cover tightly and simmer for 4 minutes or until desired doneness. Transfer to a serving dish and garnish with extra cilantro if desired.

Roasted Sweet Peppers

Pimentas Assadas
Makes 3 to 4 cups

This is a great accompaniment to fish dishes and grilled sausages. It can be served alone as an appetizer, accompanied with fresh cheese, or even popped into a sandwich. Allow the peppers to marinate in the dressing for several hours, even overnight. When I was young, we would roast these peppers over the open flame of our gas stove, turning them as they charred. It was fun peeling them, especially knowing that eating them was the final step.

6 medium sweet bell peppers, red, green, yellow, or combination
4 tablespoons Portuguese olive oil or good-quality extra-virgin olive oil
1 tablespoon red wine vinegar or cider vinegar, or to taste
3 cloves garlic, finely chopped
1 teaspoon coarse salt or to taste
1 teaspoon ground marjoram or dry oregano
¼ teaspoon fresh ground black pepper

1. Rinse the peppers and dry well. Place them on a sheet pan and broil about 4 inches from the heat source, turning often until the skin blisters and blackens. When all sides are done, remove the peppers and cool briefly. Slip off the skins and core, scraping off the seeds, then slice or leave whole.
2. Place in a bowl and drizzle with oil, vinegar, garlic, salt, marjoram or oregano, and pepper. Toss gently and chill several hours. Bring to room temperature to serve.

155

Chili Peppers in Vinegar

Malagueta na Vinagre

Makes about 2 quarts

Every culture has rituals involving food. Like drinking tequila with salt and lime, the Azoreans have a method for eating chili peppers in vinegar. It is quite simple. First you take a bite of the chili pepper. Then as quickly as you can, you chase it down with a spoonful of soup to quiet the fire. You can use you favorite chili peppers, from large to tiny, for this preparation. Recycle mayonnaise or pickle jars that have tight-sealing covers—sterilize them or wash them thoroughly. Adjust amounts of ingredients depending on the size jars you wish to fill.

1 pound red chili finger peppers (about 14)
2 clean 1-quart jars
apple cider or wine vinegar
boiling water
1 tablespoon olive oil
3 cloves garlic (optional)
1 tablespoon coarse salt
1 tablespoon marjoram (optional)
5 whole Jamaican berries or black
    peppercorns

1. Rinse the peppers and cut off and discard the green caps and stems.
2. Place the peppers in the jars. Pour equal amounts of boiling water and vinegar into the jars. Add your chosen seasonings and top off with 1 to 2 tablespoons of olive oil.
3. Allow to cool completely, then cover tightly and refrigerate for 2 to 3 weeks before using. During that time, occasionally turn the jars upside down, giving the peppers an occasional shake. Whatever variety of chili peppers you use, this preparation is colorful and can be given as gifts to friends.

Eggs with Linguiça

Ovos com Linguiça

Serves 2

Enjoy this Portuguese-style omelette for a weekend breakfast. Aromatic and flavorful, it is a wonderful way to start a Saturday or Sunday morning.

2 tablespoons olive oil
1 tablespoon finely chopped onion
2 ounces *linguiça* (page 127), sliced into ¼-inch
    rounds (about ½ cup)
3 eggs, lightly beaten
2 teaspoons finely chopped parsley

1. Heat the oil in a skillet over medium-high heat. Add and sauté the onion until a light golden color, about 10 minutes. Toss in the sausage and cook 1 to 2 minutes, lightly browning. Reduce the heat to medium-low.
2. Mix the eggs with the parsley and pour over the sausage and onions.
Cook the eggs without stirring, making a flat omelette. Invert onto a plate and slide back into the pan to cook the other side for 1 more minute. Slide onto serving dish.

Variation: Add ½ cup coarsely chopped cooked asparagus with the eggs.

156

Eggs in Broth
Molho de Ovos
Serves 4

This dish is perfect for a Saturday-night supper. It is a welcome dish after a busy day when you just don't feel like making a complicated meal. Manuel C. Silva made this, his grandmother's recipe, to feed the kitchen crew of Our Lady of Fatima Church in Peabody, Massachusetts, when they finished making 180 pounds of sausages for the church fair. The meat used that night for this stew happened to be marinated pork set aside before someone could stuff it into a casing, but Manny says, "The meat does not have to be marinated; use what you have—beef, pork, or smoked sausage."

¼ cup olive oil

1 medium onion, finely chopped (about 1 cup)

2 cloves garlic, finely chopped

1 bay leaf

¼ pound pork, beef, or sausage, cut into ½- to
    1-inch pieces

½ cup white wine

2 large potatoes, peeled and cut into 1-inch cubes

2 cups water or as needed

2 teaspoons coarse salt or to taste

1 teaspoon Hot Pepper Paste (page 167)
    or hot sauce

⅛ teaspoon black pepper or to taste

2 eggs per person

1. Heat the oil in a 4-quart saucepan over medium-high heat. Add and sauté the onion until soft and translucent, about 5 minutes. Toss in the garlic and bay leaf. When the garlic becomes aromatic, put in the meat and sauté for 3 minutes. Pour in the wine and stir, scraping up any bits of caramelized juices from the bottom of the pan.

2. Add the potatoes with 2 cups of water or enough to just cover them. Season with salt, Hot Pepper Paste, ____ ____ er. ____ tightly and bring to a boil. ____ ea_ and simmer until the potato ____ ut 20 minutes.

3. One by ___ ____ s into a shallow bowl and, nudging the p_ ____ slide the eggs into the hot broth to poach ___ 5 minutes. Ladle into serving bowls accompanied with crusty bread to dip into the broth.

157

Tortas Graciosa-Style
Tortas da Graciosa
Serves 8

The Azoreans speak fondly of tortas. *The name, which means "tart," is misleading; these are more like miniature omelettes. This traditional version is definitely for cumin lovers. Cooks would use any leftover meat or fish, season it, adding a little scallion and spice, making tasty snacks that also work well in bread as sandwich filling or alone as appetizers.*

7 large eggs, lightly beaten
1 cup leftover meat or fish, coarsely chopped
3 cups finely chopped scallions
1 cup finely chopped parsley
4 cloves garlic, finely chopped
2 teaspoons coarse salt
3 tablespoons white or yellow corn flour
    (all-purpose wheat flour can be used in a pinch)
½ teaspoon cumin powder,
½ teaspoon black pepper or hot pepper sauce
¼ teaspoon ground nutmeg
about ¼ cup olive or corn oil for frying

1. Except for the oil, combine all the ingredients in a medium bowl, stirring to blend. The mixture should be somewhat thick.
2. Heat the oil over medium-high heat, adding enough to make a shallow layer in a large skillet. Using a soup spoon, scoop some of the mixture and place in the pan, spreading it out evenly with the back of the spoon to a scant ½-inch thick. You can probably fit two or three in the pan at once. Pan-fry until golden, turning to brown the *tortas* on both sides. Make sure they are cooked in the middle. Remove to drain on paper toweling. Transfer the *tortas* to a serving dish and serve hot or at room temperature.

Mary's Tortas
Tortas à Maria
Serves 4 to 6

You don't have to wait for leftover meat to make tortas. *This version is from my sister-in-law Laraine Ortins, whose mother Mary Jodrie used canned tunafish. It is less spicy but just as tasty as the traditional recipe. It can be served as a late-night bite with a salad.*

3 eggs, lightly beaten
3 to 4 slices day-old bread, slightly moistened with water and shredded
6 ounces oil-packed canned tuna, drained and flaked (or any leftover meat, tuna, or other fish such as cod)
1 small onion, finely chopped (scant ½ cup)
1 tablespoon finely chopped parsley
1 teaspoon coarse salt or to taste
⅛ teaspoon black pepper or to taste
½ cup olive oil, or as needed

1. Except for the olive oil, combine all ingredients in a medium bowl. Mixture should be a bit thick.
2. Heat 2 tablespoons of the oil in a medium skillet over medium-high heat. Using a soup spoon, place one scoop of the mixture into the hot pan and using the back of the spoon, spread it out evenly to about ¼-inch thick or a little thicker, like a small pancake.
3. Cook for 2 minutes. When the *torta* is golden underneath, turn and cook an additional minute or two, making sure the egg is cooked, especially in the middle. Repeat, frying 2 to 3 at a time. Transfer to a serving dish. Serve warm or at room temperature.

158

Salads Portuguese-Style

Portuguese salads, especially in the early part of the growing season, are a simple combination of tender spring garden lettuce, a bit of onion, perhaps watercress and cilantro. With our year-round availability of tomatoes, occasionally Portuguese families adopt the American custom of adding tomatoes and cucumbers to salads. Before supermarkets, what was being harvested from the garden dictated the contents of a salad. Prepared salad dressings were unheard of; one simply drizzled a salad with olive oil and vinegar to taste, a habit which is still popular.

Remember to drain the excess water from the greens, blotting with a clean kitchen towel if necessary.

Sweet Pepper Salad
Salada de Pimenta Doce
Serves 4

This "salad" is really just the accompaniment that we usually serve alongside boiled potatoes and grilled sardines. Consider the quantities merely as a guide; you can adjust the ingredients' quantities to your preference.

1 large sweet green pepper, cored, seeded, and
    thinly sliced (about 1 cup)
1 large tomato, sliced (about 1 cup), optional
1 medium onion, peeled and thinly sliced in
    rounds (about ½ cup)
¼ cup black olives
½ cup olive oil, or to taste
¼ cup red wine or cider vinegar, or to taste
1 teaspoon coarse salt, or to taste
⅛ teaspoon ground black pepper, or to taste
1 tablespoon finely chopped parsley

1. Arrange the pepper, tomato, and onion slices on a serving platter or on individual salad dishes, ending with the olives arranged on top.
2. Drizzle oil and vinegar over the salad, season with salt and pepper, and garnish with parsley.

159

Fresh Cheese

Requeijão/Queijo Fresco

Makes 2 one-pound cheeses

In my family, we always made our own molds for this cheese. They must be perforated to allow the liquid whey to drain. Now I use small-mesh plastic baskets (pint or half-pint size), but when I was young, we used cleaned shallow, perforated tin cans—the ones that held tunafish or pineapple rings. You can fashion molds easily and inexpensively from deli, margarine, cream cheese, or other plastic food containers. Using a sharp utility knife, make slashes in the bottom and sides of the container for drainage. Or use a hole puncher to make small holes instead of slashes. Wash well and your molds are ready. Place filled cheese molds in a shallow pan. In the refrigerator, place the pan on a slight tilt so that the whey drains away from the molds.

Some brands of whole milk don't work as well as others. Milk with a minimum of 3 percent fat straight from a local farm without additives is best. You may need to experiment with different brands. Some people use as few as 2 tablets of rennet, but bear in mind that less rennet means longer processing.

Equipment:
a 4-quart pot
an instant-read thermometer
a stainless-steel fine-mesh strainer
two 16-ounce or four 8-ounce cheese molds

5 rennet tablets
1 gallon whole milk
⅓ cup coarse salt or to taste

1. Place the rennet tablets in a small dish or a mortar. Break into tiny pieces.
2. Pour the milk into a 4-quart saucepan and place over low heat. Heat the milk to lukewarm (78 degrees F).
3. While you are warming the milk, remove ½ cup of the milk from the pot and transfer to a cup. Dissolve the ground rennet tablets in the ½ cup of milk. Quickly return the rennet mixture to the pan of milk. Add the salt and stir well with a wooden spoon.
4. When the temperature of the milk reaches 78 degrees, remove the pot from the heat. Be careful to not overheat it.
5. Cover the pot with a lid and place a towel over it. After 20 minutes, give the milk a turn with the wooden spoon and re-cover. Let stand for about 1 to 1½ hours longer, or until the milk mixture springs back when pressed. The curds should have the texture of semifirm custard, and the whey should be visibly separate with the edge of the curd defined.
6. Suspend a large fine-meshed strainer or sieve over a deep bowl or pot. Use a small-mesh hand strainer or slotted spoon to carefully transfer the curds into

the large strainer or sieve, allowing the whey to drain away. You may lose some bits of curd if you use a slotted spoon. Let the curd stand in the strainer for 15 minutes, or until the draining slows to a mere trickle. Tilt and roll the strainer back and forth to assist the draining. The cheese will reduce in size and thicken as the whey is drained.

7. Place the molds in a shallow pan. Spoon the curds into the molds, pressing lightly to push out more whey. Repeat until they are completely filled. The whey will continue to drain for several hours.

8. Refrigerate for at least 24 hours, occasionally draining the whey from the pan as needed. The cheese is ready when no more whey drains out and the cheese is fairly firm. It will keep for about 4 to 5 days in the refrigerator. Serve with crusty bread as accompaniment to a meal or as an appetizer. Season with additional salt to taste if needed. Makes 2 one-pound or 4 eight-ounce cheeses. (Weights are approximate.)

Serving Suggestion: The following is adapted from a dish served at the Atasca Restaurant in Cambridge, Massachusetts. Cut the cheese into ½-inch slices; serve with chopped tomato and red onion. Add finely sliced *presunto* ham. Drizzle with olive oil and wine vinegar. Serve chilled or at room temperature.

Note: To make this cheese for *Queijadas* (page 212), omit the salt.

Old-Fashioned Cheese-Making

In Portugal the age-old method of making fresh cheese used unpasteurized milk straight from the sheep and goats. My great-grandfather Luis Elvas, who was a shepherd in the Alentejo region, would milk the sheep and goats. Together, he and my great-grandmother Ana Maria would make cheese to sell. They would gather *alcachofra* (*cynara scolymus*), an artichokelike flower of the wild thistle plant called *cardo* (field eryngo), which grows wild in Portugal. The tips of the flowers were cut by hand and dried. For cheese-making, the dried flowers were tied into little bundles and soaked in water. The liquid squeezed from the plants went into the warm milk to curdle and ferment it. The curds were placed in molds made from leaves and cloth. When the cheese was ready, my great-grandmother would make her rounds to sell them. The process of cheese-making may seem daunting but do not be intimidated by the instructions. The steps are detailed and easy to follow. The process is certainly easier today than it was for my great-grandparents!

Although the centuries-old tradition of using wild thistle to curdle milk for cheese may continue in areas of Portugal, here in the United States, rennet has gained popularity as a curdling agent. Keeping sheep and goats in our backyards is no longer a common practice, so pasteurized cow's milk is used. The cheese has the flavor of cottage cheese, but with a firmer texture that allows it to be sliced.

161

Hot Pepper Paste (page 167), Sweet Red Pepper Paste (page 166), and Marinated Chili Peppers

7

MARINADES,
CONDIMENTS,
& SEASONINGS
Vinha d'Alhos, Condimentos,
e Temperas

Essential to Portuguese cooking are the wine-and-garlic marinades, *vinho d'alhos,* that flavor beef, pork, chicken, game, seafood dishes, and the famous sausages. Variations on the basic components of wine and garlic may be as subtle as using red wine in place of white. Although red wine is most often used with beef and sausages, it is also used on occasion with rabbit and chicken, turning the meat a darker color. It is also not uncommon for white wine to be used for marinating beef. White wine is frequently used for pork, poultry, seafood, and sausages. Alternatively, some cooks use equal amounts of both in a single marinade, especially in sausage making (see Chapter 5). A rule of thumb I like to follow is white, light-bodied wines for delicate-flavored meats and fish and red wine for full-flavored meats.

Optional ingredients in marinades include hot chili peppers, onions, bay leaf, cilantro or parsley, paprika, lemon juice, wine vinegar, and olive oil. Choices and quantities are dictated by the item being marinated and, as always, personal taste.

The amount of marinade is determined by the amount of wine needed to partially or completely cover the item to be marinated.

In Portuguese cooking, fish—especially fried fish—is often served with a tangy vinegar sauce. In the Azores the sauce is called *molhanga* or *molho cru* (raw sauce) and on the mainland it's *escabeche.* Raw vinegar sauces are similar to vinaigrettes, but with more zest. It makes for one of the most extraordinary ways of enjoying fried or grilled fish. The olive oil used in preparing the sauce can be the same oil that was used to fry the fish; just be sure that the oil is not too brown with excess flour, in which case I suggest using fresh olive oil.

There are many variations for this tangy sauce, each one having its own special flavor. If the garlic is lightly browned in a bit of olive oil before the remaining ingredients are combined, the sauce is considered cooked. These sauces, which are typically prepared without cooking, can be served on the side as a dipping sauce or poured over the fried fish before serving. The sauce is even poured over boiled potatoes if they are served with the fish. Sometimes the cooked fish is left to marinate in the vinegar sauce for 2 to 3 days in the refrigerator, then brought to room temperature and served.

164

Aunt Custodia's Tomato Sauce
Tomatada à Tia Custodia
Makes about 5½ cups

My Uncle Ilidio nods his head in praise of his aunt Custodia's tasty sauce. Aunt Custodia often spooned it over boiled potatoes. Made from his recollections and her instructions, the sauce pleases us as well. Vegetarians might agree.

¼ pound salt pork or 4 slices bacon, coarsely
    chopped, or ¼ cup olive oil
1 medium onion, finely chopped (about 1 cup)
1 to 2 cloves garlic, coarsely chopped
6 large very ripe tomatoes, peeled, seeded, and
    coarsely chopped (about 6 cups)
2 teaspoons coarse salt, or to taste
⅛ teaspoon pepper

1. Heat the salt pork, bacon, or olive oil in a 2-quart saucepan over medium-high heat. Sauté the salt pork or bacon until the fat has been rendered. Discard the solid pieces.
2. Add the onion to the pan and sauté until translucent, about 5 minutes. Toss in the garlic and cook until it is aromatic, about 1 minute. Mix in the tomatoes, cover, and bring to a boil. Reduce the heat to medium-low and gently simmer, partially covered for 1 hour. Even after the tomatoes have cooked down, the sauce should still have some texture and not be too thick. Season with salt and pepper. Use immediately or refrigerate for future use.

Variation: Give the sauce some zing by adding 1 teaspoon or more of Hot Pepper Paste (page 167). If you prefer a smoother texture, simply purée it using a hand-held blender. This sauce can be used to flavor stews and other dishes.

165

Sweet Red Pepper Paste

Massa de Pimentão

Makes about 2 cups

Massa de pimentão is a very important and frequently used ingredient in Portuguese dishes. Because of its salt content, a little bit goes a long way, and additional salt is not usually necessary. I remember my father leading me through the simple steps of its preparation. Together we washed, quartered, and seeded the peppers. Using a wooden vegetable crate with narrow spaces between the slats, he would cover the bottom with a thick layer of coarse salt and place a single layer of pepper slices, skin side up, on the salt, flattening any curves in the peppers. He would then cover the peppers with another layer of salt. A second and sometimes a third layer of peppers was made, ending with a covering of salt. He would weigh it down, pressing with two or three heavy dinner plates, and the box was tipped slightly so that the juice from the peppers would drain away. It would remain like this for a few days or until the peppers stopped draining and were somewhat thin. He would remove them from the box, shake off the excess salt and process them through a hand-cranked grinder. We packed the peppers in sterilized baby-food jars, poured olive oil over the top to cover, and stored away our treasure to enjoy in future dishes.

You will need a freestanding stainless-steel sieve or footed colander with small holes or mesh. A cheesecloth can be used to line a colander that has large holes. This makes enough to fill two 8-ounce jelly jars, which should be sterilized. They should have tight-fitting lids.

166

4 large red peppers, cored, seeded, and quartered
5 pounds coarse salt (not pickling salt; it is too fine)
½ cup good-quality imported olive oil

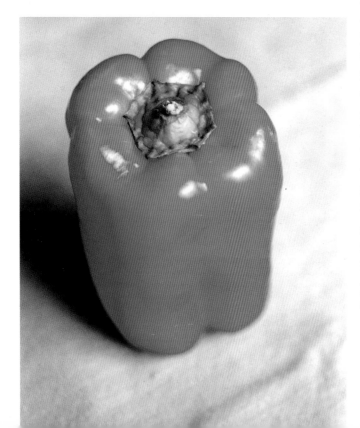

1. Set the colander inside a large noncorrosive pan or dish with sides.
2. Pour a 1-inch layer of salt into the colander to form the base. (Some salt will seep out.)
3. Place a layer of peppers, skin side up, on the salt, pressing the peppers into the salt. Be sure to uncurl even the smallest part of the pepper, otherwise mold will form.
4. Cover with a ½-inch layer of salt and the remaining peppers, ending with another ½-inch layer of salt. Place a heavy dish or bowl on top to weight it down. Let stand for up to 5 days to allow the moisture to drain from the peppers. After the fourth day, the peppers should thinner, about ¼-inch or less. The salt will be damp and the amount of liquid draining will be barely a trickle.
5. Shake off the excess salt and process the peppers briefly with either a hand-cranked grinder, food processor, or blender. The texture will not be smooth—more like coarsely ground tomatoes.

6. Fill the jars, leaving about an inch at the top. Pour olive oil over the top to a depth of ½ inch. Close the jar tightly and refrigerate.

7. To use *massa de pimentão,* simply push aside the congealed olive oil with a spoon, remove what you need, replacing the oil and adding more, if necessary. Use sparingly.

Note: *Massa de pimentão* and *massa de malagueta* (following recipe) will keep several months in the refrigerator when stored as directed. The salt acts as a preservative. I do not recommend adding garlic to these pastes. Instead, use fresh garlic recipes calling for pepper paste for optimum garlic flavor.

Tip: You can sometimes still find wooden produce crates. Check your local produce market.

Hot Pepper Paste
Massa de Malagueta
Makes about 2 cups

Making this paste is so easy, and the peppers keep for at least six months, if refrigerated. Some versions add a touch of lemon juice or vinegar and garlic, but this simple paste adds heat to a dish while allowing you to add lemon or garlic to your taste, depending on the dish. The method is different from the sweet pepper paste because water is not drained off and the seeds are retained to ensure the fire of the chili peppers.

1 pound hot red finger peppers, rinsed and
    patted dry
½ cup coarse salt
⅓ cup olive oil

167

1. Remove and discard the green caps and stems of the peppers, but do not discard the seeds. Finely chop the peppers either by hand, or in a grinder or food processor. Transfer the peppers to a medium bowl. Stir in the salt, mixing thoroughly. Let stand in this bowl for 8 days in the refrigerator, giving the mixture a few turns every day.

2. On the eighth day, pack the mixture into a sterilized jar, top it off with ½-inch of olive oil and refrigerate.

Note: When adding *massa de malagueta* to recipes, keep in mind that it is quite salty. Taste the dish before adding any additional salt.

Variation: Some versions contain vinegar to taste, about 1–2 tablespoons.

Wine and Garlic Marinade

Vinho d'Alhos

Makes about 1 cup

This marinade can be used for chicken, pork, or beef.

3 to 4 cloves garlic
1 tablespoon paprika
1 teaspoon coarse salt or to taste
6 black peppercorns
1 tablespoon olive oil
1 cup red or white wine or equal amounts of both

1. Using a mortar and pestle, mash the garlic and add the dry ingredients one at a time, blending well. Drizzle in 1 tablespoon of olive oil.
2. Rub the meat with the spice mixture and place in a nonreactive dish. Pour the wine over meat to partially or entirely cover it, depending on the recipe.
3. Marinate the meat, turning occasionally, for several hours or overnight in the refrigerator.

White Wine Marinade

Vinho d'Alhos

Makes about 1 cup

This is best for fish, chicken, or pork.

1 to 2 cloves garlic
3 green or black peppercorns
1 bay leaf
1 cup white wine, or as needed
1 medium onion, thinly sliced
1 tablespoon finely chopped parsley

1. Using a mortar and pestle, mash the garlic and grind in the peppercorns and the bay leaf. Stir in the wine. Transfer to a bowl or shallow dish, add the remaining ingredients with the item to be marinated. Let stand overnight, chilled.

White Wine and Garlic Marinade

Vinho d'Alhos

Makes 2 cups

This marinade uses the Sweet Red Pepper Paste of the Alentejo. We use this for pork and beef.

4 peppercorns
6 cloves garlic, coarsely chopped
2 bay leaves, crumbled
1 tablespoon Sweet Red Pepper Paste (page 166)
pinch crushed red pepper (optional)
2 cups red or white wine, as needed

1. Using a mortar and pestle, grind the peppercorns finely. Add and mash the garlic with the peppercorns, blending well. Incorporate the bay leaf, sweet red pepper paste, and pepper, mixing until well blended.
2. Coat the meat and place in a nonreactive dish. Pour the wine over the meat. Marinate overnight, chilled.

Marinade for Seafood

Vinho d'Alhos para Frutos do Mar

Makes about 2 cups

This marinade is especially good with swordfish or tuna steaks.

1 to 2 cloves garlic, finely chopped
1 teaspoon coarse salt
¼ cup finely chopped cilantro
1 tablespoon lemon juice
½ bay leaf
⅛ teaspoon crushed red pepper
3 white peppercorns or ⅛ teaspoon ground white pepper
1 cup light white wine, such as *vinho verde* or light chablis
½ cup olive oil

1. In a mortar, combine garlic, salt, and ¼ cup cilantro and mash well. Add lemon juice, bay leaf, crushed red pepper, and white pepper, continuing to blend. Drizzle in 1 tablespoon of olive oil and incorporate thoroughly.
2. Coat fish fillets or steaks and place in a nonreactive dish. Combine the remaining wine and oil. Pour over the fish and marinate for 1 hour, chilled.

Note: For shrimp, whisk the wine and oil together with the garlic and lemon mixture and pour over the shellfish. Marinate for 1 hour. Be sure to use a nonreactive bowl.

169

Vinegar Sauce

Molhanga

Makes about 1 cup

Our cousin Evelina Ortins Cunha shares her wonderful recipe for molhanga, *which packs extra tang and stands out among the best. If you use the oil remaining from frying fish, make sure it is not too dark. If it is, use fresh olive oil.*

1 teaspoon cumin seed or ¼ teaspoon cumin powder
6 cloves garlic, finely chopped
½ teaspoon coarse salt or to taste
¾ teaspoon safflower (page 13) (if unavailable use paprika)
¼ teaspoon ground black pepper
¼ teaspoon sugar
1 teaspoon Hot Pepper Paste (page 167)
3 tablespoons finely chopped parsley
1 tablespoon olive oil, fresh or leftover from frying fish
¼ cup water
¾ wine vinegar

1. Using a mortar and pestle and blending well after each addition, combine the cumin, garlic, salt, safflower or paprika, pepper, and sugar. Follow with the hot pepper paste and parsley.
2. Transfer to a bowl. Stir in the water and vinegar and whisk in the olive oil. To use, pour over the cooked fish or serve on the side.

Note: The use of whole cumin seed is traditional when making *molhanga*. Cumin powder may be substituted if cumin seeds are not available.

Variation: Our other cousin, Noelia, makes her *molhanga* very much like Evelyn's. While the amounts of the same ingredients are different, the method is the same. Noelia's variation includes a dash or two of freshly ground nutmeg. The nutmeg adds another dimension to the sauce.

170

Vinegar Sauce with Tomato

Molhanga com Tomate

Makes about 1¼ cups

This is another variation of vinegar sauce from my husband Philip's roots in Graciosa, Azores. Today's convenience of tomato paste gives a deeper dimension of tomato flavor to this sauce. Before the availability of tomato paste, a peeled, seeded, and chopped tomato was used. This recipe works well as a "cooked" sauce served on the side with, or drizzled over, boiled and cracked soft-shell crab.

1 head of garlic, the cloves peeled and finely chopped
1 teaspoon coarse salt
1 teaspoon ground safflower (page 13) (paprika may be substituted)
¼ cup finely chopped parsley
1 tablespoon tomato paste
½ cup wine vinegar
½ cup olive oil

1. Using a mortar and pestle, mash the garlic with the salt and safflower, forming a paste. Blend the parsley and tomato paste into the garlic mixture. Mix in the vinegar and transfer to a medium bowl.
2. Gradually whisk in the olive oil. Pour over the fish or serve on the side.

Variation: For a cooked sauce, just sauté the garlic, salt, safflower, and tomato paste in the olive oil over medium-low heat until the tomato paste is blended in. Remove from the heat and whisk in the vinegar. Serve with boiled soft-shell crabs.

Vinegar Sauce

Molho Escabeche

Makes about 1¼ cups

This Continental version of vinegar sauce can be used to marinate fish that has been fried or grilled. Refrigerate for two to three days in the sauce, then serve.

½ cup olive oil, left over from frying fish, or fresh
1 small onion, finely chopped (about ½ cup)
6 cloves garlic, finely chopped
1 bay leaf
¼ cup finely chopped parsley
1 tablespoon paprika
½ cup cider vinegar or red wine vinegar
½ teaspoon coarse salt or to taste
¼ teaspoon white or black pepper

1. In a skillet, heat the oil over medium-high heat and fry the onion until translucent. Reduce the heat, add the garlic, and cook until it becomes aromatic, about 2 minutes.
2. Add the bay leaf, parsley, and paprika.
3. Heat through and remove from the heat.
4. Add the vinegar, salt, and pepper. Mix well and pour over cooked fish or serve on the side.

171

Clockwise from the bottom: Crusty Rolls (page 181), Homestyle Bread (page 179), Corn Bread (page 175), and Baked Flat Bread (page 178)

8

BREAD

Pão

Some of the first breads in Portugal and the Azores were made of cornmeal, which had to be softened with hot water before baking. Once the method of leavening was learned, new types of breads were created. While most Portuguese bread is made with wheat flour alone, some varieties, especially from northern mainland Portugal, contain wheat flour combined with rye and corn flours. These rustic, peasant-style breads are still made in the homes of Portuguese immigrants and their descendants in America. The resulting breads taste a little different from those made in Portugal, due to the differences in the flour and cornmeal available here. The most common types of bread found in Portuguese homes in the United States are the crusty rolls called *papo-secos,* cornmeal breads (called *broa* or *pão de milho,* depending on their region of origin), and homestyle bread, *pão caseiro.*

The difference between the traditional Portuguese breads made in Portugal and those made in the United States goes beyond the difference in flours. Traditional methods do not incorporate sugar with the yeast when a sponge (*fermente*) is prepared. Nor do they add fat to the dough for *papo-secos* or *pão caseiro.* Small batches of dough starter, made days in advance, or sponge fermentations are more traditional.

Some cooks have adopted the use of sugar and fat to assist fermentation, give color, and prolong shelf life while making the bread more tender. Before you embark on making the bread recipes in this chapter, here are some points to remember:

- Have your ingredients at room temperature.
- Yeast comes in different forms—fresh cake, dry, rapid rise, and active instant. One block of fresh cake yeast weighing 0.6 of an ounce is equal to one package (2¼ teaspoons) dry active yeast, or one package rapid-rise yeast, or 1½ to 2 teaspoons instant yeast. Do not use rapid-rise yeast for the breads in the following recipes.
- Water that is too hot will kill the yeast before you have begun. For Portuguese rustic breads requiring a slow rise for flavor development, water temperature should be 65 to 70 degrees F.
- Do not add salt during the proofing stage, the first mixing of the yeast with a warm liquid.
- Store freshly baked breads wrapped in clean kitchen towels made of broadcloth or in cloth bags. Plastic bags ruin what is supposed to be a crisp crust and also promote spoilage in breads that have a moist interior.
- Once baked breads have cooled completely, they can be wrapped tightly in plastic to seal out air, followed by a layer of aluminum foil, then frozen. Allow to thaw at room temperature, then warm in a moderate oven for a few minutes.

174

Corn Bread

Broa/Pão de Milho

Makes 4 loaves

Reflecting the type of corn grown in each region, the cornmeal bread of the mainland, called broa, *calls for yellow cornmeal, while the Azorean version,* pão de milho, *uses a finely ground white cornmeal. Today, Portuguese home cooks and some Portuguese bakeries in America, use a very fine white or yellow corn flour. The corn flour or cornmeal needs to be scalded before it is combined with the other ingredients. The ratio of corn flour to wheat flour can vary: 40 percent corn flour to 60 percent wheat flour is typical. This Azorean-style recipe uses white corn flour and requires only one rising before baking. The original method of baking in stone ovens has been adapted for the home oven, using pans. The dough will somewhat sticky and heavy, but it should not be too soft. Allow 2 hours for rising. The finished product should be a medium heavy bread, with a fine, somewhat moist interior.*

Sponge:

2 tablespoons dry yeast
½ cup warm water (between 90 and 112 degrees F)
1 tablespoon all-purpose flour

1. Dissolve the yeast in the water and set aside for 10 minutes. Mix in the flour, cover and set aside for 1 hour.

Dough:

2 pounds white corn flour (*not* the same as fine cornmeal)
6 to 6½ cups boiling water, divided
1¾ tablespoons table salt
2 pounds fine unbleached all-purpose flour

1. Place the corn flour in a large bowl. Dissolve the salt in 5 cups of the boiling water. Pour the salted water over the corn flour and, stirring quickly with a wooden spoon, mix them thoroughly, making sure all flour is moistened. It will take about 5 minutes. It should look like lumpy mashed potatoes. Set aside until it is cool enough to handle, about 15 to 20 minutes.

2. When the corn flour has cooled sufficiently, gradually mix in the all-purpose flour, the yeast sponge, and an additional ½ cup of remaining water, which should be just tepid at this point. Mix until the dough comes together. If the dough seems a little dry, mix in ½ cup of the remaining water to make the dough more pliable. Use the last ½ cup only if necessary. Do not use more water than called for. Knead the dough in the bowl for about 10 minutes. It will be wet enough to stick to your hands a little. Dust the dough with flour and cover with a clean towel. Set the dough aside in a warm, draft-free spot to rise until double, about 2½ hours.

Preheat the oven to 500 degrees F.

continued on next page

175

3. When the dough has doubled, do not punch down, but cut the dough into 3 or 4 equal parts, and briefly set aside on a floured work surface without shaping. You don't want to deflate the risen dough.

4. Swirl some water in a 1-quart bowl, empty it, and then without drying it, immediately dust the bowl with about 1 tablespoon of flour.

5. Place one part of the dough into the bowl taking care not to compress it. Holding the bowl with both hands, swirl the dough once or twice to shape it. Quickly invert the bowl, emptying the dough into a floured aluminum pie plate or 8-inch round cake pan. Shape the remaining dough.

6. Place the pans on the middle rack of the preheated oven and bake for 35 to 45 minutes, depending on the size of the loaves. Turn the loaves out of the pans. Bottoms should sound hollow when done. Wrap with a tea towel until needed.

176   **Note:** For a drier interior, bake at 500 degrees for 15 minutes, then lower the heat to 375 degrees for the remaining 35 to 40 minutes.

If you are proficient at baking bread with an oven stone, go ahead and bake the following bread on a preheated oven stone. Just make sure to place enough cornmeal on the peel under the loaf to insure effortless sliding of the dough. Before you put the peel in the oven, brush off any excess cornmeal, so it doesn't fall into the oven and burn.

Fried Flat Bread

Pão de Sertã

Makes 2 eight-inch loaves

Long before the knowledge of leavening, breads were flat. Today Portuguese Americans from the Azores continue to make these unleavened breads. My friend Marguerite remembers her mother cooking this particular flat bread in a long-handled cast-iron frying pan. The dough, which does not contain yeast, is made of corn flour and wheat flour fried in corn oil. It should be served hot, accompanying a hearty meal.

Equipment:
10-inch cast-iron frying pan
tongs and spatula

2 cups white or yellow corn flour
2 teaspoons table salt
1¾ cups boiling water
1 cup all-purpose flour
⅓ cup lukewarm water
corn oil for frying

1. Place the corn flour and salt into a large bowl and mix so the salt is evenly distributed throughout the flour.
2. Pour about one half of the boiling water over the corn flour. Using a wooden spoon, quickly stir, blending thoroughly. Add remaining hot water. It will look like lumpy mashed potatoes. Set aside for 20 to 30 minutes or until it is cool enough to handle.
3. Mix in the all-purpose flour, alternating with the now tepid water, gently cutting it into the corn flour. Knead lightly without working the dough too much, for about 5 to 10 minutes, making sure all the flour is incorporated. The dough should be a little lumpy, soft, and not very elastic. Let the dough rest for 10 minutes.
4. Divide the dough into two equal parts. Gather and gently shape each part into a ball. Dust one ball with flour and, holding it in the palm of one hand, pat it with your other hand, gently flattening to a maximum thickness of ½ inch, about the same diameter as the pan or a little smaller. It is important to press the dough gently.
5. Pour enough corn oil into the frying pan to cover the bottom ¼-inch deep. Heat the oil until it is hot, but not smoking. Place the flattened dough carefully into the hot pan. The oil should not rise over the top of the bread.
6. Fry for about 5 minutes or until the bottom is evenly golden. Using tongs or a fork and wide spatula, lift the dough to check the bottom. When it is golden, turn to cook the other side. When the other side is golden, about 5 minutes more, transfer the fried bread to paper toweling to drain. Repeat with the second ball of dough. Serve while still warm. The texture will be slightly crisp, with a very moist interior. This is usually served with stews, as an accompaniment to fried marinated pork, or enjoyed on its own.

177

Baked Flat Bread
Pão Estendido

Makes 2 eight-inch loaves

This version of Portuguese flat bread from the island of Pico is one of my favorites. The difference lies in the ratio of the ingredients and the fact that it is baked. Not only does it have a crunchy texture and drier interior, but it is fat-free. It is best to bake this bread on a preheated oven stone. It can easily be reheated in an oven the next day. This bread is perfect to serve with most anything.

Equipment:
oven stone and wooden peel

1⅔ cups white or yellow corn flour (not cornmeal)
1½ teaspoons table salt
2¼ cups boiling water
1½ cups all-purpose flour

1. Set an oven (or pizza) stone in the cold oven and preheat to 450 degrees F. Combine the corn flour and salt in a medium-sized bowl and mix thoroughly.

2. Pour 1 cup of the water over the corn flour and, using a wooden spoon, mix thoroughly, making sure that all of the corn flour is moistened. Stir in the remaining hot water and mix well. It will look like lumpy mashed potatoes. Set aside for 20 to 30 minutes or until it is cool enough to handle.

3. Mix in the all-purpose flour and, without overworking the dough, knead gently for about 5 minutes. Divide into two equal parts and gently shape into balls.

4. Take one ball of dough and dust it liberally with corn flour. Holding the dough in the palm of one hand, use the other hand to gently flatten the dough, rotating to shape it to about ½-inch thick. It doesn't need to be perfectly round. When it bakes, any uneven peaks or ridges add extra crunch and character to the bread.

5. Place the dough on the peel, which has been liberally dusted with cornmeal. Stretch the loaf a little, but not so that it is less than ½-inch thick. Place the tip of the peel at the far edge of the stone. Pull back with slight jerks to make the dough slide off the peel. It won't slide if there is insufficient cornmeal on the peel.

6. Bake until a rich brown, about 45 minutes. Using tongs or the peel, remove the bread. If it seems too soft, return it to the oven to bake for up to 5 minutes longer. Repeat with the second ball of dough. (If your stone is large enough, the two loaves can be baked simultaneously.) The long baking time is needed to insure that the interior is done. Allow to cool slightly, then cut into wedges and serve immediately. The crust should be very crunchy with a slightly moist, chewy interior.

Homestyle Bread

Pão Caseiro

Makes 2 large or 4 small loaves

This bread cannot be rushed. Patience and gentle handling go a long way in creating this rustic homestyle bread. Cool water, not warm, is mixed with the yeast to allow flavor to develop fully. Usually a small part of the dough from a previous bread-making is used as the starter of the new dough. (You can store dough in the freezer or buy some from your local bakery or pizza shop.) Since not everyone has leftover dough at their fingertips, however, these recipes are made with the dry or fresh yeast available in supermarkets. A minimal amount of yeast is used to create a sponge, or fermente, *that is left to rise overnight. If you are in a hurry, more yeast can be used, and the* fermente *is ready in about 5 to 6 hours. For the best results, I highly recommend using an oven stone and peel, like those used to make pizza. You can also use a cornmeal-coated sheet pan with good results. You can mix the dough by hand, but I prefer and recommend using a free-standing mixer, if possible. It is a sticky dough (drier than the cornbread dough), and using your hands or spatulas dipped in water will make handling and shaping easier. This type of rustic, peasant-style bread reflects the typical wheat-flour breads made in Portuguese homes. Here in the United States some Portuguese bakers—like Alex Couto, owner of Central Bakery, in Peabody Massachusetts—produce this bread with some modification of ingredients and modernization of methods. The recipe that follows is adapted from an old one, but includes beaten egg white, as suggested by Alex, for added protein as well as to open the grain. Read the recipe through before beginning.*

179

Equipment:

free-standing electric mixer (optional)

sheet pan or oven stone and peel

pastry brush

bottle for spraying water or pan to hold water on
    rack below baking bread

instant-read thermometer

Day ahead, make the sponge:

½ teaspoon dry yeast

1 cup water (65 to 70 degrees F)

1 cup unbleached all-purpose flour

1 teaspoon sugar (optional)

1. Dissolve the yeast in ¼ cup of the water in a large bowl, set aside for 10 minutes. Mix in the flour, sugar (optional), and remaining water, stirring until well blended. Cover with plastic, let rise overnight (7 to 8 hours) or let rise for about 2 hours then cover with plastic and refrigerate overnight. Remove from the refrigerator 2 hours before using to bring the sponge to room temperature. Don't be alarmed if the sponge has collapsed during its stay in the refrigerator; it will foam up again as it warms.

continued on next page

Make the dough:

6½ to 7 cups bread flour (12 percent gluten)
  or unbleached all-purpose flour
1 tablespoon table salt
1¾ teaspoon dry yeast or ⅔ teaspoon fresh yeast
¼ cup egg white (room temperature)
prepared sponge
2 cups water (room temperature 70 degrees F)
  as needed
cornmeal as needed

1. Combine 6 ½ cups of the flour with the salt in the bowl of a free-standing electric mixer. Using the dough paddle, mix to distribute the salt throughout the flour, 1 minute on low speed.

2. Using a fork, lightly beat the egg white in a small bowl until very frothy. Change the attachment to the dough hook. Make a well in the middle of the flour and pour in to the mixer bowl the yeast, the beaten egg white, the sponge, and the water. Mix on low speed long enough to fully incorporate the ingredients, then let the dough rest for about 10 to 15 minutes to give the flour time to take in the water. Increasing the speed to the maximum speed of your home mixer, continue to mix for 15 minutes. The dough will be of a slightly sticky consistency.

3. Using a wet hand to keep the dough from sticking, reach deep into the bowl and scrape the bottom and sides. Mix for another 5 minutes. Remove the dough hook and set a kitchen towel rinsed in warm water under the bowl. Cover the bowl with a dry kitchen towel, followed by a sheet of plastic. Place another larger towel over the bowl. (I always double-cover rising dough to insure consistent temperature and protection against drafts from doors opening and closing.) Let rise until double, about 2 to 2½ hours. Dough temperature should be about 75 to 84 degrees F.

4. Using a wet hand, again reach down to the bottom of the bowl and lift the dough, folding it onto itself. Cover and let rise again until double, about 1 more hour.

5. Do not punch down. Turn the dough out onto a well-floured work surface. Dust flour lightly over the top of the dough. Using a wet dough scraper or kitchen knife, divide the dough into 2, 3, or 4 equal parts. Using wet hands, gently shape into rounds or logs stretching gently and folding the dough over and onto itself. Let the dough rest again, about 1 hour, until it has risen to about a ¾ rise (almost double). Meanwhile (with the stone in place, if using) preheat the oven to 450 degrees F.

6. Dust the sheet pans or wooden peel with coarse cornmeal and place the readied pan or peel close to the shaped dough. Carefully lift the loaves onto the sheet pan or peel. You might need a dough scraper to lift and support the unbaked breads. Lightly dust the tops with flour. Make a couple of slashes across the top of the breads with a dough razor or very sharp knife.

7. Place a pan of hot water on the bottom oven rack. Slide the breads onto the preheated oven stone or place the sheet pan in the oven. Squirt the oven walls with water using a spray bottle and quickly close the oven door to trap the steam. You can even toss a few ice cubes onto the stone or oven floor. Bake for 35 to 45 minutes. Add another 5 minutes for larger loaves. The breads should feel fairly light and the bottom of breads should sound hollow when tapped. Cool slightly before cutting.

Crusty Rolls

Papo-secos

Makes about 2½ dozen

When my father made these rolls at his bakery, they practically flew out of the bin. These traditional rolls are delicious simply slathered with butter or eaten with grilled sausages or sardines. The old method of making these rolls and some of the other breads takes a long time—three days or more. Bakers made sponges and dough starters before mixing the final dough. The slower fermentation creates a fuller flavor. John M. Silva, owner of Danversport Bakery, in Danvers, Massachusetts, explains that bakeries, especially in the last twenty years, have adopted dough accelerators and conditioners to hasten production while attempting to maintain the flavor of the traditional recipes.

A former baker, Manuel Galopim, helped me convert the type of recipe used in my father's bakery—and in his own—to one without preservatives that is suited to home baking. Like the old method, this recipe requires patience to allow the flavor to develop. The amount of yeast, salt, and sugar for these rolls is based on the amount of flour used, not the amount of water. The addition of a fat (lard or shortening), which can improve shelf life and flavor, is optional. Try it with and without. Water, which can be soft or hard depending on where you live, can affect the dough. The best flour to use is hard spring-wheat flour with high gluten content (14.5 percent), which will hold the shape of the dough and give a better crumb. High-gluten flours also absorb more water. Some flours are cured or dried longer than others, reducing moisture and flavor in the product. Check with your local bakeries; sometimes they will sell bread-baking flour in small quantities. Also, baking catalogs and health-food stores sometimes carry high-gluten flour. A second package of yeast is added during the mixing of the dough. This gives a boost to the strong flour. If you make these rolls with other flours, you will probably enjoy the result, but you will miss out on the uniquely delicious texture and flavor that comes from high-gluten flour.

Equipment:
oven stone and wooden peel or metal sheet pan
pastry brush
shallow pan to hold water on oven rack below rolls
free-standing mixer (optional, but recommended)
4 kitchen towels
instant-read thermometer

Make the sponge at least 6 hours ahead:
1 package dry yeast
1 cup water (65 to 70 degrees F)
1 cup high-gluten flour (about ¼ pound)

1. Dissolve the yeast in the water in a medium bowl. Mix in the flour until blended. Cover with plastic and set aside at room temperature for a minimum of 6 hours, up to 7 or 8 hours. If you plan to start the dough in the morning, mix the sponge just before you retire the night before, cover, and chill overnight. Bring the sponge completely to room temperature (it will take about 2 hours), before using.

continued on next page

181

Make the dough:

6 cups (about 1½ pounds) high-gluten (14.5
    percent) hard spring-wheat flour
2 scant tablespoons lard or shortening (optional)
2 scant tablespoons (1 ounce) table salt
2 scant tablespoons (1 ounce) sugar (optional)
1 package dry yeast
1½ to 2 cups water (65 to 70 degrees F)
rice flour (optional, see Note at end of recipe)

1. Place the flour in a large bowl. Rub the shortening, if using, into the flour to distribute throughout. Transfer the flour to the bowl of a free-standing mixer and add the salt, and (optional) sugar, and the yeast. Using the paddle, mix on low speed for 1 minute to distribute the added ingredients throughout the flour.

2. Add the sponge and pour in about 1½ cups of the water, reserving the remaining ½ cup of water to add as needed. Change to the dough hook and mix on high speed for 15 minutes to develop the gluten. If the dough seems stiff after 5 minutes, add some of the remaining water, a little at a time, until you see the dough ease up. After 15 minutes the dough should be smooth and elastic, springing back when pressed with your finger. (The dough should be a little stiff.) Cover with a kitchen towel, followed by plastic wrap.

3. Set in a warm, draft-free place until double, about 2 hours. When the dough is ready, an indentation will remain when it is pressed lightly with your finger. Punch down to redistribute the yeast and let the dough rise for 1 more hour.

4. Punch down the dough, then turn out on a lightly floured work surface. Divide the dough into 24 to 36 equal-sized pieces, about 2 to 3 ounces each, or the size you prefer.

5. On an almost flour-free area of the work surface, use the palm of your hand with slightly curled fingers and medium pressure, to rotate the pieces of dough against the work surface until each piece is a smooth, fairly tight ball. Set 2 inches apart on a floured surface, covering with a towel, to relax for about 30 minutes.

6. On the floured work surface, flatten each ball into a disk about 3 inches in diameter. Dust the surface of the dough facing you with some all-purpose or rice flour. Using the outside edge of your hand, press a crease into the dough, as if you're going to cut it in half, but don't go completely through.

7. Fold the disks in half along the crease and pinch the ends firmly, giving the dough a slight lengthwise stretch and at the same time twisting or rolling the ends to a point.

8. Place the rolls, smooth side up, crease side down, on lightly floured towels, 2 inches apart, in rows. Pull the toweling up slightly between rows, so the rolls won't touch. Cover with another towel, top with plastic wrap, and let rise to nearly double, about 45 minutes to 1 hour. Meanwhile, place an oven stone on the middle shelf of the cold oven and a shallow pan on the bottom shelf. Preheat the oven to 400 degrees F.

9. Lightly dust the wooden peel or baking pan with fine cornmeal. Remove 6 rolls from under the toweling and place crease side up on the peel, forming two rows toward the edge farthest away from the handle. Or place rolls on the baking sheet and place on middle rack of oven. Pour hot water into the pan on the lower shelf, then quickly place the tip of the wood peel at the far edge of the hot stone. Using smooth, small jerking motions, pull back the peel while sliding the rolls gently onto the stone. They should stay upright. Bake for 15 to 20 minutes. They will be a rich golden color and sound hollow when tapped on the bottom. Remove, shoveling them up with the peel. Repeat, baking the remaining rolls six at a time.

Note: Although my father and I never used rice flour, Alex Couto suggests using it to help maintain the center crease of the rolls; it prevents them from ballooning out, which is an effect of the humidity in the oven.

CRUSTY ROLLS TECHNIQUE

Photographs illustrate steps five through nine

Rotate piece of dough into smooth, fairly tight balls

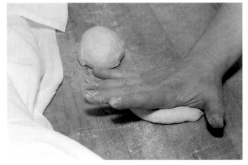

Flatten each ball into a disk about 3 inches in diameter

Using outside edge of palm, press a crease into the dough

Fold the disks in half along the crease

Pinch the ends firmly, giving a slight stretch and roll

Roll ends to a point

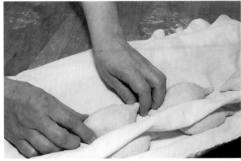

Place rolls, smooth side up, crease opening down on lightly floured towel

Place rolls facing up on lightly cornmeal-dusted wodden peels or baking pan

183

Clockwise from bottom: Pastry Tartlets with Muddled Filling (page 212), Baked Fritters (page 208), and Custard Cream Pastries (page 209)

9

SWEETS

Doces

Portuguese desserts, usually quite sweet and high in egg content, have never been a nightly habit. The more common ending to a typical family meal is a serving of cheese and fresh fruit. Despite, or perhaps because of this, Portuguese hold their desserts, homespun as they may be, in very high regard. I can remember as a young girl looking forward the vast array of sweets that graced the Portuguese dessert table. Today, dessert habits have not changed much. Weekends, holidays, and special occasions still bring out a wide variety of sweets that, I must admit, we are very happy to indulge in. With so many to choose from, I have had to relegate certain desserts to particular holidays. In our home, Thanksgiving has a more American theme, but when it comes to Christmas or Easter, the richer desserts come forth. Although I always like to include something new, the traditional ones are expected. Delectable lemon- or orange-infused cookies, creamy rice puddings, lusciously smooth caramel-custard flans, egg-rich sweet bread, tasty cakes, and, especially, brandy-flavored fried squash fritters, are sure to grace the table. At Easter time, in addition to the sweet breads and rice puddings, sweetened egg-white meringue puddings and pastry tarts are included in the array.

The majority of the desserts, as you will notice, are flavored with lemon or orange peel (interchangeable, as you wish), and occasionally vanilla. Feel free to use extracts, but keep in mind the depth of flavor will suffer. Cinnamon, caramelized sugar, and occasionally brandy and port wine are also used for flavoring.

The common method for cakes is the separation of eggs and the folding of stiffly beaten egg whites into the batter. For best volume of the egg white, make sure the bowl and beaters are clean and free of any trace of fat. It is also not unusual to combine sugar and butter with milk and heat until the butter is melted and the sugar is dissolved before incorporating them with dry ingredients.

Cookies are usually just brushed with egg wash before baking, but can be decorated with nonpareils. Recipes made with American flour have a somewhat different texture from those made in Portugal. While heirloom recipes of cakes and cookies that relied on a large quantity of eggs for leavening are made here in the same way, there are some that now include baking powder. The recipes that follow are representative of the traditional desserts that have continued to satisfy the Portuguese sweet tooth. More than one version has been given for some recipes to show the possibilities of texture and taste. My favorite —it's so very hard to choose!—would probably be *farofias* (Meringue Puffs, page 199), but then again, it could be . . . .

These recipes can easily be modified to be less sweet. I suggest that you follow a recipe as directed the first time, and then adjust the amount of sugar to your preference thereafter.

Washboards

Lavadores

Makes 4½ to 5 dozen

When I was in Portugal, I washed clothes outdoors, without hot water, in a soapstone washtub that had a washboard attached at one end. How we scrubbed those clothes on the washboard to get them clean! These cookies, marked horizontally with the tines of a fork to resemble the lines of washboards, are appropriately named. Possessing a delicate lemon flavor, these are especially delicious with tea.

½ cup butter, softened
1½ cups sugar, divided
4 eggs
grated peel of 1 lemon
about 4 cups all-purpose flour
1 tablespoon baking powder

Preheat the oven to 350 degrees F.

1. Using medium-high speed on an electric mixer or by hand, mix the butter with 1 cup of the sugar, about 1 minute. Beat in the eggs, one at a time, blending well after each, until the mixture is fluffy and pale yellow, about 2 to 3 minutes. Stir in the grated lemon peel.

2. In a medium bowl, whisk together the flour and the baking powder, stirring to distribute the ingredients evenly. Fold the flour into the butter and egg batter, using a wooden spoon or spatula. Mix the ingredients together well, gently kneading the dough in the bowl for about 5 minutes.

3. Place the remaining ½ cup of sugar in a shallow dish. Shape pieces of dough into 1½-inch balls. Roll in the sugar and place on parchment-lined or lightly greased cookie sheets, 2 inches apart. Flatten gently with the tines of a fork to make horizontal lines, like those of a washboard.

4. Bake for 20 to 25 minutes or until a light golden color.

187

Clockwise from top: Washboards, Dry Rings (page 189), and Orange Biscuits (page 188)

Orange Biscuits

Biscoitos de Laranja

Makes about 5 dozen

Children big and small love biscoitos de laranja. *Festively colored with nonpareils for special occasions, these keep well for 3 to 4 weeks stored in plastic containers. They are especially popular at Christmas time.*

6 cups all-purpose flour
2 teaspoons baking powder
½ teaspoon baking soda
¼ teaspoon salt
1½ cups sugar
1 cup butter plus 2 tablespoons, softened, divided
3 eggs, room temperature
4 ounces orange juice (commercial juice is fine)
1 egg, lightly beaten
colorful nonpareils (optional)

Preheat the oven to 350 degrees F.

1. In a medium bowl, sift together the flour, baking powder, baking soda, and salt. Set aside.

2. Using the high speed of an electric mixer or mixing by hand, beat the sugar with 1 cup of the butter in a large bowl until smooth. Mix in the eggs, one at a time, alternating with the orange juice and blending well after each egg. The texture will look muddled, not smooth and emulsified.

3. Fold in the flour mixture, then knead briefly in the bowl, about 3 minutes.

4. Lightly grease your hands with some of the remaining butter. Roll a quarter-sized piece of dough into a ½-inch diameter rope about 5 inches long. Shape into a coil. (These can also be made into twists by folding the length of rolled dough in half, then twisting a few times. This shape produces a crisper cookie.) Repeat with the remaining dough.

5. Place on parchment-lined or lightly greased baking sheets 1½ inches apart and brush with the beaten egg. Sprinkle with nonpareils. Bake for 15 to 20 minutes or until the bottom is lightly browned and the top is a light golden color, or for a crisper cookie, bake a few minutes longer until a rich gold color.

188

Dry Rings
Rosquilhas Secas

Makes about 3 dozen

These popular Azorean cookies have very little sugar in them; in fact, they are more of a dry biscuit and are frequently dunked into coffee, hot chocolate, even wine. They are made from a yeast dough and, while they are very simple to make, they require extra oven time to dry after baking.

2 packages (2 tablespoons) dry yeast
½ cup water, 110 degrees F
1 cup milk
2 sticks (1 cup) butter or margarine, softened
3 rounded tablespoons sugar
2 large eggs, room temperature
5 to 5½ cups all-purpose flour

1. In a small cup, dissolve the yeast in the water and set aside for 10 minutes. Meanwhile, combine the milk with the butter and sugar in a 1-quart saucepan. Place over medium-low heat until butter is melted and the sugar is dissolved.
2. Beat the eggs in a large bowl. Gradually whisk in the hot milk. Mix in 2 cups of the flour. Add the dissolved yeast and enough of the remaining flour (3 to 3½ cups) to form a medium-textured dough. Knead in the bowl until smooth and elastic, about 10 minutes. Cover well and set aside in a warm place to rise until double in size, about 2 hours.
3. Punch down and let the dough rise once more until double. Preheat the oven to 350 degrees F.
4. When the dough is ready, an indentation should remain in the dough after lightly pressing with your finger. Pinch off walnut-sized pieces of dough. Using a gentle hand, roll them into balls, then into ½-inch thick, 6-inch ropes. Press the ends firmly together, forming a ring. Stretch the rings slightly to open the center hole. Place on a parchment-lined or lightly greased baking sheet, 1½ inches apart. Place in the preheated oven.
5. Bake at 350 degrees for 15 minutes, reduce the oven temperature to 300 degrees and continue to bake until the rings start to color. Reduce the oven temperature to 250 degrees and continue to bake for 1 more hour. Turn off the oven and let the cookies remain in the oven until they are dry. Depending on the dough and the weather, it may take as long as it takes for the oven to cool down, but do not let the cookies get deep brown. They should be crisp and dry, not hard and overbaked.

Variation: You can dress these up with a sugar glaze. Combine 3 cups confectioner's sugar and ½ cup of water until smooth. Add a touch of flavoring. Drizzle over the rings and allow the glaze to dry completely before storing or serving.

189

Lizards

Lagartos

Makes about 4 dozen

Impressions made in the dough of these cookies are supposed to represent the ridges on a lizard's back. It is important to have egg whites at room temperature to obtain the best volume.

1¼ cups sugar
2 sticks (½ pound) butter, softened
4 eggs, separated, room temperature
grated peel of 1 lemon
1 teaspoon baking soda
4 cups all-purpose flour

Preheat the oven to 350 degrees F.

1. Using the high speed of an electric mixer or mixing by hand, beat the sugar with the butter in a large bowl, about 1 minute, until smooth. Beat in the egg yolks and grated lemon peel and mix until fluffy and pale yellow, about 2 to 3 minutes.
2. In a separate bowl and using clean beaters, beat the egg whites at high speed until stiff peaks form. Then fold into the butter-and-sugar mixture.
3. Blend the baking soda with the flour, distributing it throughout. Mix the flour into the batter and blend well. Gently knead in the bowl for about 5 minutes, thoroughly incorporating the flour to form a medium-textured dough.
4. Pinch off walnut-sized pieces of dough, roll into balls, then into ½-inch thick, 4- to 5-inch cylinders, tapered at one end. With the edge of a fork, make 3 vertical lines down the length of dough.
5. Place the "lizards" on parchment-lined or lightly greased baking sheets, 2 inches apart, giving them a slight S shape. Bake until golden, about 20 minutes.

Baking-Soda Cookies

Bolachas de Bica Bernato

Makes about 4 dozen

These tasty cookies from the Azores can be decorated with colored sugar or other decorative sprinkles. These, like most Portuguese cookies, are very simple to make and fun for children to shape.

1 cup sugar
½ cup butter, softened
1 egg
6 tablespoons milk
1 teaspoon vanilla (optional)
1 teaspoon baking soda
⅛ teaspoon salt
4 cups all-purpose flour
2 egg yolks, lightly beaten. for brushing
decorative sugar for sprinkling (optional)

Preheat the oven to 350 degrees F.

1. With an electric mixer at high speed or by hand, beat the sugar with the butter in a large bowl for about 1 minute. Stir in the egg, milk, vanilla (if using), baking soda, and salt, mixing at medium speed until well blended, about 2 to 3 minutes.
2. Using your hands, mix in the flour. Then knead in the bowl for about 5 minutes to form a medium-textured dough.
3. Divide the dough into four equal parts. With a lightly floured rolling pin on a lightly floured work surface, roll out one part until ¼-inch thick. Cut into triangles or circles 2½ to 3 inches in size. Repeat with remaining dough.
4. Place on parchment-lined or lightly greased baking sheets. Brush the tops with beaten egg yolk and sprinkle with white or colored sugar. Bake 15 to 20 minutes until golden.

Spikes of Corn

Espigas de Milho

Makes about 5 dozen

Azoreans shape these cookies with an ingenious method. Using a die plate like a six-pointed star inserted into an old-fashioned meat grinder, they extrude the dough into a ridged rope. The rope is cut into 5- or 6-inch lengths, placed on cookie sheets, and shaped into an S. A pastry bag with a 6-pointed star tip or a cookie press can create the same effect. You can also drop the dough by spoonfuls onto greased baking sheets.

1 pound (4 sticks) butter
1 tablespoon lard or shortening
1 pound (about 3¾ cups) fine white corn flour
   (not cornmeal)
1 dozen eggs
4 cups sugar
2 pounds (about 7½ cups) all-purpose flour
1 tablespoon baking powder
grated peel of 1 lemon
1 teaspoon table salt
½ teaspoon cinnamon

Preheat the oven to 350 degrees F.

1. Place the butter and lard in a 1-quart saucepan over medium-high heat until melted. Put the corn flour in a medium bowl and pour the hot melted butter over it. Mix until thoroughly blended. It will look like lumpy mashed potatoes. Set aside to cool to room temperature.

2. Put the eggs in a medium bowl and, using the high speed of an electric mixer or mixing by hand, beat the eggs until frothy. Gradually beat in the sugar, beating for about 3 minutes.

3. In a large bowl, combine the all-purpose flour, baking powder, grated lemon peel, salt, and cinnamon. Stir with whisk or fork to blend thoroughly.

4. When the corn flour has cooled, incorporate it into the egg and sugar mixture. Blend well, then add to the large bowl of dry ingredients. Using your hands, gently turn the ingredients completely, incorporating all the flour and forming a fairly soft dough.

5. Use a cookie press or pastry bag and star tip to make a rope of the dough. Cut the rope into 5- to 6-inch lengths, then place on baking sheets that are greased and floured or lined with parchment, shaping into an S. (Alternatively, you can simply pipe the cookies directly onto the prepared baking sheet or make simple drop cookies.) Bake until just light golden, about 15 to 20 minutes.

191

Fluffy Bread

Pão de Lo

Serves 10 to 12

Light and sometimes flavored with lemon, this sweet bread requires no icing. Typically served plain, it is eaten in some parts of Portugal with the very soft and mild cheese called queijo da serra *(page 4). Recipes differ across Portugal with varying amounts of eggs and sugar. The volume is obtained from the eggs themselves, the number of which can range from as few as 6 to as many as 12. Some versions, called* alfeizerão, *are only partially baked, having a maximum baking time of 15 minutes in a very hot oven. The result is more of a pudding cake and is eaten the day after baking. Don't be disappointed by its plain appearance. You can dress it up with a custard sauce or a fruit sauce, but I think you will enjoy it just the way it comes out of the oven. You will need a 10-inch tube pan.*

8 large egg yolks, room temperature
1½ cups sugar, preferably extra fine
grated peel of 1 lemon or orange (optional)
1¼ cups all-purpose flour
6 egg whites, room temperature

Preheat the oven to 325 degrees F.

1. Using the high speed of an electric mixer or mixing by hand, beat the egg yolks in a large bowl until frothy, then gradually beat in the sugar. Continue beating until the eggs are thick and pale yellow, at least 5 minutes. Stir in the lemon peel.
2. Add the flour to the egg batter and mix on medium speed until thoroughly incorporated.
3. In a separate bowl, free of any grease or yolk, beat the egg whites, using clean beaters and the mixer's high speed, until quite stiff. Gently fold the whites into the yolk batter, turning the ingredients carefully, so volume is not lost, until the egg whites are thoroughly incorporated.
4. Pour immediately into a greased tube pan. (If the batter is allowed to sit, it will begin to deflate and will not reach its maximum height.) Bake at 325 degrees for about 1 hour or until the cake is golden brown and the top springs back when lightly pressed.
5. Remove from the oven and allow to cool for about 5 to 10 minutes. Loosen all around the sides of the cake with a thin spatula. Invert on a flat plate, then invert again onto a serving dish so that the cake is upright. Use a serrated knife for slicing.

Note: This can also be baked at 350 degrees F for 40 minutes.

Beer Cake

Bolo de Cereveja

Serves 10 to 12

This recipe comes from the archives of Senhorina Bettencourt as it was given to her by Senhora Aurora of Carapacho, Graciosa, in the Azores. Light or regular beer works equally well in this cake.

2 cups sugar
1 cup butter, softened
4 eggs, separated, room temperature
1 cup beer
3 cups all-purpose flour
1 teaspoon baking powder

Preheat the oven to 350 degrees F.

1. In a large bowl, using the high speed of an electric mixer or mixing by hand, beat the sugar with the butter, until smooth, about 1 minute. Beat in the egg yolks, at medium speed, until the ingredients are fluffy and pale yellow, about 2 to 3 minutes.
2. Pour in the beer, mixing to blend. Add the flour and the baking powder and mix thoroughly, about 1 minute.
3. In a separate clean bowl and using clean beaters, beat the egg whites until stiff. Gently fold into the batter. Pour into a lightly greased and floured 10-inch tube pan and bake in the preheated oven until a wooden skewer comes out clean and the cake springs back when lightly pressed with your finger, about 50 minutes. Cool about 5 minutes before removing from pan.

Coimbra Cake

Bolo de Coimbra

Serves 10 to 12

This recipe comes from northern Portugal, named after the city of Coimbra. Excavated from the recipe archives of Senhorina Bettencourt, it proves to have been a worthy find.

2 sticks butter, softened
2 cups sugar
8 eggs, separated, room temperature
2½ cups cake flour
2 teaspoons baking powder
1 teaspoon cinnamon
grated peel of 1 lemon

Preheat the oven to 325 degrees F.

1. Place the butter in a large bowl and, using the high speed of a mixer or mixing by hand, gradually pour in the sugar, beating until fairly smooth. Add the egg yolks, one at a time, beating well after each one. Set aside.
2. Put the egg whites in a clean medium-sized bowl and beat them with clean beaters on high speed until stiff peaks form. Set aside.
3. In another large bowl, combine the flour, baking powder, cinnamon, and grated lemon peel. Blend well to distribute the ingredients evenly. Fold the dry ingredients into the bowl containing the egg yolks, making sure all the flour is well blended.
4. Using a rubber spatula, gently and completely fold the stiff egg whites into the batter. Pour the batter in a lightly greased and floured 10-inch tube pan. Bake at 325 degrees for about 45 to 50 minutes. Cake will spring back when lightly pressed with your finger. Cool about 5 minutes before removing from pan.

193

Orange Squares
Quadradas de Laranja
Makes about 1½ dozen

This is one of the few Portuguese cakes that are baked and cut into squares and then glazed with syrup—a technique more common in eastern Mediterranean countries. The flavor of oranges adds another dimension.

1 cup sugar
2 sticks (1 cup) butter, softened
6 eggs, separated
grated peel of 2 oranges
1 cup milk
2 cups all-purpose flour
2 teaspoons baking powder
¼ teaspoon salt

Preheat the oven to 350 degrees F.

1. In a large bowl, using the high speed of an electric mixer or mixing by hand, beat the sugar with the butter until it is fairly smooth, about 1 minute. Add the egg yolks, one at a time, beating well after each one. Stir in the grated orange peel and the milk.
2. In a separate clean bowl, using the high speed of the mixer and clean beaters, beat the egg whites until stiff peaks form, about 4 to 5 minutes. Fold the egg whites into the batter.
3. In a separate bowl, combine the flour with the baking powder and salt, mixing well. Fold the flour into the batter, gently mixing to incorporate all of the flour. Transfer to a lightly greased and floured 9 x 13-inch baking pan and spread evenly. Bake at 350 degrees for 35 to 40 minutes.

Glaze:
1 cup sugar
juice of 4 oranges

1. While the cake is baking, combine 1 cup of sugar with the orange juice in a small saucepan and place over medium-high heat. Bring to a boil and reduce the heat to medium-low. Simmer for 20 to 30 minutes, or until the sugar is dissolved and a medium syrup thickly coats the spoon.
2. When the cake is done, remove from the oven. With a toothpick or skewer prick holes in the cake. Then spread the syrup evenly over the cake. If you wish, you can place the cake, still in the pan, briefly under the broiler or use a chef's torch to heat the glaze just until it starts to bubble. Cut into squares and serve.

194

Sweet Rice Pudding

Arroz Doce

Serves 4 to 6

This age-old pudding goes hand in hand with Massa Sovada, *a traditional sweet bread (see page 203). We would eat the sweet bread topped with the rice pudding. One of my earliest memories is of my grandmother sprinkling cinnamon in the pattern of a cross onto platters of* Arroz Doce *for Easter. There are many variations, since this dish is on the table at every Portuguese event, but the version that follows is the one I knew growing up. Covering the chilling pudding with plastic wrap keeps the surface from drying. Bring almost to room temperature before serving.*

2 cups water
1 cup short-grain rice (such as Italian arborio rice
    or the River Rice brand found in U.S. markets)
¼ teaspoon salt
2 cups milk, scalded
peel of 1 lemon, without pith, in large pieces
1 cup sugar
ground cinnamon for decorating

1. Pour the water into a 2½ quart saucepan, cover, and bring to a boil over medium-high heat. Stir in the rice with the salt and reduce the heat to medium-low. Cover and simmer the rice for 25 to 20 minutes or until the water is nearly evaporated. Rice will be barely tender.

2. Stir in the warm milk and add the pieces of lemon peel. Stirring constantly, continue to simmer until the mixture starts to thicken slightly, about 20 to 25 more minutes.

3. When the rice is well cooked, stir in the sugar and continue cooking until the sugar is dissolved and the pudding has thickened to the consistency of oatmeal, about 5 to 10 minutes more. The rice should be very tender. Remove from the heat. It will continue to thicken as it cools.

4. Remove the pieces of lemon peel. Pour the pudding onto a large flat serving platter or individual flat plates to a thickness of not more than about ¾ inch.

5. Taking a pinch of ground cinnamon between thumb and forefinger, rub thumb and finger together gently close to the surface of the rice. Dust the surface of the rice in a design of your choice, perhaps forming the initials of a guest. (If fingers are held too high, cinnamon will scatter over a wider area.) Cool and serve or chill the rice to serve later. (See Health Note on page 141.)

Variation: Beat 3 or 4 egg yolks in a small bowl. When the pudding is done but still hot, remove ¼ cup of pudding and gradually mix into the egg yolks. (This will temper the egg yolks and prevent curdling.) Add the yolk mixture to the pudding and quickly blend in, stirring constantly for 1 minute to cook the eggs. Pour onto platters as above. This version will be thicker and tinted yellow, with a custardy texture and flavor. Some versions from the Azores are so thick they can be cut into wedges and eaten like slices of pizza.

195

Mrs. Nogueira's Sweet Rice

Arroz Doce à Senhora Nogueira

Serves 4 to 6

Note that in all recipes for Portuguese rice pudding, the amounts of sugar and rice are equal. Despite the similarity of ingredients, the preparation method and quantity can vary. In this recipe from Isaura Noguiera, the rice is cooked amost entirely in milk. For an extra-large batch, just triple the quantities.

5 cups milk
1 cup short-grain rice
½ teaspoon salt
water
peel of 1 orange, without pith, in large pieces
1 cup sugar
ground cinnamon for dusting

1. Pour the milk into a 2½-quart saucepan and heat over medium-high heat until little bubbles form around the edges and the milk starts to steam. Remove from the heat.
2. Put the rice and salt into a separate 2½-quart saucepan. Add enough water to just cover the rice. Place over medium-high heat, cover, and bring to a boil. Reduce the heat to medium-low and stirring constantly, cook the rice just until the water evaporates, being careful not to burn it.
3. Stir the scalded milk into the rice and add the orange peel. Cover and continue to simmer the rice for another 20 to 25 minutes until it is almost done.
4. When the rice is tender, remove the orange peel and add the sugar. Continue to simmer for 5 more minutes, stirring constantly, until the sugar is dissolved. The pudding should be somewhat thick, like oatmeal. It will continue to thicken as it cools.
5. Pour onto flat platters or individual serving dishes and garnish with cinnamon in the Portuguese style: pinching some cinnamon between the index finger and thumb, dropping it close to the surface of the rice, in a design or initials of a guest of honor. Chill. Serve chilled or bring to room temperature for serving. (See Health Note on page 141.)

Tip: Use a vegetable peeler and light pressure to remove peel from lemons and oranges without removing the pith.

Creamy Flan Pudding
Pudim Flan
Serves 6

Flan makes an elegant dessert and yet it is simple to prepare. This version is particularly rich and creamy. It is rare that this luscious treat fails to make an appearance, especially for holidays. Condensed milk gives it a creamy texture. Extra flavoring is not needed, although a touch of lemon can be added. It is not unusual for a Portuguese cook to make the caramel sauce without adding any water at all, but it only takes a momentary distraction to make a beautiful golden color turn too dark, giving a burned taste. Even with the addition of water, care must be taken to obtain the right color. Additional care should be taken in handling the very hot sugar syrup. If you get burned, immediately immerse in cold water.

Caramel sauce:
1 cup granulated sugar
⅓ cup water

1. Combine the sugar and the water in a 2-quart saucepan, stir, and bring to a boil over medium-high heat.
2. When the sugar is dissolved, reduce the heat and simmer without stirring until the syrup turns golden, about 15 minutes.
3. Remove the syrup from the heat once the desired color is reached. Use a pot holder to hold the mold, especially if it is made of metal. Carefully pour the hot caramel into the bottom of a 1½-quart oven-proof mold, turning the mold to coat the bottom, then the sides. Don't worry if the sides do not get completely coated. Set the pan aside to cool thoroughly.

Custard:
14 ounces sweetened condensed milk
14 ounces whole milk
4 eggs, lightly beaten

Preheat oven to 350 degrees F.

1. In a large bowl, combine the condensed milk, the whole milk, and eggs. Mix well, strain if you wish, and pour into the cooled mold.
2. Set the mold into a larger pan and place in the oven. Carefully pour hot water into the larger pan so that it comes halfway up the side of the mold.
3. Bake for about ½ hour or until a knife, inserted into the middle of the custard comes out clean.
4. Carefully remove the custard pan from the larger pan and chill for several hours. Before serving, loosen the edges with a spatula. To serve, place over the mold, a serving plate that has a rim around the edges to catch the sauce. Invert the mold and plate and shake gently. Remove the mold; the caramel will flow over the custard. Garnish with a sprig of mint or a lemon curl.

197

Custard Flan Pudding

Pudim Flan

Serves 10

The version of flan that I grew up with is not as rich as some. It is made the old-fashioned way with whole milk and lots of eggs. I often serve this on Christmas day or Easter. Pick one of the flavor options to suit your taste

Caramel sauce:

1 cup sugar

⅓ cup water

1. Combine the sugar and the water in a 2-quart saucepan, stir, and place over medium-high heat.
2. When the sugar is dissolved, lower the heat and simmer without stirring until the sugar syrup turns golden color, about 15 minutes.
3. Using a pot holder to hold the mold, especially if it is made of metal, carefully pour the hot caramel into the bottom of a 2-quart oven-proof mold, a tube pan, or a 10-inch by 2-inch-deep round pan, quickly turning the mold or pan to coat the bottom, then the sides. Don't worry if the sides do not get completely coated. Set the pan aside to cool thoroughly. The caramel will crackle as it cools.

Custard:

8 whole eggs

2 egg yolks

½ teaspoon cinnamon

1¼ cups sugar

1 quart whole milk

1 tablespoon port wine, Beirão brandy, or the
    peel, without pith, of 1 whole lemon or
    orange, in large pieces

Preheat the oven to 350 degrees F.

1. Using the high speed of an electric mixer or mixing by hand, beat whole eggs, the egg yolks, and cinnamon in a large bowl until frothy.
2. Place the sugar and milk and choice of flavoring into a 2½-quart saucepan. Place over medium-high heat and warm until the sugar is dissolved. While stirring with a whisk, gradually pour the warm sweetened milk into the eggs and cinnamon.
3. Remove the zest, if used, strain if you wish, then pour into the prepared mold or pan. Place the mold into a larger pan and place on the middle rack of your preheated oven. Add enough hot water to the larger pan so that it comes about halfway up the side of the custard pan. The water bath is called a *banho maria* in Portuguese.
4. Bake in the water bath at 350 degrees for about 35 minutes or until a knife inserted into the middle of the custard comes out clean.
5. Chill thoroughly before serving. To unmold, run a knife around the edges and invert onto a rimmed serving dish, letting the caramel sauce cascade over the top and sides. Cut into wedges to serve.

Note: Use a serving dish that has raised sides (about ¾-inch high) to prevent syrup from overflowing. Flans can also be made in individual serving molds, but it's traditional to make this in a single mold and serve it—like most Portuguese food—family style, whether on a buffet table or the family dinner table.

Meringue Puffs

Faròfias

Serves 4 to 6

I was visiting cousin Marguerida at Quinta Vale dos Moinhos, her family's farm near the village of Almoster in the Atlentejo region, when I tasted this cloudlike dessert for the first time. When I was thirteen, Aunt Ana taught me how to make it, and I've made it often ever since. This melt-in-your-mouth dessert isn't that difficult to make and is actually fun to do! It teases us with lightly sweetened meringue that has been poached in milk, then set afloat in a lemon-flavored custard sauce. It is a perfect dessert to satisfy a sweet tooth even after a heavy meal.

4 large eggs, separated, room temperature
¾ cup sugar, divided
2 teaspoons cornstarch
2 cups whole milk
peel of 1 lemon, without pith, in large pieces
ground cinnamon for dusting

1. Beat the egg whites in a medium bowl, by hand or using the high speed of an electric mixer, until soft peaks form. Gradually add ¼ cup of the sugar and continue to beat until the whites are stiff. Set aside.
2. Place the cornstarch in a small cup and gradually mix in ¼ cup of the milk. Combine the yolks and lemon peel in a small bowl and stir in the cornstarch mixture. Set aside. (If you are planning to make the meringues a day ahead, then postpone this step until you make the sauce.)
3. Heat the remaining milk with the remaining sugar in a 2½-quart saucepan, over medium-high heat. When the milk is about to boil, reduce the heat to maintain a simmer.
4. Using a slotted spoon, place 1 or 2 large spoonfuls of meringue into the simmering milk. Poach for about 1½ minutes in the steaming milk. The meringues may rise like they're going to boil over, but do not let the milk boil or it will curdle. Turn the puffs over to cook the other side, 1½ minutes; the meringues should be slightly firm. With a slotted spoon, remove the meringues to a colander set in a shallow bowl to capture the milk that drains off. Allow the meringues to drain well. Repeat with the remaining egg white

mixture. Reserve the drained milk.
5. Transfer the cooked and well-drained puffs to a deep serving platter or individual serving plates. At this point, the puffs can be covered with plastic and refrigerated to serve later the same day or the next day.

Make the sauce:
1. Transfer the milk captured from draining the meringues, plus any milk remaining in the pan, to a clean 1-quart saucepan. Stir the egg yolk mixture, then quickly add it to the milk. Over medium-low heat, cook, stirring constantly, until the custard sauce thickens slightly. Do not boil. Remove lemon peel. Drizzle the sauce over the puffs or pool it around them. Sprinkle with cinnamon and serve at room temperature or chill for 20 minutes.

Notes: If the milk has been allowed to boil during poaching, add ½ cup of cold fresh milk when you make the sauce or use 1½ cups of fresh milk instead. If you plan to make the meringues a day ahead, make the sauce the next day using fresh milk.

Molotoff Pudding

Molotoff

Serves 10 to 12

Airy meringue desserts are very popular with the Portuguese. This recipe comes from Maria Fidalgo, whose version is the best I have ever had. It calls for caramelized sugar syrup, which sounds more difficult than it actually is, so don't let that intimidate you from making this heavenly treat. An electric mixer is essential unless you are proficient at beating meringue by hand.

Meringue:
16 egg whites, room temperature
1 cup plus 3 tablespoons sugar

Preheat the oven to 350 degrees F.

1. Beat the egg whites in a large bowl, using the high speed of an electric mixer, until frothy. Continue beating while gradually adding 1 cup of the sugar. Beat until stiff peaks form, then set aside.
2. Melt the remaining 3 tablespoons of sugar in a 1-quart saucepan and heat with out stirring, until lightly caramelized, about 10 to 15 minutes. While it is still hot, quickly whisk half of the caramelized sugar syrup into the egg whites.
3. Butter a 3-quart tube pan or domed mold (available in kitchen specialty stores or see Resource Guide at the end of the book). Carefully transfer the meringue to the pan. Set the pan of meringue in a larger pan. Pour enough hot water into the larger pan to come halfway up the side of the meringue pan, forming a water bath, *banho maria*. Set the pans into the preheated oven and bake for 20 minutes. *Do not open the oven door.* Turn off the oven and leave the meringue in the oven for another 20 minutes. Carefully remove the pans from the oven. Remove the mold from the larger pan and set aside to cool.

Sauce:
2 cups whole milk
5 tablespoons sugar
grated zest of 1 lemon
remaining caramelized sugar
6 egg yolks

1. Combine the milk, sugar, and lemon zest in the same small saucepan holding the remaining caramelized sugar (sugar will be hard). Warm over medium-high heat, stirring until the caramelized sugar is dissolved and the milk is scalded. Turn off the burner and allow pan to cool slightly.
2. Beat the egg yolks in a medium bowl, then quickly whisk a small amount of the milk into the yolks. Transfer the mixture back to the pan of milk. Reheat the milk slowly over medium-low heat, stirring constantly, until it becomes the consistency of heavy cream. Chill until ready to serve.
3. Unmold the meringue by dipping the bottom briefly in a bowl of hot water. Invert onto a rimmed serving platter and chill. Drizzle some of the sauce over the meringue. Slice into wedges as you would a cake and drizzle additional sauce over each serving or pass the sauce around.

200

Ideal Dessert
Sobremesa Ideal
Serves 8 to 10

The people from the island of São Miguel have their own special meringue dessert. This lemon-flavored pudding, which floats in a caramel sauce topped with airy meringue, is a specialty brought from her homeland by Maria Coimbra, who made sweet bread in my father's bakery.

Caramel sauce:

½ cup sugar
¼ cup water

1. Place the sugar and water in a 1½-quart saucepan and stir well. Without stirring, warm over medium-low heat until the sugar dissolves and becomes a rich golden color, about 10 to 15 minutes. Quickly pour the caramel sauce into a 9 x 13-inch ovenproof serving dish, tilting it back and forth to coat as much of the bottom as you can. Don't worry if it doesn't cover completely.

Pudding:

4 egg yolks, room temperature
3 tablespoons sugar
peel of 1 lemon, without the pith, in large pieces
14-ounce can sweetened condensed milk
4 tablespoons cornstarch
1 quart whole milk

Preheat the oven to 300 degrees F.

1. Place the egg yolks, 3 tablespoons of sugar, and the lemon peel in a heavy-bottomed 2½-quart saucepan. Using a wooden spoon, stir in the condensed milk and cornstarch, mixing thoroughly. While stirring, gradually pour in the milk.

2. Heat the ingredients, stirring constantly, over medium-low heat until the pudding starts to bubble, about 20 to 25 minutes. The pudding will have thickened enough for a spoon to leave a swirl when it is drawn through it. (Don't leave this pudding to simmer without constantly stirring and don't rush it by raising the heat because it can easily burn.) Remove the lemon peel and pour the pudding into the serving dish over the cooled caramelized sugar, spreading evenly.

Topping:

4 egg whites, room temperature
7 tablespoons sugar

1. Beat the egg whites in a small bowl and gradually add the 7 tablespoons of sugar until very stiff peaks are formed. Spread evenly over the pudding layer, pulling up little peaks with the tines of a fork. Bake in the preheated oven until the peaks start to turn golden, about 15 to 20 minutes. Cool gradually at room temperature before chilling well. Serve this treat with a glass of port wine.

Pasta Pudding

Aletria

Serves 6

This pudding, which is similar to rice pudding, makes use of angel-hair pasta, but vermicelli can also be used. I find the best way to make this pudding come together is to cook the pasta in the milk, not separately in water.

6 cups milk
2 tablespoons butter
2 cinnamon sticks
whole peel of 1 lemon, without pith
¼ teaspoon salt
2 cups broken (1- to 2-inch pieces) or crushed
    angel-hair or vermicelli pasta (about 6 ounces)
1 cup sugar
6 egg yolks
ground cinnamon for sprinkling

1. Combine the milk with the butter, cinnamon sticks, lemon peel, and salt in a 4-quart saucepan and bring to a high simmer over medium-high heat. Do not boil.
2. Add the pasta, stir, and reduce the heat to medium-low. Simmer until the pasta is slightly tender, but not so that it is mushy, about 3 to 5 minutes, depending on the type of pasta. You want the integrity of the strands of pasta to be maintained.
3. Stir the sugar, then continue to simmer until the pasta is completely cooked, the sugar is dissolved, and the pudding starts to thicken, about 10 to 15 minutes. Remove the pan from the heat.
4. Beat the egg yolks in a small bowl. To temper them, take about ¼ cup of the hot pudding and add it to the yolks, stirring quickly. Add more pudding in small quantities until the eggs are quite warm.
5. Quickly whisk the egg mixture into the pan of remaining pudding, stirring thoroughly to cook the eggs. Remove the cinnamon sticks and the lemon peel and discard. Then pour the pudding onto a platter or individual dishes. Sprinkle with ground cinnamon.

202

Sweet Bread
Massa Sovada
Makes about 4 loaves

Many years ago, when I learned to make this sweet bread I learned the old way. (Massa sovada literally means "beaten dough," in reference to the method of kneading it.) With both hands suspended over a mixing bowl containing a large quantity of eggs, I spread my fingers wide. Plunging my outspread fingers into the bowl, I beat the eggs, whipping my fingers through them in a rotating motion. Another person stood ready to add the next ingredient, and when the flour was added, I used my palms and fists (the "beating") to incorporate the flour and form a dough. It was hard work! If large batches of dough were needed, women took turns mixing and kneading the dough. Today's heavy-duty mixers make the job much easier, but something special had been lost in the process.

Nothing can take the place of Portuguese sweet bread! It perfectly complements Sweet Rice Pudding (pages 195–96), of course, but toasted sweet bread, with a little butter and cup of strong coffee, is an indescribable pleasure. It also makes delicious bread puddings. This recipe is time-consuming, so start early! Traditionally, after setting the dough to rise, we bless it so that it really will rise. Sweet bread recipes differ in the amount of eggs and sugar they call for—some less, some more. The length of pre-fermentation varies as well. Delta Ortins, who provides the following recipe, is considered one of the best makers of sweet bread. This recipe requires patience and a very slow rising time—but that is the secret to the bread's flavor.

Two days ahead, make the sponge (*fermente*):
1 package dry yeast
¾ cup warm water, 110 degrees F
3 eggs, room temperature and lightly beaten
5 tablespoons flour
3 tablespoons sugar

1. Combine the yeast with the water in a medium bowl and stir well. Set aside for 10 minutes. Mix in 2 tablespoons of the flour and allow to rise for 3 hours. To complete the sponge, add the eggs, the remaining 3 tablespoons of flour, plus the sugar, mixing thoroughly. Cover and set aside in a cool, not cold, place for 3 days. The sponge will appear to have settled, with some froth on top.

Day ahead, make the dough:
1½ pounds (3½) cups sugar
1¼ pounds (5 sticks) butter, divided
2 cups milk
1 tablespoon table salt

2 dozen eggs, room temperature
2 tablespoons lard, melted
5 pounds (about 22 cups) all-purpose unbleached bread flour
2 teaspoons cinnamon
2 eggs, lightly beaten, for egg wash (optional)

1. In a 2-quart pot, combine the sugar, 4 sticks of the butter, the milk, and the salt and bring just to the edge of a boil. Set aside.
2. Place the 2 dozen eggs and melted lard in a extra-large bowl and whisk until quite frothy. While quickly stirring, slowly pour in the warm milk.
3. Stir up the sponge and add to the eggs. Fold in the flour with the cinnamon, mixing well. Knead in the bowl until smooth and elastic, about 15 minutes. Melt the last stick of butter, pour it over and around the dough. Give the dough a few more turns to incorporate the butter completely. Cover well and set to rise in a draft-free place for about 12 hours.

continued on next page

Next day:

1. Butter your hands and punch down the dough. The punching will remove excess gases and redistribute the yeast.

2. Lightly butter your work surface. Divide the dough into about four equal parts, more if you wish the loaves to be smaller. Then shape into balls or rings or put into lightly greased and floured loaf pans. To shape into rings, take one portion of dough (it will be close to a cantaloupe in size) and stretch it into a log about 24 inches long and 5 inches in diameter. Pat the dough lightly with your hands until it is of even thickness. Starting in the middle of the log of dough, lift and twist one half, as if you're wringing a towel. Put that half down. Go back to the middle and lift and twist the other half, twisting in the opposite direction. Bring the ends together to form a circle, pinching together or tucking them under one another. Place the ring of dough on a lightly buttered and floured or parchment-lined sheet pan, stretching the hole in the center to make sure it doesn't close up.

6. Depending on the size of your sheet pan and rings, two loaves may fit on one pan, but leave at least a 4-inch space between them. (To make other shapes, see instructions at end of the recipe.) Shaping the rest of the dough. Cover and set aside in a draft-free area to rise a second time until nearly double (¾-proofed), about 4 hours. The dough will finish springing in the oven.

Preheat the oven to 350 degrees F.

7. Just before baking, using clean kitchen shears, make four evenly spaced snips, about 2 inches long, in the surface of the dough. If you make simple rounds, cut a cross in the center top. Brush the bread surface with egg wash, if desired. Then bake in the preheated 350-degree oven. After 20 minutes, reduce the heat to 325 degrees and continue baking until a long wooden skewer comes out clean, about 25 to 30 minutes more. Times will vary depending on the size and shape of the loaves, but the skewer should come out clean. Remove the bread from the oven and brush with melted butter.

Shaping the loaves:

Shape a 2-pound piece of dough (grapefruit size) into a ball, rotating and pulling the dough across the work surface to make it tight and smooth. Set the dough into greased round pans for the second rising. Sweet bread is traditionally round, but I also use loaf pans (aluminum or steel is better than glass for this bread). The resulting bread is perfect for slicing and toasting. For round shapes, use flat sheet pans lined with buttered and floured foil, or even buttered and floured aluminum pie plates. Parchment paper also works perfectly well on sheet pans.

Note: When we make sweet bread for Easter, we reserve a small amount of dough, roll it into strips, and criss-crossed them over raw eggs that have been set into the surface of the dough after the dough has been shaped and risen for the second time. The strips are brushed with egg wash and baked on the bread. These breads should be kept refrigerated if the eggs will be eaten later. For safety, discard eggs that have been at room temperature for more than two hours.

Squash Fritters

Beilhoses

Makes about 5 dozen

Christmas Eve dinner would not be complete without these tasty fried puffs. In fact, I cannot remember a single Christmas without them. This dessert and the name belhoses *are unique to the Alentejo region. The delectable fritters are also known as* filhos de Natal *(Christmas fried dough). The squash is puréed by hand or with the help of a food mill. The squash should be cooked with just enough water to cover. If you have time, cook the squash early in the day or the night before to give it enough time to drain well. The nutrients in the cooking water are not wasted because the liquid is used in the dough. When you add the yeast to the cooking liquid, the liquid must be below 110 degrees F, but not less than room temperature.*

1 pound (about 2 cups) Blue Hubbard squash or
    pumpkin, peeled and cut into chunks
1½ cups water
1 package dry yeast
1 cup squash cooking water, divided
4 large eggs, room temperature
¼ cup orange juice
2 tablespoons brandy (optional)
½ teaspoon cinnamon
½ teaspoon table salt
4½ cups all-purpose flour, as needed
corn oil for frying
1 cup sugar
½ to 1 teaspoon cinnamon

1. Place the peeled squash in a 3-quart saucepan with the water. Cover tightly and bring to a boil over medium-high heat. Reduce and simmer until the squash is very tender. Reserving 1 cup of the cooking liquid, drain the squash well by setting it in a colander. When the squash is well drained, purée and set aside.
2. Dissolve the yeast in ¼ cup of the cooking liquid once it has cooled to between 90 and 110 degrees F; set aside for 10 minutes to proof.
3. Using the high speed of your electric mixer or by hand, beat the eggs in a large bowl until light and frothy. Mix in the dissolved yeast and 2 cups of puréed squash, blending thoroughly. Stir in the juice, brandy, cinnamon, and salt.
4. Mixing thoroughly, add enough flour to form loose dough, like a very thick batter. Add about ½ cup more cooking liquid if needed. Dust the top of the dough liberally with flour, cover with a towel, and set aside in a warm, draft-free spot to rise until double, about 2 hours. Punch down and let it rise for 1 more hour.
5. Heat 5 to 6 inches of oil in a deep 3- to 4-quart saucepan over medium-high heat until it seems to shiver, about 350 degrees F. Using two teaspoons dipped into the hot oil, scoop scant walnut-sized balls of dough (1½ inch diameter) with one spoon, removing with the other and drop carefully into the oil. Oiling the spoons first helps the dough slide into the oil. Fry just a few puffs at a time until they are golden brown. Remove with a slotted spoon, roll in cinnamon and sugar, and serve warm.

Note: If too much water or flour is used, the dough will be too heavy. When you fry the puffs, they will brown on the outside but will not be cooked all the way through. Make sure that you let this dough rise sufficiently.

Fried Dough

Malassadas/Filhoses

Makes about 2 dozen

This Azorean recipe for Fried Dough, Malassadas, *does not include squash or pumpkin: It is more like sugared, raised donuts or the fried dough sold at country fairs. They are very popular at Carnival festivals and Christmas time. In some regions of continental Portugal, these would be called* filhoses—*except the* filhoses *of the Alentejo are crisp and delicate.*

Sponge:

1 package dry yeast
¼ cup warm water, 110 degrees F
1 tablespoon flour
1 tablespoon sugar

1. Dissolve the yeast in the water in a small bowl. Set aside for 10 minutes. Mix in the flour and the sugar, stirring to blend. Cover and set aside.

Dough:

4 eggs, room temperature
6 ounces (¾ cup) sugar
½ cup milk
4 tablespoons (½ stick butter), softened
1¼ pounds (3¾ cups) all-purpose flour
¼ teaspoon salt
corn oil for frying as needed
1 cup sugar
1 teaspoon ground cinnamon

1. Crack the eggs into a large bowl. Beat until frothy at medium-high speed of a mixer or by hand, until they are light and pale yellow, about 3 minutes.

2. Heat the sugar, milk, and butter in a 1-quart saucepan over medium-low heat until the butter is melted and the sugar is dissolved.

3. Alternating with the milk, add the flour and salt to the eggs. Add the yeast sponge and mix thoroughly, forming a medium-textured dough. Knead in the bowl for 10 to 15 minutes. Cover and set aside in a warm, draft-free spot to rise until double, about 1 hour. Punch down to redistribute the yeast and cover. Let rise again for 1 more hour.

4. Pour corn oil to a depth of 5 inches into a deep 3- to 4-quart saucepan. Heat over medium-high heat until the oil starts to quiver or shake. Pinch off a 3-inch piece of dough and flatten it slightly with your hands. You can shape it in the style of Graciosa by using your thumb to poke a hole in the middle, then stretch and pull it into a doughnut shape about 4 to 5 inches in diameter. Or shape it São Miguel style by simply stretching the piece of dough into a ½-inch thick square or triangle before frying. Whatever shape, deep-fry until golden brown, drain on brown paper or paper towels. Mix the cinnamon and sugar in a bowl and toss the warm pastries to coat.

Dreams

Sonhos

Makes about 3½ dozen

After you eat one of these delightful puffs, you may think you are dreaming. These always put a smile on my father's face. The puffs are made basically as a choux pastry dough, which is then deep fried and drizzled with a syrup flavored with orange and brandy or rolled in cinnamon and sugar. You can use Grand Marnier instead of plain brandy.

Syrup:
½ cups sugar
1 cup water
2 tablespoons brandy
peel of 1 orange

1. Combine ingredients in a saucepan and simmer for 15 minutes. Remove orange peel and set aside for drizzling over puffs.

Dough:
1 cup water
½ cup butter
¼ teaspoon salt
1 cup flour
4 eggs
corn oil for frying

1. Bring the water, butter, and salt to a boil in a 2-quart pan. When the butter is melted, reduce the heat and add the flour. Using a wooden spoon, beat thoroughly until a dough forms. Keep stirring until the dough leaves the sides of the pan.
2. Add the eggs one at a time, beating well after each one. Remove from the heat.
3. Deep fry rounded teaspoonfuls or walnut-sized balls until golden. Drain on paper towels, then arrange in a mound on a serving dish. Allow to cool completely.
4. Drizzle with syrup.

Variation: You can omit the syrup and coat the balls in cinnamon and sugar instead. Mix 1 cup of sugar and 1 teaspoon of cinnamon in a shallow dish. Do not drain the hot puffs on paper towels. Roll them in the sugar mixture and mound attractively in a serving dish. Do not cover them while they are hot or they will get soggy. Best eaten fresh.

207

Baked Fritters

Filhos do Forno

Makes about 3 dozen pastries

There is much music and dancing—and eating—during Carnival time, which occurs three days prior to Ash Wednesday. These fritters, similar to cream puffs, and Malassadas *(page 206), are popular pastries enjoyed by all.*

2 cups water
½ pound (2 sticks) butter
2 cups all-purpose flour
8 eggs
¾ cup sugar
¼ cup plus 1 tablespoon cornstarch
4 cups whole milk
6 egg yolks
1 teaspoon vanilla or whole peel of 1 lemon,
    without the pith

Preheat the oven to 425 degrees F.

1. In a 3-quart saucepan, combine the water and butter and bring to a boil over medium-high heat. The butter will melt in the boiling water.

2. Place the flour in a large bowl. Pour the hot water and butter over the flour, stirring thoroughly until the mixture pulls away from the sides of the bowl, forming a medium-textured dough.

3. Add one egg at a time, beating well after each.

4. Spoon the thick batter into greased and floured or paper-lined muffin tins until ¾ full. Bake 40 to 45 minutes. Do not open the oven door during baking. Fritters should be nicely golden. Remove and allow to cool fully.

5. Meanwhile make the filling: In the top of a double boiler, combine the sugar and cornstarch. Gradually stir in the milk. Mix in the yolks and the lemon peel, if using. Place the double boiler over medium-high heat and, stirring constantly, bring ingredients to the edge of a boil. Reduce the heat and continue to simmer without boiling until thickened. Remove from the heat and transfer the filling to a bowl. Stir in the vanilla if using, and allow to cool fully. If you added lemon peel, remove it at this time.

6. When the pastries are fully cooled, slice off the top third of each and add some cream filling. It is best to fill these shortly before serving so they don't become soggy.

208

Custard Cream Pastries
Pasteis de Nata
Makes about 30 to 36 2½-inch tarts

These delightful custard-cream tarts are baked in flaky puff-pastry shells for a magnificent dessert. Served with or without a dusting of cinnamon, slightly burned on top or not, they are sure to be popular with your family. It is best to make the pastry one day ahead to give it time to relax completely. The pastry dough requires patience: it must be chilled between each of six rollings. Albert F. Cunha, who made extraordinary pastry for many years at a local bakery, shares this long-sought-after recipe, in which he uses a combination of bread flour and pastry flour.

Because American flour is different from that used in Portugal, various formulas attempt to replicate the old-world flavor and texture of puff pastry. Bakers commonly use 100-percent bread flour (which is 12 percent gluten) to make puff pastry. You can use half bread flour and half pastry flour or, if you do not have access to pastry flour, a mixture of three parts all-purpose flour to one part cake flour. This adaptation uses real butter instead of the special shortening used by bakeries.

Keep the following points in mind:
- Be careful not to overwork the dough; overworking toughens the pastry.
- Lemon juice is added to relax the gluten in the dough.
- Let the dough rest before rolling and cutting; the dough will stretch more easily and there will be less shrinkage during baking.
- Use cold fat when rolling; fat should be firm, but not hard. If it is room temperature, it is too soft.

Equipment:
pastry brush
rolling pin
36–60 pastry tins*
large sheet pan.
candy thermometer

*The tart tins I use are 2½ inches across at the top, 1½ inches at the bottom, and about 1 inch deep with flat, not fluted, sides. Disposable aluminum tart tins work well, too.

Day ahead, make the dough:
Makes about 2½ pounds puff pastry, enough to line about 36 2½-inch pastry tins.

12 ounces (2½ cups) all-purpose flour
1¼ cups cake flour
1¼ cups ice-cold water, as needed
½ teaspoon salt
2 teaspoons lemon juice
1 pound (4 sticks) unsalted butter, very cold and
    firm but not hard

1. Sift the flours together into a large bowl or a mound on your work surface. Make a well in the center of the flour. Combine the water, salt, and lemon juice together in a cup. While pouring the water mixture into the well in the flour, use the outstretched fingers of one hand to draw the flour into the water, turning the ingredients gently to mix. Continue mixing until you have a rough dough; it should not be smooth at this point. Shape the dough into a ball and place in a bowl. Cover and set in the refrigerator to rest for about 15 minutes.

2. Meanwhile, prepare the butter: Make sure the butter is chilled and firm, but not hard. Unwrap the sticks of butter and lightly dust with flour. Place the sticks side by side on a sheet of waxed paper or plastic wrap on a pastry board. Using a long 1-inch dowel or thin rolling pin, gently flatten the butter, shaping it into a neat 6-inch-square block. It should end up being about 1 inch thick. Set aside.

3. On a well-floured surface, roll out the dough into a 10-inch square, also about 1-inch thick. The object is to enclose the butter in the dough. Place the block of butter diagonally on top of the dough so the corners of butter fall inside the edges of dough. Fold the corners of the dough over the

butter to meet at the the center. Pinch the seams and make sure the butter is completely enclosed by the dough.

4. To roll out the dough: Keep your work surface and rolling pin well floured. Place the block of dough in front of you. Use a rolling pin without handles. Begin at the end of the block farthest from you and gently press into the dough. Next, press the rolling pin into the middle of the dough and then closest to you. Continue to make horizontal ridges at even intervals (like speed bumps). This spreads out the butter and dough evenly.

5. Using small strokes, roll out the dough, extending it in one direction (away from you) to about three times the length of the original block of dough, to a thickness of ½ inch. Using a pastry brush, dust off any excess flour. Fold the dough into thirds: first bring one third over. Brush off any excess flour. Fold the other end over, aligning the sides to make a neat rectangle. (If the dough seems to be getting too soft, chill for about 20 minutes before continuing.)

6. Begin each rolling with the rectangle of dough extending lengthwise away from you. Roll out the dough four more times, for a total of five, chilling in between. After each roll out, make light impressions in the dough with the tip of your finger to remind you how many times you have rolled out the dough.

7. On the sixth roll-out, roll out the dough to ¼-inch thick. This time, do not fold. Instead, turn the dough so that the long edge faces you. Roll the dough towards you, creating a long, approximately 22-inch, jellyroll shape. Keep the rolling even and firm. (If it is difficult to manage, cut the roll in half and roll each half separately.) The diameter of the final roll should be about 2½ inches to match the diameter of the tart tins. Wrap the rolled dough tightly in plastic wrap and refrigerate for 24 hours.

Next day, make the filling and assemble:

1. Unwrap the dough and, using a very sharp knife, cut the dough into a thumb's nail width, scant ¾-inch-thick slices. (If you are using larger tins, thicker slices of dough are needed.) Place one slice over the top of each ungreased pastry tin and let rest for about 20 to 30 minutes, while you start the filling.

Filling:

½ cup all-purpose flour
1½ teaspoons table salt
1⅜ cups whole milk, divided
2 cups sugar
1 cups plus 1½ tablespoons water

1. Combine the flour and salt in a 2-quart saucepan. While stirring, slowly pour in ⅜ cup of the milk, whisking to blend thoroughly, creating a thick slurry.

2. Heat the remaining milk in a 1-quart pan until it is quite hot, but not scalding. Slowly, while stirring quickly and constantly to avoid burning, pour the hot milk into the slurry. Place the pan over medium heat and simmer the white sauce 2 to 3 minutes to cook out the starch. Remove from the heat and set aside, keeping hot.

3. Make a sugar syrup: Combine the sugar and water in another 1-quart saucepan over medium-high heat. When bubbles start to form, reduce heat to medium-low. Do not allow to turn color, but heat until the sugar dissolves and the syrup reaches the pearl stage (230 degrees F) and drips slowly from the spoon, like honey. Remove from heat. While slowly pouring, fiercely whisk the hot syrup into the hot white sauce. Simmer for 2 to 3 minutes over medium-low heat. Remove from the heat and allow to cool slightly.

Complete filling and assembly:

5 egg yolks
1 whole egg
1 teaspoon vanilla or lemon extract

1. Moistening your thumb with water, press the center of each slice of dough straight down into the middle of the tin making sure bottom has a fairly thin ⅛" covering without bumps. Keeping your thumb slightly moistened, pull the dough against and up the sides of the tin to the top edge, forming a lip. Repeat, working your way around the tin, each time pulling from the center outward, until the tin is evenly lined with the pastry dough. The pastry should look as though even rings line the tin. Place the lined tins on a large sheet pan. Cover with plastic and let them rest another 30 minutes, chilled. Preheat the oven to 500 degrees F (525 degrees if your oven goes that high).

2. Lightly beat the yolks and whole egg in a medium bowl. Just before filling the lined tart tins, quickly whisk in enough of the warm sauce, a little at a time, to temper the eggs. Once the yolks have become quite warm, immediately whisk them fiercely into the remaining sauce, stirring constantly to blend thoroughly. Stir in the vanilla or lemon. You should have about 1 quart of filling.

3. Using a small ladle, fill the shells a scant ¾ full. Take care not to spill any of the filling on the edges of the pastry, which would prevent the pastry from puffing. This yields enough filling for 30–34 warm tarts. *Important:* The sauce must be warm when you beat in the eggs yolks in order to cook them. The filling then only needs to be browned in the oven during the short baking time.

4. Place the pastries immediately onto the middle shelf of the preheated oven. Bake at 500 degrees until pastries are a rich golden color, 15 to 20 minutes. (Filling will puff up during baking and deflate as it cools.) Cool for about one minute then remove from the pastry tins. If they are allowed to cool too long, they will stick to the tins. Best served warm or at room temperature. The most luscious way to serve them is slightly warm, with a dusting of cinnamon and a little splash of Beirão, a Portuguese brandy. The tarts can be refreshed in toaster oven the next day, then flavored with the brandy if desired.

211

Pastry Tartlets
Pasteis/Queijadas
Makes about 48 tartlets

Dilia Luz, who is constantly sought after to supply her friends and family with these popular dainty pastries, shares her wonderful recipes for the pastry and three fillings. She takes advantage of an Italian pasta machine to make the labor-intensive rolling of the dough a breeze. The term queijadas *is sometimes used loosely to include tarts that have fillings without cheese, even though the name implies cheese. The following recipe makes enough dough to line about 48 2½-inch tart tins. The pastry dough can be used for any of the filling recipes that follow, all of which can be made a day ahead or early on the day of baking.*
Just make sure the fillings are cooled completely before using.

Equipment:
hand-cranked dough sheeter
48 2½-inch diameter fluted tart tins
pastry brush

Tip: Make your choice of filling first

Dough:
3⅔ cups all-purpose flour
¼ teaspoon table salt
1 to 1¼ cups water
4 tablespoons soft butter, plus butter for the tins
3 tablespoons sugar

1. Combine the flour and salt in a large bowl, mixing to evenly distribute the salt.
2. In a small bowl, mix 1 cup of the water, the butter, and sugar together, then pour into the middle of the flour. Using one hand, draw the flour into the water and mix until the dough leaves the sides of the bowl. Knead in the bowl about 5 minutes, until a smooth soft dough forms. Cover and set aside to rest for about 20 minutes. (If the weather is warm or the flour very dry, you might need the remaining ¼ cup of water.) Preheat the oven to 350 degrees F.
3. While the dough is resting, use the pastry brush to butter the tins. Remove a lump of dough, about 4 inches in diameter, place it in a small bowl of flour, and set aside. You will use it as a press to form the pastries. Line up about 6 tins in a single row, end to end.
4. Pinch off a lemon-sized piece of dough from the main batch. Set the dial on the machine to #3 and roll out the dough. Turn the dial to #5 and roll the sheet of dough through again. It should be almost as thin as filo dough. (Not all pasta machines use the same numbering system. You may need to experiment to achieve a dough that is slightly thicker than filo pastry.) Let the sheet of dough rest for 10 minutes.
5. Drape the sheet of dough over the lined-up, buttered tins. Take the reserved floured ball of dough and press it gently but firmly into each tin. Pull away the excess dough. Place the tins on a baking sheet and repeat with the remaining dough until all the tins have been lined. Fill each tin a scant ¾ full with filling, about 2 full tablespoons. Place in the preheated oven and bake for 15 to 25 minutes, until golden. (Cheese filling will cook more quickly than other fillings.) Remove tarts from the tins while they are still warm or they may stick.

Note: The shape and size of the tart tins you use will determine the number of pastries you get. The tins we use range in size from 2 to 2½ inches wide by 1 inch deep. Scraps of dough may be re-rolled to line more tins.

Muddled Filling

Atrapaladas
Fills 24 tartlets

Not quite cheese, the milk is "muddled" with vinegar and has a surprising and delightful taste. Since this filling takes time, make it before the dough, even a day ahead.

4 cups milk
2 cups sugar
1 tablespoon vinegar (cider, wine, or white)
10 large egg yolks, lightly beaten
1 tablespoon butter
¼ teaspoon lemon extract

1. Combine the milk with the sugar in a 5-quart pot. Place over medium-high heat and bring to a boil. Drizzle the vinegar over the milk and reduce the heat. Simmer on medium-low heat for about 2 hours, until the milk is reduced and somewhat thickened and 90 percent of the clear liquid has evaporated. The milk will be curdled. Break up the large curds with a spoon and mix in the butter.
2. Slowly pour some of the hot milk into the yolks while quickly stirring. Transfer the yolks to the pot while whisking vigorously. Return the filling to a simmer. Cook until it is thickened and is just ready to boil, about 10 minutes. Remove from the heat. Stir in the lemon flavoring. Allow to cool completely before using. Makes about 3½ cups.

Pastry Tartlets with Muddled Filling

Bean Filling

Feijão

Fills 24 tartlets

Some versions of this filling include finely ground almonds.

1 cup milk
4 cups sugar
2 cups cooked and drained white or red kidney
    beans or chickpeas, puréed (Progresso or
    Goya brand canned beans may be used)
16 egg yolks
grated peel of 1 lemon or ½ teaspoon lemon
    extract

1. Combine the milk, sugar, and puréed beans in a 4-quart pot. Place over medium-high heat and bring to a boil. Reduce the heat and simmer, stirring frequently, for 30 minutes.
2. In a medium bowl, mix the yolks with the lemon peel or extract. While whisking vigorously, slowly pour some of the hot bean filling into the yolks to temper them. Gradually add more of the filling to the yolks until they are quite warm. Transfer the yolk mixture into the pan. Return the filling to a simmer, stirring constantly, just to the point of boiling. Remove from the heat and cool completely before using.

Cheese Filling

Queijadas

Fills about 30 tartlets

Queijadas or cheese pastries are extremely popular in Portugal, especially those from the town of Sintra. The recipe in Sintra is very secret, so we must make do with this tasty substitute.

2 whole eggs
5 egg yolks
¾ pound (12 ounces) Fresh Cheese (page 160)
    (or substitute farmer's or ricotta cheese)
1 cup sugar
scant ½ teaspoon cinnamon
½ teaspoon vanilla or lemon extract
2 tablespoons butter, softened

1. In a medium bowl, mix together the whole eggs and yolks. Using a whisk, beat in the cheese, sugar, cinnamon, vanilla, and butter.
2. Strain the filling through a fine mesh strainer to break down any large lumps.

214

São Miguel, Azores

215

10

WINES

Vinhos

When the Portuguese tasted the first drop of wine brought by the Phoenicians, at least 600 years B.C., they did not realize where this encounter would lead. Wine eventually became the national drink and was consumed judiciously, but also creatively. Like spices, wine was originally used to preserve meats and mask the off flavor of spoiling meat. From that functional beginning, wine has evolved into marinades for meat that enhance flavor and tenderness.

Since the initial popularity of port, Mateus, and Lancers wines, the art of wine making in Portugal has improved tremendously. Before the revolution of 1975, wine cooperatives were controlled by the government. With no incentives, almost all estate bottling disappeared. Although the government sent out inspectors to insure that vineyards replaced weak vines with strong, high-yielding, disease-resistant stock, it paid the wine producers only for the quantity, not the quality of the grapes produced. Today, estate bottling is back and growing rapidly.

Local homemade wines in Portugal were often sold by the barrel, never reaching the point of bottling. And most of the barrels were purchased

by local taverns frequented by farmers and townsmen. They would gather to drink their local wines and discuss local issues, munching on boiled lupini beans *tremoços,* and eating *petiscos* and savory *salgadas.* (See Chapter 1.)

In these gathering spots, wine was ordered by the *meia bola* or *bola* (half or full glass). It was served in tumblers, not fancy wine glasses, then drunk tavern-fashion, like shots, not sipped. Even in America, my father wasn't the only one who continued to drink his wine in juice tumblers, a charming and unpretentious custom. One of my favorite Italian restaurants served wine in small tumblers as well. But recently, much to my dismay, it caved in to social pressures and replaced the tumblers with wine glasses.

Both in the old days, and now in the United States, Portuguese homemade wines can be stronger or lighter—depending on the maker—than commercial wines. Some wine makers add sugar or a touch of brandy to increase the strength of their wine, particularly if a weak grape is used; others use only grape juice, minimizing contact with the grape skins, in order to make a lighter wine. Of course, not every Portuguese household in Portugal or the United State makes its own wine. Augusto Gabriel, originally from Terceira in the Azores, remembers his boyhood. At the age of eleven, when his family wanted wine for their midday meal, Augusto would be sent to the local tavern to purchase wine. He would take a five-liter jug to be filled. There wasn't such a thing as an age requirement to enter a tavern and purchase alcohol.

Homemade or not, wine is also used by the Portuguese for medicinal purposes. A concoction of warm water, sugar, and wine was a simple remedy. To help me with my childhood anemia, my father would often take an egg yolk, mix it with a teaspoon or so of sugar, then stir in a small amount of red wine. He would then turn to me and say, "Take this; it will build up your blood."

Agapito Figueira, originally from the island of Madeira, recommends a digestive popular in his homeland. The *ponche* is made by macerating sugar with lemon juice and a touch of honey. The lemon and sugar mixture is then stirred into a small glass of *cachaça,* a white rum distilled in Madeira from sugar cane.

After 1975, Portugal became more conscientious about growing

grapes and wine making, which was, however, not supported by a consumer demand for quality. Wine continued to be produced for regional local markets such as taverns. In 1986, the European Union opened Portugal to a global market, stimulating a revolution in Portuguese wine making. Money became available, not only for equipment upgrades and irrigation systems for the vineyards, but for education as well. Enologists needed to learn about better ways to grow the grapes, about the characteristics of grape varieties, and about improved methods of making wine. This type of education made it necessary to travel outside the country.

Those wine makers who first broadened their horizons are now teachers of a new generation of wine makers. The up-and-coming wine makers need to accommodate two types of wine consumers, the new generation and the old generation. "Old" here does not necessarily mean

old age. People who drink the Lancers or Mateus wines of the world, have always done so and will continue to do so. The new generation of wine drinkers, however, is looking for something different. They want to know the story behind the wine. This trend is more apparent in America. Europeans drink wine as a beverage the way Americans drink soda. They are not so interested in what went into it. Here, in contrast, not only do wine enthusiasts think about the grape, they want to know *what* grape—to break it down and scrutinize it. With this demand from consumers, it is only natural that Portuguese wine makers have adjusted their thinking toward the global market, not just the local consumer. Today more than ever, you'll find interesting articles in the world's leading wine magazines about Portuguese wine-making. Having found its own little niche at the dining tables of the world's gourmets, Portuguese table wine no longer sits in the shadow of the world-renowned port.

In Portugal, as in other wine-producing countries, wine is designated by region. When it comes to food, there is a natural tendency to pair wine with dishes of the same region. Since the same soil that flavors the ingredients of a dish, flavors the grapes of the same region, the resulting wine complements the food. Portuguese custom throws the red-wine/red-meat white-wine/fish rule right out the window. Balance should be the goal of pairing Portuguese wines with food. The tannin in red wine, as we know, definitely goes well with red meat, and white wine with fish and its natural oils. But most Portuguese cooking involves fish, while most of our wines are red. How to reconcile the two? The trick is to find a red wine with low tannin content. Low maceration (contact) of the grape juice with the skins, produces less tannin, resulting in a more acidic red wine with less tannin—a perfect match for fish. Such a fruity, light-bodied, and acidic wine is the Quinta da Romeira "Tradicão" from the Palmela region. It uses 100 percent Periquita grapes.

In making a wine selection, you must pay attention to the flavors of the spices and seasoning in the juices or the sauce of the dish as well as the kind of protein it is based on. The acidity of a medium- to full-bodied red wine will certainly stand up to a seafood dish with a spicy, tomato-based sauce without overpowering it. *Caldo Verde* (page 23), a traditional soup, is especially nice with a fine drizzle of Madeira wine over it and a glass of Madeira wine served on the side. This illustrates the idea that when a particular wine is used in a dish—as a marinade or sauce—that same wine should be drunk with that dish.

Grape varieties that were introduced by the Phoenicians long ago are still grown in Portugal today. Portuguese wines today encompass light, effervescent *vinho verdes* and smooth and refined ports and a range in between. The following list is an overview of wines by region, with some suggestions for pairing with food.

Vinho Verde: *Vinho verde* wines come from a region located in the northwest corner of Portugal. The name "green wine" does not reflect the color of the wine; it is made from immature grapes that have not yet developed a high sugar content. The wine is fresh, uncomplicated, and fruity. It has a low alcohol content (9 to 10 percent), with varying degrees of fizziness, depending on the grapes used. In some locales, dryer *vinho verdes,* like the Alvarinhos, may have 11 to 12 percent alcohol. *Vinho verdes* can also be red, although whites are more commonly imported to the United States. Lightly chilled, the lively *vinho verde* wine not only is a perfect aperitif and a good partner to shellfish dishes; it also stands very well on its own as a refresher on a hot summer's afternoon. Prominent names of *vinho verdes* are Casal Garcia, Aveleda, Casa Vila Verde, Gatão, Alvarinho, Quintas do Malgaço, Alvarinho Palacio da Brejoiera, Grinalda, and Quinta da Aveleda.

Douro: The Douro wines, which at one time were consumed mainly by locals, are produced from grapes grown in the Douro River valley in northern Portugal. Grown in poor soil and under stressful conditions, the grapes from the lower slopes produce wines of low acidity and full flavor and body—the wines with which to make port. The precise blending of these grapes with those of higher acidity from the hills above the river also produces some of Portugal's finest red table wines. The medium- to full-bodied Douro wines can be paired perfectly with full-flavored red meats, especially lamb or game and spicy dishes. Some names to check out are Charamba (one of my personal favorites), Duas Quintas, Barca Velha, Calços do Tanha, Sogrape Douro Reserva, Quinta do Crasto, Quinta da Gaivosa, Quinta de Covelos, Quinta do Vale Da Raposa (Touriga National), Quinta do Côtto, and Quinta do Portal, to mention just a few.

Dão: Like the Douro, the Dão region is protected from the effects of the Atlantic Ocean, giving it a more Mediterranean climate. Consistent temperatures are ideal for slow wine fermentation, which gives rise to medium to heavy, full-bodied wines with good balance and a wonderful aroma. Popular selections are the Grão Vasco, Duque de Viseu, Porta dos Cavaleiros, Quinta dos Carvalhais (Touriga National), Casa de Santar, Meia Encosta, and Caves Aliança Partigular. These wines are perfect for the heartiest dish you can make.

Bairrada: These wines are made from grapes grown in the clay soil of the Bairrada region. The Baga grape, which is considered difficult to tame, produces very hearty wines. But take care—Bairrada wines can vary from a very light-bodied and harsh wine to a beautiful full-bodied, well-balanced wine like the Luis Pato. This region also produces some of Portugal's best sparkling wines. Drink them with braises and roasts of lamb, roasted suckling pig Bairrada-style, and root-vegetable dishes. Some names to choose are Luis Pato, Caves São João, Caves Prima Vera, Aliança, Caves São Jorge, Casa de Saima, and Quinta das Bageira.

Alentejo: Some of the country's more complex, well-balanced, and full-bodied wines are produced in the Alentejo region of southern Portugal. The predominant grapes grown in these plains and hills are Periquita, Aragonez, and Trincadeira Preta. Font Roupeiro is the dominant grape for the Alentejo's white wine. The estate-bottled wines tend to be more full bodied, good for cellaring. Suggested wines from this region are Borba, Esporão, Requengos, Quinta de Terrugem, Quinta do Carmo (part of the Rothschild family), and João P. Ramos, a noted top-quality, light-bodied, well-balanced wine that pairs very well with the region's popular Carne de Porco à Alentejana (page 98).

On a side note: In addition to its wine, wheat, olives, and pork, the Alentejo area is well known for cork, supplying a large demand in the global market. On cork farms like the one owned by my cousin Senhor Jose Oliveira, the harvested bark of the cork trees is piled high, leaving the naked trunks of the trees blushing with a cinnamon color—an unforgettable sight. Cork trees take nine years to produce bark, which is used for wine-bottle corks, insulation, wall and floor tiles, cork liners in shoes, and so on. Usually a cork farm has several groves that are harvested in rotation; a different one each year. The year is marked on the trees of a freshly harvested grove to keep track of when their next harvest will be ready.

221

The upcoming trend in Portuguese wines is the single-grape varietal wines we refer to as *monocasta*. Top-quality wineries are now concentrating on producing small batches of wine made of a single grape variety. Some varietal red wines go by the names Touriga Naçional, Tinta Roriz, Tricadeira, Aragonêz, and Baga. Alvarinho and Arinto are varietal whites. These are the new generation in Portuguese wines. They are more expensive than the average regional wines, but they are of superb quality. Small amounts are now available in the United States, but the future bears watching. (Some of these grapes are already grown in California and are used for the state's port wine.) Most regions in Portugal produce white wines along with their reds, but there are only a few regions that specialize in white wine: Vinho Verde, which is in a category by itself; Boucelas, which produces some of the best Arinto grape wines; and Terra do Sado, which produces the fabulous dry muscat João Pires. Dry muscat pairs nicely with dishes that are lightly spiced.

Sangria Atasca

Sangria Atasca

Serves about 12

Owners of the Atasca Restaurant in Cambridge, Massachusetts, Joe and Maria Cerqueira, share their very popular drink. Joe suggests using your favorite full-bodied red wine.

2 cups ice cubes
8 ounces orange juice
5 ounces of either soda water, tonic water, ginger ale or Sprite
1½ ounces Triple Sec
1½ ounces brandy of choice
½ medium apple, peeled, cored, cut into cubes
½ medium orange, peeled, cut into cubes
1½ bottles (about 1 quart) of your favorite full-bodied red wine

1. In a punch bowl or 2-liter pitcher, combine the ice, orange juice, soda water, Triple Sec, and brandy. Stir to blend. Mix in the fruit, top off the ingredients with the wine, and stir. Serve immediately.

Ponche

Ponche

Serves 1

This typical digestive from the island of Madeira can be drunk warmed, like a hot toddy. Be sure to use rum that is made from sugar cane.

2 tablespoons lemon juice or to taste
1 teaspoon sugar or to taste
1 teaspoon honey or to taste
6 ounces *cachaça* (Madeira rum)

1. Using a mortar and pestle, mash the sugar with the lemon juice. Transfer to an 8-ounce glass. Add the remaining ingredients and stir.

223

HOMEMADE WINE

The art of making Portuguese wine is so old it is one of the strands that make up the fabric of Portuguese culture. Continentals and Azorean Portuguese alike transplanted their craft to their new homeland, teaching it to their children in the hopes of a continuing tradition. Wooden grape boxes piled high on neighborhood sidewalks during early fall are a dead giveaway that wine is in the making. Some home wine makers use the grapes grown on their backyard vines; others purchase California grapes or combine the two. A few months later, the work gives way to wine-tasting socials, at which delicious dinners are enjoyed accompanied by the age-old debate of who made the best wine this year.

Like other culinary traditions, wine-making techniques are handed down through the generations. Our friend Manuel Santos Silva came to the United States in 1968 from the town of Luz on the island of Graciosa in the Azores. He brought with him his family's wine-making techniques that have been carried on for generations. His wife Maria, whom he married in Portugal in 1971, joined him here in 1972, and together they raised a family in which cultural traditions remain strong.

Manuel learned to make wine as a small child, when he helped crush the grapes. Over the years, he has perfected the art of wine-making. Though he does have a vineyard in his backyard in eastern Massachusetts, he chooses to purchase the grapes he needs each fall in the wholesale markets of Boston.

The process begins some three months before he makes the wine when Manuel cleans his oak barrels, using the old-world method. He inserts clean stones into each barrel and adds cold water. He corks the side hole in each barrel and rolls the barrels around to loosen sediment and residue. (In the Azores it is common to see the barrels being rolled on the road.) After that, he removes the corks, rinses the barrels well, removing the stones. He then turns the barrels on their sides to dry for three days.

The barrels are then given a final cleaning. Manuel folds a teaspoon of Sulphur Sublime in a three-inch square of broadcloth tied to a thin wire. Holding the wire, he places the cloth near the opening, ignites the cloth, and quickly inserts it into the barrel. He corks the hole and lets the sealed barrel sit. The barrels will be ready for use in three months.

In the fall, Manuel goes to Boston to taste different varieties of grapes before making his selection. Recently his preference has been Uva de Collina, a Select Alicante Bouchet, marked California Special. This grape is also used in Portugal. One box of grapes (42 pounds) yields about 3½ gallons of grape juice. Manuel purchases 33 boxes to obtain approximately 112 gallons of wine.

As a child in the Azores, Manuel used his feet to crush grapes. Now he uses a hand-cranked grape crusher instead. Since fermentation begins as soon as the grapes are crushed, the grapes are placed immediately in a large, upright barrel and allowed to ferment for three or four days. The barrel is not filled to the top because space is needed for the skins and pulp that will rise to the surface during fermentation. Near the bottom of the barrel is a corked opening 1 inch in diameter.

225

When the level of juices has increased sufficiently and the pulp and skins have all risen to the surface, the cork is replaced by a 5-inch-long wooden spigot. The juice is poured into a large container and strained before being transferred to the clean barrels Manuel prepared three months ago. Filled to within six inches of the top, the barrels are left uncorked and lying on their sides during fermentation, to permit accumulating gases to escape. Otherwise, the tops would blow off. In the Azores, an apple is placed over the hole, allowing ventilation while preventing contamination, and Manuel continues to use this custom. Extra grape juice is held in glass bottles and used to replenish the volume lost in the barrels during fermentation.

The skins and pulp are removed from the large barrel and placed in a press, where any remaining juices are extracted, strained, and added to the fermenting juice. The compacted pulp is then removed from the press, and may be reserved for distilling *cassis*.

After two or three weeks, when fermentation stops (Manuel knows this because the sound of the fizzing stops!), the apples are removed and the barrels are corked. When the wine is ready, in two or three more months, Manuel will draw first from the smallest barrel, refilling from the next, until the wine is consumed. And the tradition of making homemade wine continues as Manuel teaches his son.

If you are interested in making your own wine at home, there are many suppliers now selling equipment and information with which you can produce wines that not only capture the essence of late summer's sweet harvest but also put you in contact with this age-old tradition.

RESOURCE GUIDE

Cataplana *pans, tableware, chef's torch:*
    Sur La Table
    410 Terry Avenue North
    Seattle, Washington 98109
    Tel: 800-243-0852
    www.Surlatable.com

    Williams Sonoma
    Catalog Department
    P.O. Box 7456
    San Francisco, California 94120-7456
    Tel: 800-541-2233
    www.williams-sonoma.com

Cheeses, wines, seasonings, sausages, kale cutter
(by special order):
    Tremont Market
    70 Tremont Street
    Peabody, Massachusetts 01960
    Tel: 978-531-2764

    Maria's Portuguese-American Market
    57 Union Square
    Somerville, Massachusetts
    Tel: 617-623-7630

Portuguese cheeses, sausages, and wines:
    New England Meat Market
    60–62 Walnut Street
    Peabody, Massachusetts 01960
    Tel: 978-531-0846

    New England Meat Market
    465 Broadway
    Cambridge, Massachusetts 02138
    Tel: 617-547-2333

Grand Central Market
500 Main Road
Tiverton, Rhode Island
Tel: 401-624-9914

Mello's Portuguese Market
477 Milford Road
Swansea, Massachusetts 02777
Tel: 508-676-0167
www.portuguesefood.com

Pottery, tableware:
    3 Wellington Street, Suite 1
    Boston, Massachusetts 02118
    Tel: 617-536-8226
    www.Importugal.com
    E-mail: kcosta@importugal.com

Tableware, pottery, kale cutter, linens:
    Casa Portugal
    96 Tremont Street
    Peabody, Massachusetts 01960
    Tel: (978) 531-5525

Wines:
    Whitehall Imports
    750 Everett Street
    Norwood, Massachusetts 02062
    Tel: 800-370-6500
    www.wcltd.com

For complete sausage-making supplies:
    The Sausage Maker, Inc.
    1500 Clinton Street, Building 123
    Buffalo, New York 14206
    Tel: 716-824-5814
    Fax: 716-824-6465

226

REFERENCES

For Azeitão *artisan cheese:*
> Dean & Deluca
> 560 Broadway
> New York, New York, 10012
> Tel: 800-221-7714
> www.deandeluca.com

In the Ironbound section of Newark, New Jersey, Ferry Street, often referred to as "Little Portugal," possesses the widest variety of products imported from Portugal:
> Seabra's Market
> 260 Lafayette Street
> Newark, New Jersey
> Tel: 973-587-8606

> Ferry Wine and Liquors
> 158 Ferry Street
> Newark, New Jersey
> Tel: 973-589-8251

> Lisbon Liquors
> 114 Ferry Street
> Newark, New Jersey
> Tel: 973-344-0139

> Oporto Liquors
> 178 Ferry Street
> Newark, New Jersey
> Tel: 973-589-3325

Açores, by Francisco Carreira Da Costa. Lisbon: Editorial de Publicações Turistas, R. DeSanta Barbara, 81 5°D, 1967.

Dicionário Português Inglês, P. Julio Albino Ferreira. Porto, Portugal: Editorial Domingos Barreira de Manuel Barreira, Rua Oliveira, Monteiro, 1965.

Fava (Broad) Beans—General Information, Michigan State University Extension, Data Base 01 March 9, 1998. E-mail: wrublec@msue.msu.edu

The Complete Book of Herbs, by Lesley Bremness. New York: Viking Penguin, 1988.

Great Sausage Recipes and Meat Curing, by Rytek Kutas. Buffalo, NY: The Sausage Maker Company, 1984.

Food and History, by Eduardo Mayone Dias. LusaWeb Comunidades Project, 1997. www.lusaweb.com/comunides/foods

Food in History, by Reay Tannahill. New York: Crown, 1988.

The Way to Cook, by Julia Child. New York: Albert A. Knopf, 1989.

Wines of Portugal, by Pasquale Iocca. New York: Portuguese Trade Commission.

227

INDEX

228

229

231

232

233

234

235

236

Óbidos rooftops

NOTES

NOTES

NOTES

NOTES

AAY 0520

AAY 0520

The Other Ducks

Ellen Yeomans   Pictures by Chris Sheban

A NEAL PORTER BOOK
ROARING BROOK PRESS
NEW YORK

This one is for Mom and Dad who mostly managed to keep their ducks in a row. —E.Y.

To the duck I ate that one time. I'm sorry. —C.S.

Text copyright © 2018 by Ellen Yeomans
Illustrations copyright © 2018 by Chris Sheban
A Neal Porter Book
Published by Roaring Brook Press
Roaring Brook Press is a division of Holtzbrinck Publishing Holdings Limited Partnership
175 Fifth Avenue, New York, NY 10010
The art for this book was created using watercolor, colored pencil, and graphite.
mackids.com

Library of Congress Control Number: 2017957295
ISBN: 978-1-62672-502-7

Our books may be purchased in bulk for promotional, educational, or business use. Please
contact your local bookseller or the Macmillan Corporate and Premium Sales Department
at (800) 221-7945 ext. 5442 or by e-mail at MacmillanSpecialMarkets@macmillan.com.

First edition 2018
Printed in China by RR Donnelley Asia Printing Solutions Ltd., Dongguan City, Guangdong Province
1 3 5 7 9 10 8 6 4 2

This Duck and That Duck were the best of friends.

They played all spring as
the rushes grew high and lush
beside the wadey-water of
the Little Puddle.

One day,
This Duck
and That
Duck went
waddling
through the
rushes.

"At a time like this there should be Other Ducks," This Duck said.

"What's Other Ducks?" That Duck asked.

"Like us, only not us," This Duck answered. "If there were Other Ducks, we would waddle in a line."

"Aren't we in a line? After all, I go where you go," That Duck said.

This Duck stopped. "Two is not a line. Two is a *follow*. A line is better. A line is more ducky. We need Other Ducks for that. Right now, we're just a couple of ducks out for a waddle."

They continued waddling in a not-quite-line until they
came to a Big Puddle full of cool, clear, wallow-water.

This Duck splashed and splished, she dipped and dunked.
"I'm swimming!" she called.
"How do you know?" That Duck asked.

"It just feels like swimming,"
This Duck answered.

That Duck dipped his webbed foot into the Big Puddle
and pulled it right back out.

"And what exactly is swimming?" That Duck asked.

"This," said This Duck. "It's like waddling but in the water. I don't think my feet are touching bottom."

"Not touching? Oh dear!" That Duck fretted.

This Duck looked down to check and saw . . .
another duck looking up at her.

"Come on in!" This Duck called to That
Duck. "There's a wonderful surprise in here!"

"Is it safe? That's an awfully big puddle."

That Duck was worried but finally flip-flap followed. He paddled and paddled, and then looked down to see if his feet were touching the bottom and saw . . . another duck looking up at him.

"Are these—?" That Duck began.
"The Other Ducks," This Duck finished.

As summer warmed the world around them, The Other Ducks swam whenever and wherever This Duck and That Duck swam. They dipped and dunked at the same time, too.

If only The Other Ducks weren't always upside down. And though This Duck and That Duck tried, they could never get The Other Ducks behind them so they could all swim in a line.

They never waddled in a line, either, because
The Other Ducks never got out of the Big Puddle.
It was nice to have them around, but it was not
as ducky as it might have been.

And then one windy, rainy day The Other Ducks disappeared.
This Duck and That Duck called and called for them.
They swam through the choppy water
to the far side of the
Big Puddle. But
they didn't
find them.

The next day was sunny and bright and The Other Ducks
were back. Soon, autumn claimed the world all
around them. More and more days were
windy, rainy, and cold. The
Other Ducks were
not there as often.

One day, This
Duck said, "I think
they've left us."

"Is that them?" That Duck asked.

"Bug," said
This Duck.

"Is that them?" That Duck asked.
"Falling leaves," This Duck said. She
was beginning to wonder if That Duck
had learned anything all summer.

"How about that?" That Duck asked.

"Birdy-bird," This Duck answered.

"How do you know?" That Duck asked.

"It just looks like a birdy-bird." This Duck stretched her wings and pretended to be a birdy-bird.

"What do they do?" asked That Duck, pretending the same thing.

"They fly high and they fly far," This Duck said.

And then, This Duck ran . . .

and . . . flew.

and hopped . . .

"Look! My feet aren't touching. Be a birdy-bird, too,"
This Duck called down.

And though That Duck wasn't at all sure he wanted to be one, he ran and hopped and flew. This Duck and That Duck flew around their Big Puddle. They searched for The Other Ducks but they did not see them. Still, the flying was fun.

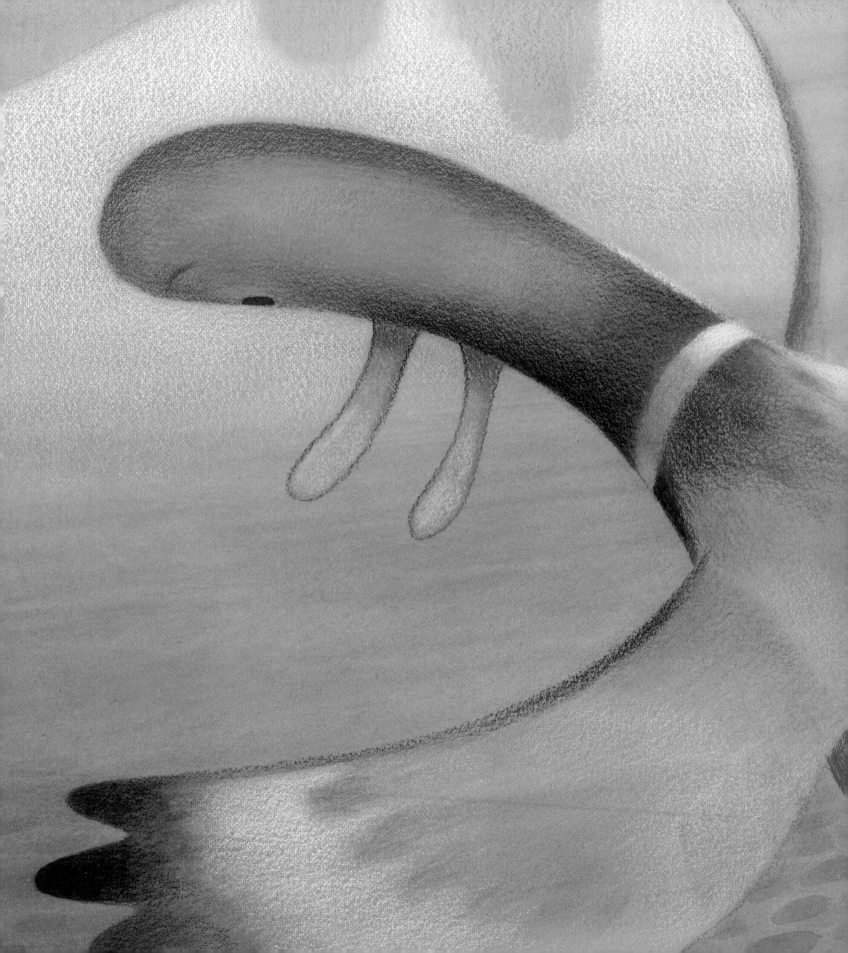

One day, This Duck did not want to play with That Duck. She was restless. "My feathers itch," she said.

The next day That Duck felt the very same way.

"We need to go," This Duck said.
"Where to?" That Duck asked.
"To South."
"Where is that?"
"We'll figure it out."

That Duck looked into the Big Puddle. "I wish The Other Ducks could go with us."

"Maybe The Other Ducks are already there," This Duck said. "Let's fly instead of waddle."

"Because we don't quite make a line?" That Duck asked.

"Yes, and because I think we need to get to South faster," This Duck said. "Look, so many birdy-birds. Let's follow them to South."

This Duck and That Duck took to
the air right behind the birdy-birds.
When they caught up, they found
that the birdy-birds were . . .
Other Ducks!

This Duck and That Duck
joined a line. A line!
   "Like us, only not us," This Duck
called to That Duck. And all
together they flew to South.

Winter settled itself over the
Big Puddle and the Little Puddle,
but there weren't any ducks to see
it, or feel it, or hear how very
quiet it was.

When spring arrived, This Duck and
That Duck flew home.
   This time, as the rushes grew tall
and lush beside the Little Puddle, a
lively line formed behind them.

This Duck led the way to the Big Puddle.
"Keep the line, everyone," she called.
"Why are they so small?" That Duck asked.

"It's the way everything starts," This Duck answered.
"How do you know?" That Duck asked.
"I just pay attention," This Duck said.

This Duck and That Duck and The Little Other Ducks waddled in a line to the cool, clear, wallow-water. And every single one of them felt downright ducky.